First Lieutenant J. Ogden Murray
7th Virginia (1862)

THE IMMORTAL SIX HUNDRED

A Story of Cruelty to Confederate Prisoners of War

by
Major John Ogden Murray
One of the Six Hundred

THE CONFEDERATE
REPRINT COMPANY
☆   ☆   ☆   ☆
WWW.CONFEDERATEREPRINT.COM

The Immortal Six Hundred
by John Ogden Murray
(Second Edition)

Originally Published in 1911
by The Stone Printing and Manufacturing Company
Roanoke, Virginia

Reprint Edition © 2015
The Confederate Reprint Company
Post Office Box 2027
Toccoa, Georgia 30577
www.confederatereprint.com

Cover and Interior by
Magnolia Graphic Design
www.magnoliagraphicdesign.com

ISBN-13: 978-0692365625
ISBN-10: 0692365621

DEDICATION

To the dead and living comrades of the Immortal Six Hundred – Confederate officers, prisoners of war – who were confined in the stockade on Morris Island, South Carolina, under fire of our own guns shelling that island; and who were subsequently starved on rations of rotten corn meal and onion pickle at Fort Pulaski, Georgia, and Hilton Head, South Carolina, 1864-65, by order of Edwin M. Stanton, United States Secretary of War – to all who remained true unto the end, under the terrible ordeal of fire and starvation, this history is affectionately inscribed with a comrade's love.

J. Ogden Murray

CONTENTS

☆　☆　☆　☆

PREFACE

☆　☆　☆　☆

In presenting this Second Edition of the history of the Six Hundred Confederate Officers, Prisoners of War, who were placed on Morris Island, S.C, under fire of their own guns shelling that island in 1864-65, and the wanton cruelty subsequently inflicted upon them by order of the United States Government, it is told without malice. But it is told to refute the slanders made by the pulpits and press of the North that the Confederate Government was inhuman and cruel to Union prisoners of war in Southern prisons. We shall tell the story truthfully and backed, as the story is, by the official orders and records of the United States Government. We do hope to prove the South was not guilty of the charges made against it. But that the real culprits guilty of inhumanity to prisoners of war, were the Secretary of War, Edwin M. Stanton, and his colleagues in Washington City, in 1861-1865. The charges of cruelty, made against President Davis and the Confederate Government, to the Union prisoners of war in Southern prisons, were made by these officials to hide from the people of the North those really guilty of the inhumanity, and shift from their own shoulders the responsibility of violating the cartel of exchange, which was the cause of all the suffering of Union prisoners of war in Southern prisons. The Confederate authorities did all they could do, to alleviate the lot of the unfortunates that the fate of war threw into their hands. Whatever the Confederate soldier received in the field as ration, was given to the Union prisoners of war, and Mr. Edwin M. Stanton was fully informed, officially and otherwise, of this fact. The charges that the Confederate authorities refused to make exchange of prisoners of war, were made at a time when passion was at fever heat in the North, and the charges were made and circulated to conceal from the people of the North, the real culprits who were responsible for the home sickness, and troubles of the Union prisoners of war confined in the South.

Capt. James Madison Page, 2d Wisconsin Volunteers, U.S.A., a gallant Union soldier, in his book, *The True Story of Andersonville Prison,* charges all the discomforts of the Union prisoners of war to Mr. Stanton and the Washington authorities, for violating the exchange cartel; surely this gallant soldier's word will be accepted by the North. Read what Mr. Charles A. Dana says. He was Stanton's Assistant Secretary of War, 1861-65. Read what the commission appointed by the United States Government to investigate Northern Military prisons say of the conditions they found, and see where the blame of cruelty rests. Read General Grant's request and order to stop exchange and why he wanted exchanges stopped. Read General Henry W. Halleck's, U.S.A., order to stop all exchanges of prisoners of war, and we think this alone should convince those who slander Mr. Davis and the Confederate authorities just where the responsibility rests. It was the inhuman orders to stop exchanges, issued by the Washington authorities that made both Union and Confederate prisoners of war suffer. The Confederate authorities had no say in these orders. Read D.A.M. Clark's, U.S.A., report on Northern Military prisons. Read General J.G. Foster's, U.S.A., authority to place Confederate prisoners of war on Morris Island, S.C, under fire of their own guns shelling that island. Read what General Scammell, et al, U.S. officers confined in Charleston, S.C., prisoners of war, tell General Foster of their treatment, and the letter is official. And when you read these proofs, honestly say who was guilty of inhumanity to helpless prisoners of war.

All we ask is that the truth shall be told. If the truth shows the South or Confederate authorities to have been guilty of cruelty to prisoners of war, then they should be held up to the scorn of the civilized world. We cannot change the Record now, it must stand. And we say without the least fear of contradiction, that the Confederate Government never by order, fed Union prisoner's of war on rotten corn meal and acid pickle, the corn meal ground in 1861, and when fed to the Six Hundred, was filled with bugs and worms. Who was responsible for this cruelty? Let's have the truth and fix the responsibility for this cruelty; that if it was not inflicted by order of the United States Government, she may purge herself of this crime before the world. Let's have the truth that the future historians may be able to place before the world the men guilty of inhumanity to prisoners of war. Find, if it is possible to do so, such an order to feed men on rotten corn meal and acid pickle, in the Records of the Confederate Government, as this order of Stanton, Foster, et al. Read the report of General C. Grover, U.S.A., on condition of the Six Hundred Confederate prisoners of war at Fort Pulaski, Ga.:

Headquarters, Dist. of Savannah.
Savannah, Ga., Feb. 7, 1865.

Asst. Adjt. General. Headquarters Department of the South:

My medical director yesterday inspected the condition of the Rebel prisoners confined at Fort Pulaski, and represents that they are in a condition of great suffering and exhaustion for want of sufficient food and clothing; also, that they have scurvy to a considerable extent. He recommends, as a necessary sanitary measure, that they be at once put on full prison rations; and, also, that they be allowed to receive necessary articles of clothing from friends. I would respectfully endorse the surgeon's recommendation, and ask authority to take such steps as may be necessary to relieve actual sickness and suffering.

C. Grover, U. S. A.,
Brev. Maj. Gen. Commanding.

(See *War Record*, Vol. XXXV, p. 162).

To-day there is abundant proof to show the most biased

mind, that President Jefferson Davis and General Robert E. Lee, did protest against the violation of the cartel of exchange, and did offer, for humanity's sake, to turn over to the United States all the wounded and sick Union prisoners of war held in the South, if the United States would send transports and take them away, and finally, General Robert E. Lee, in humanity's name, said, "Come and get all your prisoners of war, we cannot feed them, nor get medicines to keep them in health." All offers to exchange or send for their prisoners were rejected by Mr. Secretary Stanton, on part of the United States Government, and this as every one now knows was the cruelty inflicted on the prisoners of war in the South, and was not inflicted nor sanctioned by the Confederate Government.

There never was a Union soldier, prisoner of war, in the South placed under fire of his own guns by order of any one, and there is not one particle of proof that can show there was, but there is an abundance of proof to show the wanton cruelty of the United States to its prisoners of war, 1864-65, and the above is proof from their own records.

And it is a fact, proven beyond all question of doubt, that notwithstanding the South had no medicines, and could get none, to cure the sick, and keep men in health, that only nine (9) in each one hundred Union prisoners of war died in Southern prisons, while twelve (12) in every hundred Confederate prisoners of war died in the prisons of the North, where medicine and food were abundant to keep men in health. This should be a vindication of the South and her people from the slander of cruelty, and would be, but for the persistent slander of some of the pulpits and press of the North, that make the charges, to keep alive the hatred en-gendered by the war, which are used for political purposes, by the corrupt politicians who live politically on sectional hate.

We want only the truth; we ask for nothing else. We want to refute the slanders against the South and her people. Neither Jefferson Davis, President of the Confederate States, nor General Robert E. Lee, were ever cruel to any human being. But Secre-tary of War Stanton and his colleagues in power at Washington,

1861-65, were and they were guilty of all prisoners of war suffering on both sides, by stopping exchanges of prisoners of war.

– the Author

Major J. Ogden Murray
(1905)

CHAPTER ONE

History of the Incidents Leading Up to the Retaliation Measures Inflicted Upon the Six Hundred Confederate Officers With Official Correspondence Between Gen. J. G. Foster, U. S. A., Department of the South, and Gen. Samuel Jones, C. S. A., Commanding Charleston, S. C. Violation of the Cartel, etc.

There is no apology to be made by me for the publication of this work or history of the six hundred Confederate prisoners of war confined on Morris Island by order of the Federal government. It is put in print for two reasons: First, to preserve the record of this gallant band; second, to give to the world a true history of the wanton cruelty inflicted upon helpless prisoners of war, without the least shadow of excuse. The only information that the United States government had that there were six hundred Union soldiers, prisoners of war, under fire in Charleston, S.C, was based upon the word of runaway negroes, Confederate deserters, Union scallawags, and such people, whose word should not have been taken by any decent man without corroboration; yet Gen. J. G. Foster, U. S. A., commanding Department of the South, headquarters, Hilton Head, S. C., accepted the word of these creatures without question, and inflicted upon helpless prisoners of war cruelties that would have shamed Nero.

There never were any Union prisoners of war under fire of their own guns in any part of the South; there were never any prisoners of war treated with harshness or cruelty by order of the

Confederate government authorities; but on the contrary all was done to lessen the burden of prison life that could be done by the Richmond government, and men of the highest rank in the United States Army attest this fact. The cruelty charged against the South is as false as the tongues that utter it, and it has been proven false time and time again. Even Andersonville, that much maligned prison, has been proven to have been a very paradise in comparison to Camp Chase, Rock Island, Elmira, and other Yankee prisons.

The treatment meted to the six hundred Confederate officers, prisoners of war, confined on Morris Island, S. C, by the United States Secretary of War, is a blot upon the escutcheon of the United States that can never be blotted out nor removed. It was cowardly, it was inhuman, and cruel. The names of the men responsible for this cruelty must be written – and they will be written – upon history's blacklists of cruel men. Stanton, Foster, and Halleck, are names that must always cast a shadow upon the days of 1861-65.

There can be no excuse given for cruelty. There is no justification for it under the laws of God or man, and it has never been proven, yet, that the Confederate authorities treated or allowed to be treated harshly or unkindly Union prisoners of war. The stories told of cruelties to Union soldiers in Confederate prisons were the offsprings of the brains of perjured men, some of them never in a Confederate prison, nor never south beyond Washington city. The word of an ignorant negro or a Confederate deserter was given credence by the Washington authorities, when the testimony of, and letters of, such men as Generals Wessells, Scammon, and other honorable officers of the United States army, who were prisoners of war, was ignored. The records show most conclusively there were never any Union prisoners of war under fire in Charleston city or at any other point in the Confederacy; and, further, there never was any premeditated and planned cruelty perpetrated upon Union prisoners of war in Southern prisons like that inflicted upon Confederate prisoners of war in Northern military prisons. There were men, no doubt, both in the

North and South, who took delight in treating prisoners of war cruelly. Such men were both moral and physical cowards, and acted upon their own responsibility; but I do say the authorities at Washington city did plan, order, and execute wantonly, cruelties upon Confederate prisoners of war that can not be justified under any pretext; and I claim that no proof can be produced that the Confederate government did at any time countenance the slightest cruelty to its prisoners of war. The same rations given to the Confederate soldier in the field were issued to the Yankee prisoners of war in Confederate prisons. The greatest cruelty inflicted upon the Union prisoners of war in the South was inflicted by Edwin M. Stanton, United States Secretary of War, and Gen. U. S. Grant, when they refused to exchange prisoners of war. The records show that General Grant, by order of Stanton, stopped exchange and inflicted whatever hardships upon their own men they did suffer by this suspension of exchange; and it is a matter of recorded proof that both President Davis and Gen. Robert E. Lee, to alleviate the suffering of the prisoners of war in Southern prisons, offered, if the United States government would send transports, to turn over all prisoners held by the Confederate authorities, in humanity's name.

Here are two extracts from Union witnesses to prove on which side cruelty shall be charged, and I do not hesitate to say these witnesses do most effectively offset Libby or Andersonville if the stories of the prisons be true.

On February 9, 1862, Judge Ould, Confederate States Commissioner of Exchange, wrote Colonel Ludlow, United States Exchange Commissioner:

> I see from your own papers that some dozen of our men, captured at Arkansas Pass, were allowed to freeze to death in one night at Camp Douglas. I appeal to our common instincts against such atrocious inhumanity (*War Records*, p. 257).

There is no denial of this charge to be found in the *War Records*. On May 10, 1863, Dr. William H. Van Buren, of New York, on behalf of the United States "Sanitary Commission," reported to the Secretary of War at Washington the condition of the hospitals of the prisoners of war at Camp Douglas, near Chicago, and Gratiot Street prison, St. Louis. In this report he incorporates the statements of Drs. Hun and Cogswell, of Albany, N.Y., who had been employed by the "Sanitary Commission" to inspect hospitals. And Dr. Van Buren commends these gentlemen as men of high character and eminent fitness for the work to which they had been assigned. It is from the statement of these Northern gentlemen that I quote. They caption their report from Albany, April 5, 1863, and say, among other, things as follows:

> In our experience, we have never witnessed so painful a spectacle as that presented by these wretched inmates; without change of clothing, covered with vermin, they lie in cots, without mattresses, or with mattresses furnished by private charity, without sheets or bedding of any kind, except blankets, often in rags; in wards reeking with filth and foul air. The stench is most offensive. We carefully avoid all exaggeration of statement, but we give some facts which speak for themselves. From January 27, 1863, when the prisoners (in number about 3,800) arrived at Camp Douglas, to February 18th, the day of our visit, 385 patients have been admitted to the hospitals, of whom 130 have died. This mortality of 33 per cent, does not express the whole truth, for of the 148 patients then remaining in the hospital a large number must have since died. Besides this, 130 prisoners have died in barracks, not having been able to gain admission even to the miserable accommodations of the hospital, and at the time of our visit 150 persons were sick in barracks waiting for room in hospital. Thus it will be seen that 260 out of the 3,800 prisoners had died in twenty-one days, a rate of mortality which, if continued, would secure their total extermination in about 320 days.

Then they go on to describe the conditions at St. Louis, showing them to be worse than at Chicago, and after stating that the conditions of these prisons are "discreditable to a Christian people," they add:

It surely is not the intention of our government to place these prisoners in a position which will secure their extermination by pestilence in less than a year.

See also Report of United States Surgeon A. M. Clarke, Vol. VI, Series 71, p. 371, p. 113.

Now let me ask this question: Why did not the representatives of this same "Sanitary Commission," when they were publishing their slanderous report of September, 1864, as to the way Union prisoners were treated in Southern prisons, which report they illustrated with skeletons alleged to have come from Libby, Andersonville, and other prisons in the South, make at least mention of the condition of the things found by them in Camp Douglas and Gratiot Street prison hospitals?

One word on violation of the exchange cartel: On May 13, 1863, Judge Ould wrote Colonel Ludlow, calling his attention to the "large number of Confederate officers captured long since and still held by the United States," threatened retaliation if the unjust and harsh course then pursued by the Federals towards our officers was persevered in, and concluded as follows:

Nothing is now left as to those whom our protests have failed to release but to resort to retaliation. The Confederate government is anxious to avoid a resort to that harsh measure. In its name I make a final appeal for that justice to our imprisoned officers and men which your own agreements have declared to be their due (*War Records*, p. 607).

Again on May 14, 1863, Judge Ould wrote, naming several of Mosby's men who had been carried to the Old Capitol prison. He then said:

They are retained under the allegation that they are bushwhackers and guerillas. Mosby's command is in the Confederate service, in every sense of the term. He is regularly commissioned, and his force is as strictly Confederate as any in our army. Why is this done? This day I have cleaned every prison in my control as far as I know. If there is any detention anywhere, let me know and I will rectify it. I am compelled to complain of this thing in almost every communication. You will not deem me passionate when I assure you it will not be endured any longer. If these men are not delivered, a stern retaliation will be made immediately (Id., p. 632).

This being the condition of things, on May 25, 1863, the following order was issued by the Federals:

War Department, Washington, D. C.,
May 25, 1863.

General Schofield:

No Confederate officer will be paroled or exchanged till further orders. They will be kept in close confinement, and be strongly guarded. Those already paroled will be confined.

H. W. Halleck,
General-in-Chief.

Why was the cartel suspended? Surely not by request of the Confederate authorities. Who was responsible for this inhuman work that inflicted so much suffering upon the Union prisoners of war in the hands of the South that could not care for them nor feed them?

The question is asked in all honesty because this suspension of the cartel by the United States government was the cause of the suffering of the Union prisoners of war in the South.

Edwin M. Stanton, Secretary of War, and Gen. Henry W. Halleck are responsible for the suffering of Union prisoners of war in the South, and not President Davis nor the Confederate government. Mr. Charles A. Dana, the Assistant Federal Secretary of War, in an editorial in his paper, the New York *Sun*, said in commenting on a letter President Davis wrote to Mr. James Lyons in reply to some strictures Mr. Blaine had made upon the question of prisoners of war:

This letter shows clearly, we think, that the Confederate authorities, and especially Mr. Davis, ought not to be held responsible for the terrible privations, sufferings and injuries which our men had to endure while they were kept in Confederate military prisons. The fact is unquestionable, that while the Confederates desired to exchange prisoners, to send our men home, and to get back their own, General Grant steadily and strenuously resisted such an exchange. * * *

"It is hard on our men held in Southern prisons," said Grant, in an official communication, "not to exchange them; but it is humane to those left in the ranks to fight our battles. If we commence a system of exchanges which liberates all prisoners taken, we will have to fight on until the whole South is exterminated. If we hold those caught they are no more than dead men."
* * *

This evidence must be taken as conclusive. It proves that it was not the Confederate authorities who insisted on keeping our prisoners in distress, want, and disease, *but the commander of our own armies.* * * * Moreover there is no evidence whatever, that it was practicable for the Confederate authorities to feed our prisoners any better than they were fed, or to give them any better care and attention than they received. The food was insufficient, the care and attention were insufficient, no doubt, and yet the condition of our prisoners was not worse than that of the Confederate soldiers in the field, except in so far as the condition of those in prison must of necessity be worse than that of men who are free and active outside.

This is the statement of the Federal Assistant Secretary of War during the war, and he knew whereof he wrote. He was the man who ordered General Miles to put shackles on President Davis, and, as a fact, did hate Mr. Davis and all things Southern. Yet he did tell the truth, and is most conclusive, and puts the blame for the hardships of the Union soldiers in Southern prisons where it belongs, and clearly points out the guilty party.

When we add to this the pregnant fact that the report of the Federal Secretary of War, Mr. Stanton, dated July 19, 1866, shows that of the Federal prisoners of war confined in the military prisons of the South, only 22,576 died, whilst of Confederate prisoners of war confined in Northern prisons, 26,436 died; the report of the Federal Surgeon-General Barnes, published after the war, showing that the whole number of Federal prisoners captured and held in the South during the war was 270,000, while the whole number of Confederate prisoners confined in Northern prisons was 220,000 (from this report we see that while the South held 50,000 more prisoners of war than the North, the deaths in the South were four thousand less. The rate of deaths in Southern prisons was eight in each 100 men. The rate in the Northern prisons of Confederates was twelve in each 100), I think it is useless to go further into discussion of this matter, but leave our case to the bar of impartial history.

I hesitated before going into this history of the Immortal Six Hundred, but frequent requests of comrades of the six hundred who were true unto the end of the ordeal induced me to undertake the task and do the best I could in compliance with their request. I can only tell the story from a personal experience.

There were many incidents that took place that did not come under my observation, and not being able at this late date to obtain them, much must go untold. I shall tell the story without malice or bitterness against those men responsible for our bad treatment. I have no bitterness against the men who wore the blue. The story is part of the unwritten history of the Confederate States; it is the story of the men who could surrender life, but not principle to save their lives. These men were the men who made the fame of the Confederate soldier, and gave the world an example of courage equal to that of Sparta or Rome.

There shall be no exaggeration of facts. God knows the facts are ghastly enough without adding to them. I do not blame all men who wore the blue for our bad treatment. While prisoners of war we came in contact with some brave, honorable men, who appreciated our helpless condition; and they often showed us their humanity while in their custody. The bombproof fellows who were cruel to prisoners can have no part in the meetings of the brave men of to-day, who come together clasping hands over the bloody past – forgetting its bitterness.

> The man who hates knows no law but selfishness. They
> hate the precepts of the Master. They ignore His command, "love
> thy neighbor."

There is no part of the conflict of 1861-65 that has been so imperfectly told, and no subject of more importance than the history of the military prisons North and South. The story must be truthfully told by the historian. If it is not truthfully told it can not and should not have place in history. Nothing is history if it is not absolutely correct. If future generations are to sit as judges of the past we must give them data of absolute truth upon which they can base a verdict. If we in the least deviate from this line judgment must be against us.

In telling the story of the Six Hundred Immortals – the Confederate officers, prisoners of war – who were taken from Fort Delaware prison in August, 1864, by order of Edwin M. Stanton, Federal Secretary of War, and confined in a stockade on Morris Island, S. C, under fire of the Confederate batteries shelling that point, we will tell it truthfully, without the least exaggeration, that those who read may make honest judgment and render fair verdict. It is not intended that this work shall be a general history of military prisons. It is only a history of the Six Hundred Immortals that will refute, so far as it can, the repeated and almost constant charge made by the pulpit and press of the North that the Confederate authorities were cruel and inhuman to their prisoners of war. These charges of cruelty made by the North are worthy the attention of the South's historians; and now that the passions of the war have, to a great degree, cooled, the facts can be presented and the responsibility fixed, so that when the Confederate soldier of the war of 1861-65 has passed over the picket line of life into the unknown land, and the honest verdict of history is rendered, our good names and records as soldiers will not be blackened by the blot of cruelty, nor our peerless leaders be painted by the tongue of slander with cruelty to prisoners of war.

I will corroborate my story of the Immortal Six Hundred by the official records, so far as the United States government has printed the record under the supervision of the War Department.

As stated before, this history is of the Six Hundred Immortals only. What led up to this cruel retaliation upon the six hundred prisoners of war by the United States government is not very clear. From the official records we can only glean the fact that much stock was taken in the word and stories told by deserters, runaway negroes, and scallawags generally, without the least attempt by the United States officials to verify the truth of their statements. Below is the official correspondence:

Headquarters Department South Carolina,
Georgia, and Florida.

Charleston, S.C, June 13, 1864.

Maj.-Gen. John G. Foster,
        Commanding U. S. Forces, Coast of South Carolina.

General:
        Five general officers and forty-five field officers of the United States Army, all of them prisoners of war, have been sent to this city for safe keeping. They have been turned over to Brigadier-General Ripley, commanding First Military District of this department, who will see that they are provided with commodious quarters in a part of the city occupied by non-combatants, the majority of whom are women and children. It is proper, however, that I should inform you that it is part of the city which has been for many months exposed day and night to the fire of your guns.

Very respectfully your obedient servant,
Sam Jones,
Maj.-Gen. Commanding

(*War Records*, Vol. XXXV, Part 2, p. 132).

In this letter Gen. Sam Jones says most clearly where the Union prisoners of war are quartered in Charleston city: "In that section of the city where the non-combatants – women and children – are housed." On June 16, 1864, Maj.-Gen. J.G. Foster replied to General Jones's letter as follows:

Headquarters Department of the South,
Hilton Head, S.C, June 16, 1864.

Maj.-Gen. Samuel Jones,
        Commanding Confederate Forces,
        Department South Carolina, Georgia, and Florida.

General:

I have to acknowledge the receipt this day of your communication of the 13th instant, informing me that five generals and forty-five field officers of the United States Army – prisoners of war – have been sent to Charleston for safe keeping; that they have been turned over by you to Brigadier-General Ripley with instructions to see that they are provided with quarters in a part of the city occupied by noncombatants, the majority of which latter, you state, are women and children. You add that you deem it proper to inform me that it is a part of the city which has been for many months exposed to the fire of our guns.

Many months since Major-General Gillmore, U.S.A., notified General Beaureguard, then commanding at Charleston, that the city would be bombarded. This notice was given that non-combatants might be removed and thus women and children be spared from harm. General Beaureguard, in a communication to General Gillmore, dated August 22, 1863, informed him that the non-combatant population of Charleston would be removed with all possible celerity. That women and children have been since retained by you in a part of the city which has been for many months exposed to fire is a matter decided by your own sense of humanity. I must, however, protest against your action in thus placing defenseless prisoners of war in a position exposed to constant bombardment. It is an indefensible act of cruelty, and can be designed only to prevent the continuance of our fire upon Charleston. That city is a depot of military supplies. It contains not merely arsenals but also foundries and factories for the manufacture of munitions of war. In its shipyards several ironclads have already been completed, while others are still upon the stocks in course of construction. Its wharves and banks of the rivers on both sides of the city are lined with batteries. To destroy these means of continuing the war is, therefore, our object of duty. You seek to defeat this effort, not by means known to honorable warfare, but by placing unarmed and helpless prisoners under our fire.

I have forwarded your communication to the President, with the request that he will place in my custody an equal number of prisoners of like grades, to be kept by me in positions exposed to the fire of your guns so long as you continue the course stated in your communication.

I have the honor to be
Very respectfully your obedient servant,
J.G. Foster,
Maj.-Gen. Commanding.

(*War Records*, Vol. XXXV, Part 2, pp. 134-135).

General Foster, after reply to Gen. Sam Jones's letter, sent to Washington the following letter by hand of his aide-de-camp, Maj. E.W. Strong, which was wired from Fortress Monroe to Washington, D.C.:

Fortress Monroe, Va.,
11.30 p.m., June 19, 1864.

Maj.-Gen. H.W. Halleck,
Washington, D.C.

I am directed by Major-General Foster to forward to you the following dispatch.

———————

Headquarters South Carolina,
via Fortress Monroe, Va.

Maj.-Gen. Halleck,
Washington, D.C.

I have the honor to report that I have to-day received from Maj.-Gen. Sam Jones, commanding the Rebel forces in the department, a letter stating that five general officers and forty-five field officers of the United States Army – prisoners of war

– had been placed in Charleston city, to be retained there under fire. Against this wicked act I have protested. In meantime the fire on the city is continued. I respectfully ask that an equal number of Rebel officers of equal rank may be sent to me in order that I may place them under the enemy's fire as long as our officers are exposed in Charleston. I send Maj. E. W. Strong, in steamer *Mary A. Boardman*, to Fortress Monroe to await your answer and, if my request is granted, to bring the prisoners. Copies of my correspondence will be mailed to you as soon as Major Strong arrives at Fortress Monroe.

J.G. Foster,
Major-General.

E.N. Strong,
Major, and aide-de-camp.

General Foster did not state all the facts in his telegram to Washington city, nor did he think proper to await the due course of mail, but wired General Halleck a garbled and false statement of the facts in the case (see *War Records*, Vol. XXXV, Part 2, p. 141).

On June 27, 1864, the following letter was sent by General Halleck to General Foster, which shows clearly how anxious these worthies were to begin their cruelty upon helpless human beings – prisoners of war.

Washington, D.C, June 27, 1864.

Maj.-Gen. J. G. Foster,
       Department of the South.

General:

Your letter of 16th instant, transmitting the correspondence between yourself and the commanding general of the Rebel forces at Charleston in regard to confining our officers – prisoners of war – in part of that city exposed to the fire of our batteries is just received. The Secretary of War has directed an equal number of Rebel generals and field officers to be sent to you, by Major Strong, *to be treated* in precisely the same manner as the

Lieutenant John F. Lytton
5th Virginia

enemy treats ours; that is, to be placed in a position where they will be most exposed to the fire of the Rebels. In whatever position they may be placed, whether in field or in batteries or vessels, you will take every proper precaution to prevent *their escape or recapture*, putting them in irons if necessary for that purpose. The Secretary of War directs on that point you will exercise great vigilance, and that the *Rebel officers will be treated with same severity that they treat ours*.

Very respectfully your obedient servant,

H. W. Halleck,
Maj.-Gen., Chief of Staff.

(*War Records*, Vol. XXXV, Part 2, p. 143).

Had Gen. J. G. Foster, U. S. A., communicated by flag of truce, which he could have done, with his officers, the prisoners of war, in Charleston, he would have been saved the humiliation of having his letter and its statements refuted over the signatures, in a joint letter, of his own prisoners of war confined in Charleston city. They say in their letter they are not under fire, in no danger whatever, and are treated humanely, courteously by the Confederate authorities from the major-general down to the sentinels on guard.

On June 23, 1864, Major Strong was sent the following order by Colonel Hoffman, Commissary of Prisoners of War, U.S.A.:

Office of the Commissary of Prisoners,
Washington, D. C, June 23, 1864.

Maj. E. N. Strong, A. D. C,
Washington, D.C.

Major:

The Rebel prisoners of war, officers whom you are to receive to conduct to Major-General Foster at Hilton Head, S.C, are at Fort Delaware, and Brigadier-General Schoepf, the commanding officer at that post, has been instructed to deliver them to you. You will therefore proceed without delay, in the steamer provided for the purpose by the Quartermaster-General's Department, to Fort Delaware, and having received the generals and field officers referred to, you will return to Hilton Head, and deliver them to Major-General Foster, commanding Department of the South. The guard detailed to accompany you from Fort Delaware is expected to return from Hilton Head with as little delay as possible.

W. Hoffman,
Colonel 3d Infantry,
Commissary-General Prisoners.

After receipt of this order Major Strong went to Fort Delaware and the following Confederate officers were turned over to him to be, and were, taken to Hilton Head:

Maj.-Gen. Edward Johnson, C.S.A.
Maj.-Gen. Franklin Gardner, C.S.A.
Brig.-Gen. J.J. Archer, C.S.A.
Brig.-Gen. George H. Steuart, C.S.A.
Brig.-Gen. M. Jeff. Thompson, C.S.A.
Col. R. Welby Carter, 1st Va. Cav.[1]
Col. N. Cobb, 44th Inft.
Col. Basil W. Duke, Kentucky.
Col. M.J. Ferguson, 16th Va.
Col. J.M. Hanks, Kentucky.
Col. Richard C. Morgan, Kentucky.
Col. James A. Pell, Kentucky.
Col. W.H. Peebles, Georgia.
Col. A.S. Vandeventer, 50th Va.
Col. W.W. Ward, Tennessee.
Col. William M. Barbour, N.C.
Col. John N. Brown, S.C.
Col. J.A. Jaquess, C.S.A.
Col. B.E. Caudill, Kentucky.
Col. W.H. Forney, Alabama.
Lieut.-Col. James F. Brewer, Tennessee.

---

1. For some reason, Colonel Carter did not go.

Lieut.-Col. F. H. Daugherty, Tennessee.
Lieut.-Col. P. E. Devant, Georgia.
Lieut.-Col. J. P. Fitzgerald, 23d Va.
Lieut.-Col. C. L. Haynes, 27th Va.
Lieut.-Col. O. A. Patton, Kentucky.
Lieut.-Col. William M. Parsley, N. C.
Lieut.-Col. A. L. Swingley, Tennessee.
Lieut.-Col. Joseph Tucker, Tennessee.
Lieut.-Col. D. H. L. Martz, 10th Va.
Lieut.-Col. A. Dupree, C. S. A.
Lieut.-Col. Thomas C. Jackson, C. S. A.
Lieut.-Col. M. J. Smith, C. S. A.
Maj. D. W. Anderson, 44th Va.
Lieut.-Col. J. W. Caldwell, Kentucky.
Lieut.-Col. J. T. Carson, Georgia.
Lieut.-Col. W. T. Ennett, N. C.
Lieut.-Col. J. E. Groce, Mississippi.
Lieut-Col. H. A. Highley, C. S. A.
Lieut.-Col. E. M. Henry, C. S. A.
Lieut.-Col. E. A. Nash, Georgia.
Lieut.-Col. L. J. Perkins, 50th Va.
Lieut.-Col. George H. Smith, Tennessee.
Lieut.-Col. E. J. Sanders, Mississippi.
Lieut.-Col. T. Steele, Kentucky.
Lieut.-Col. Thomas B. Webber, Kentucky
Lieut.-Col. J. M. Wilson, Louisiana.
Lieut.-Col. W. H. Manning, Louisiana.
Lieut.-Col. T. E. Upshaw, 13th Va.
Lieut.-Col. F. F. Warley, S. C.
Lieut.-Col. W. L. Davidson, N. C.

These officers left Fort Delaware in June, 1864, in charge of Major Strong, U. S. A., and in due course were delivered to Major-General Foster, commanding United States forces at Hilton Head, S. C. After the arrival of these prisoners correspondence took place between Maj.-Gen. J. G. Foster, U. S. A., and Gen. Sam Jones, C. S. A., commanding Confederate forces, Charleston, S. C, which will be found in Vol. XXXV, *War Records*.

It was General Foster's intention to place these Confederate officers – prisoners of war – under fire on Morris Island. But he found, upon investigation and from correspondence, that his hasty action upon General Jones's letter had gotten him a very large elephant on his hands, which he could not control; and he also had the testimony in letters from the Union prisoners of war confined in Charleston city, that they were not under fire at all, and all Foster had to bolster up his infamous scheme and slander was the testimony of the runaway negroes and Confederate deserters. Here is the letter of protest against Foster's action:

Charleston, S.C., July 1, 1864.

Maj.-Gen. J.G. Foster,
    Commanding Department South,
       Hilton Head, S.C.

General:
    The journals of this morning inform us, for the first time, that five general officers of the Confederate service have arrived at Hilton Head, with a view to their being subjected to the same treatment that we are receiving here. We think it just to ask for these officers every kindness and courtesy that you can extend to them in acknowledgment of the fact that we, at this time, are as pleasantly and comfortably situated as is possible for prisoners of war, receiving from the Confederate authorities every privilege that we could desire or expect, nor are we unnecessarily exposed to fire.
    Respectfully, General, your obedient servants,

H.W. Wessells,
T. Seymour,
E.P. Scammon,
C.A. Heckman,
Alexander Shaler,
    Brig.-Gens. U.S. Vols.
    Prisoners of War

(*War Records*, Vol. XXXV, p. 163).

Charleston, S.C, July 1, 1864.

Brig.-Gen. L. Thomas,
    Adjt.-Gen. U.S.A., Washington, D.C.
        (Through Maj.-Gen. J.G. Foster, commanding Department of the South, Hilton Head, S.C.)

General:

We desire respectfully to represent through you to our authorities our firm belief that a prompt exchange of prisoners of war in the hands of the Southern Confederacy (if exchanges are to be made) is called for by every consideration of humanity. There are many thousands confined at southern points of the Confederacy in a climate to which they are unaccustomed, deprived of much of the food, clothing, and shelter they have habitually received, and it is not surprising that from these and other causes that need not be enumerated here much suffering, sickness, and death should ensue. In this matter the statements of our own officers are confirmed by the Southern journals. And while we cheerfully submit to any policy that may be decided upon by our government, we would urge that the great evils that must result from any delay that is not desired should be obviated by the designation of some point in this vicinity at which exchange might be made, a course, we are induced to believe, that would be acceded to by the Confederate authorities.

And we are, General, very respectfully your obedient servants,

H.W. Wessells,
T. Seymour,
E.P. Scammon,
C.A. Heckman,
Alexander Shaler,
    Brig.-Gens. U.S. Vols.,
        Prisoners of War

(*War Records*, Vol. XXXV, p. 162).

Headquarters Department of South Carolina,
Georgia, and Florida.

Charleston, S.C, July 1, 1864.

Maj.-Gen. J.G. Foster,
     Commanding Department of South
     Hilton Head.

General:

I send with this a letter addressed by five general officers of the United States Army, now prisoners of war in this city, to Brig.-Gen. L. Thomas, Adjutant-General United States Army, recommending and asking an exchange of prisoners of war. I fully concur in opinion with the officers who have signed the letter that there should be an exchange of prisoners of war and, although I am not instructed by my government to enter into negotiations for that purpose, I have no doubt it is willing and desirous now, as it has ever been, to exchange prisoners of war with your government on just and honorable plans. Our difficulty in the way of carrying out the cartel of exchange agreed upon between the two governments would not exist, that I am aware of, if the exchange was conducted between you and myself. If, therefore, you think proper to communicate on the subject with your government I will, without delay, communicate with mine, and it may be that we can enter into an agreement, subject to approval of our respective governments, by which the prisoners of war now languishing in confinement may be released. I should be glad to aid in so humane work, and, to the end that there may be no unnecessary delay on my part, I have directed an officer of my staff, Maj. John F. Lay, Assistant Adjutant and Inspector-General, charged with the delivery of this, to wait a reasonable time in vicinity of Port Royal Ferry for your answer. He is fully informed of my views on this subject, and, if you desire it, will confer with you or any officer you may designate.

Very respectfully your obedient servant,

Sam Jones,
Maj.-Gen. Commanding

(*War Records*, Vol. XXXV, pp. 161-162).

Headquarters Department of the South,
July 4, 1864.

Maj.-Gen. Samuel Jones,
   Commanding Confederate Forces,
      South Carolina, Georgia, and Florida,
         Charleston, S.C.

I have received your letter of the 1st inst. covering a letter from the five general officers of the United States Army now prisoners of war in Charleston to Brig.-Gen. L. Thomas, Adjutant-General United States Army.

I fully reciprocate your desire for an exchange of prisoners of war, but before any steps can be taken to effect it will be necessary for you to withdraw from exposure to our fire these officers now confined in Charleston. I have not yet placed your prisoners in a similar position of exposure.

Very respectfully your obedient servant,

J.G. Foster,
Maj.-Gen. Commanding

(*War Records*, Vol. XXXV, p. 164).

————————————

Headquarters Department of the South,
July 4, 1864.

Brig.-Gens. T. Seymour, H. W. Wessells,
   C. A. Heckman, E. P. Scammon, and
      Alexander Shaler.

My Dear Friends:

I have received your letter of 1st inst. and will observe your wishes in the treatment of the prisoners now placed in my hands. We all regret very much the circumstances of your being placed under our fire in Charleston, and every one feels justly indignant at this barbarous treatment of prisoners of war. I will endeavor to have your wants supplied so far as possible, and have requested the Sanitary Commission to forward what articles they have on hand suited to your necessities. I believe your exchange might be effected rank for rank provided, as a first step, General Jones should relieve you from your position of exposure to fire.

Very respectfully and truly yours,

J.G. Foster,
Maj.-Gen. Commanding

(*War Records*, Vol. XXXV, p. 164).

Headquarters Department
South Carolina, Georgia, and Florida.

Charleston, S.C, July 13, 1864.

Maj.-Gen. J.G. Foster,
Commanding United States Forces,
Hilton Head, S.C.

General:
Your letter of 4th date in reply to mine of 1st inst. has been received. I am pleased to know that you reciprocate my desire for an exchange of prisoners, but regret that you should require as a condition precedent to any negotiations for this end that I should remove from their present location the United States prisoners of war now in this city. Such a course on my part would be implied admission that those officers are unduly exposed and treated with unnecessary rigor, which they themselves assure you in their letter of 1st inst. is not the case. I regard the exchange of prisoners as demanded alike by rules of civilized warfare and the dictates of common humanity; and to require a change of location which you have every reason to know the prisoners do not themselves desire is to throw an unnecessary obstacle in the way of accomplishing this end, and thus retain prisoners of war in irksome confinement. The change I most prefer would be to send them to your headquarters and this may be done, unless defeated by obstacles interposed by yourself or your government.

I was notified of your request to send a staff officer to meet one of yours at Port Royal at 2 p.m. to-day, too late to comply therewith. I have, however, directed the officer of your staff to be informed that I would send an officer to meet him at 4 p.m. to-morrow and have accordingly directed Maj. J.F. Lay, Assistant Adjutant and Inspector-General, to take charge of this letter and deliver it at Port Royal Ferry.

I repeat that he is fully advised of my views, and, should you desire it, will confer with you or any officer of your staff whom you may designate.

Very respectfully your obedient servant,
Sam Jones,
Maj.-Gen. Commanding

(*War Records*, Vol. XXXV, pp. 174-175).

All this correspondence was forwarded by General Foster to Washington, and receipt thereof acknowledged by General Halleck:

Headquarters Department
South Carolina, Georgia, and Florida,
Charleston, S.C, July 13, 1864.

Maj.-Gen. J.G. Foster,
Commanding United States Forces,
Hilton Head, S.C.

General:
I have received your letter of the 1st inst. Mine of the 13th and 22d ult. indicate, with all necessary precision, the location of the United States officers who are prisoners of war in this city. I can not well be more minute without pointing out the very houses in which they are confined, and for reasons very easily understood I am sure that this will not be expected. If statements in my letter of the 22d ult. are insufficient the letter of the five general officers, dated 1st inst., in which they assure you they "are as pleasantly and comfortably situated as is possible for prisoners of war, receiving from the Confederate authorities every privilege that we (they) could desire or expect, nor are we (they) unnecessarily exposed to fire" gives you all the information in regard to their treatment that you can reasonably desire. In conclusion let me add that I presume from copy of your confi-

dential order of 29th ult. that you were commanding in person
the troops operating against the city, and, as you had particularly
requested me to communicate with you only by way of Port
Royal Ferry, I felt bound to delay my reply until I was assured
it would promptly reach you by route you were pleased to indicate.

Very respectfully your obedient servant,

Sam Jones,
Maj.-Gen. Commanding.

After this correspondence came the following letter, an
exchange was made of these officers, and they were not placed
under fire.

Headquarters Department South,
Hilton Head, S.C, July 29, 1864.

Maj.-Gen. Sam Jones,
    Commanding Confederate Forces,
      South Carolina, Georgia, and Florida.

General:
    I have the honor to inform you that the Secretary of War
has authorized me to exchange any prisoners of war in my hands
rank for rank or their equivalent, such exchange being a special
one. In accordance with the above I send Major Anderson to
make arrangements as to time and place for exchange.
    I have the honor to be very respectfully your obedient
servant,

J.G. Foster,
Major-General.

General Foster sent the following note to the Union generals – prisoners of war – in Charleston city:

Headquarters Department South,
Hilton Head, S. C, July 29, 1864.

General Wessels, etc., etc.

My Dear General: – I have just received authority to exchange the prisoners in my hands rank for rank or their equivalent, according to cartel. I send aide-de-camp to make arrangements for exchange.

Yours truly,

J.G. Foster

(*War Records*, Vol. XXXV, Part 2, p. 199).

On August 4, 1864, subsequent to the exchange of the general and field officers, General Foster wrote to General Halleck, chief of staff, U.S.A., Washington, D.C, that he (Foster) had obtained information from Rebel deserters and runaway negroes, and escaped Union prisoners of war, that the Confederate authorities were anxious for exchange of prisoners of war, and that he (General Foster) could manage the matter and arrange to have the exchange take place in Charleston Harbor. He also tells Halleck, in this letter, that there are six hundred Union officers – prisoners of war – brought from Macon, Ga., to Charleston to induce the United States authorities to make exchange of prisoners of war; but he (Foster) will notify Gen. Sam Jones at Charleston, that no more exchange of prisoners will be made in Charleston Harbor. Both Gen. J.G. Foster and Secretary of War Stanton knew that Federal prisoners of war were dying at the rate of seventy per day because the Confederate authorities can not furnish them proper medicine. Yet the United States government will not exchange nor relieve their own prisoners. Here is proof positive – official admission – by the highest officials of the United States that they will not exchange prisoners of war, although the Confederate government is willing to make exchange, or give up all the sick and wounded Federal prisoners in their hands if the United States will send transports and take them away.

General Grant said it was much cheaper to feed Rebel prisoners than fight them, and the Washington authorities acted upon the suggestion and broke off the exchange of prisoners of war. Mr. Stanton believed it was cheaper to starve Rebel prisoners of war than put guns in their hands. There was nothing in the way to prevent the exchange of prisoners of war except the inhu-

Captain Bruce Gibson
6th Virginia Cavalry

manity of Edwin M. Stanton, Federal Secretary of War. He did not care for the Union prisoners of war. He hated the Confederate prisoners with a deadly hate (see *War Records*, Vol. XXXV, p. 213).

After this correspondence came the call, by Gen. J. G. Foster, for six hundred Confederate officers – prisoners of war – to be tortured on Morris Island, S. C, under fire of their own guns, and be starved upon rotten corn meal and pickle at Hilton Head, S.C, and at Fort Pulaski, Ga., by order of the United States government. It can not be proven that the Confederate authorities at any time placed Federal prisoners of war under fire or treated them inhumanely; nor can General Foster's friends nor Edwin M. Stanton's friends give the least excuse for the brutality of those men. Why the exchange of prisoners was stopped is given in plain terms over Gen. U. S. Grant's signature:

City Point, Va., August 27, 1864, 5 p.m.

Secretary of War,
        Washington:

Please inform Maj.-Gen. J. G. Foster that in no circumstances will he be allowed to make exchange of prisoners of war. Exchanges simply re-enforce the enemy at once, whilst we do not get the benefit of those received for two or three months and lose the majority entirely. I telegraph this from just hearing 500 or 600 more prisoners had been sent to Major-General Foster.

U. S. Grant,
        Lieutenant-General

(*War Records*, Vol. XXXV, p. 254).

Comment upon this dispatch is unnecessary. General Grant preferred to feed Rebels to fighting them, even if his own men must suffer in Confederate prisons where there was not food to give them. Gen. J.G. Foster, on June 27, 1864, wrote this letter to General Halleck, which shows he had no proofs that Union prisoners of war were under fire in Charleston city:

Headquarters Department of the South,
Hilton Head, S.C, June 27, 1864.

Maj.-Gen. H.W. Halleck,
  Chief of Staff, Armies United States,
    Washington, D.C.

General:

I have received your letter of the 21st and will endeavor to carry out your instructions and those of the Secretary of War to the very letter. I shall first endeavor to ascertain from Gen. Samuel Jones the degree of exposure, the kind and amount of rations, the general comforts, as beds, blankets, etc., etc., which are given to our prisoners, and then give the same to the Rebel prisoners. Every precaution will be taken to prevent escape or recapture.

I have the honor to be very respectfully
Your obedient servant,
J.G. Foster,
Maj.-Gen. Commanding

(*War Records*, Vol. XXXV, p. 150).

On July 21st General Foster received reply from his own prisoners in Charleston, telling exactly how kind they were treated (see General Scammon, *et al*, letter).

CHAPTER TWO

Fort Delaware. Rumors of Exchange. Order to Get Ready For Exchange. Saying Good-Bye. Packing Us On Steamship *Crescent City*.

Fort Delaware is built upon Pea Patch Island, in the Delaware River, midway of the stream between the New Jersey and Delaware shores. The structure is of brick, strong and durable. In the years 1861-65 the United States government utilized this Fort and Island as a military prison for the confinement of its prisoners of war. On the grounds of the island were built large wooden barracks separated into compartments, one of which was occupied by the Confederate officers – prisoners of war – the other by the enlisted men of the Confederacy who were held as prisoners. In the officers' side of this huge barracks, in the month of August, 1864, there were confined about 1,500 Confederate officers, captured in different battles in the South. This prison was fairly well conducted as to quarters, but most miserably as to rations. There were two large mess halls in which the prisoners were fed twice each day. The ration for breakfast was a chunk of bread cut wedge shape, a small portion of molasses as black as it was bitter, with a tin cup of very black coffee without sugar. The dinner menu card was a tin of soup (so called), a small piece of fat meat or beef, with slice of bread. For supper, wind. General Schoepf, U. S. V., commandant of the post, was a German, in his way a very good sort of an old fellow who no doubt did all he dare do, if report is correct, to alleviate the condition of Confederate prisoners of war. But he had about him some very mean, low men and prison officials. It was the general report amongst the prisoners of war that General Schoepf's wife was a Virginia lady who was in sympathy with her State and people. For this reason the General was not given a command in the field, but assigned to command of Fort Delaware prison that he might be kept under surveillance from Washington city. Report also said Capt. A. A. Ahl, his A. A. General, was forced upon him as a spy, and was not at all agreeable to the General. Ahl was the monitor placed over him by Secretary of War Stanton. If this report be true or false I do not know; but this I do know, that Captain Ahl did most intensely hate Confederate prisoners of war, and it is susceptible of proof that all the drastic orders issued for the government of Fort Delaware military prison were the conceptions and work of this fellow Ahl, and their enforcement compelled by his diction and domination over General Schoepf. While Fort Delaware prison was a hell upon earth for both officers and men – Confederate prisoners of war – it is said by prisoners of war confined in other Northern prisons to be the best of the lot. This fact can not be denied: where large numbers of men are confined and huddled together in a small space, deprived of liberty of roaming about, poorly fed, and unprotected from the elements, there must be necessarily much suffering and always much complaint, even if those in authority and control are disposed to be humane in their treatment of those in their custody.

The assistant provost-marshal in charge of the officers' prison at Fort Delaware was a Dutchman. Lieutenant Woolf, a graduate from the slums of Philadelphia city, a coarse, brutal creature, with all the mean, cowardly, and cruel instincts of the beast from which his name was taken; a fellow without culture, refinement, or gentility, who took much delight in insulting the Confederate officers that the misfortunes of war had made prisoners. It might be charity to place this fellow's meanness to the credit of his profound ignorance and slum breeding. His assistants were as miserable fellows as himself. Aided by these assistants and some miserable scoundrels – Confederate soldiers who deserted and took the oath of allegiance to the United States government – this fellow Woolf made the prison of the Confederate enlisted men a veritable torture-house. After taps were sounded I would often, with the aid of Lieut. Bob Bowie and Capt. Tom Roche, my bunk-mates, steal into the enlisted men's camp next to ours, separated by a high board fence, and hear from the men the story of the atrocious treatment this fellow Woolf, Hackout, and the other scoundrels would inflict upon the helpless sick and poor Confederate prisoners of war, who could not make complaint, for the reason their complaints never got further than Captain Ahl, who never brought the matter to General Schoepf's attention.

Through that incomprehensible means that can not be defined nor explained, and is only known to prisoners of war, we, confined in the officers' camp of the prison, became possessed of the knowledge that there was to be an exchange of prisoners of war. We seldom saw a paper; they were not allowed us. If a letter was written a prisoner that contained the least particle of information about the outside world save that which pertained strictly to family affairs it never reached the prisoner to whom it was written. Yet news would get into our camp, and we called such news "grape." One day in August, 1864, news spread over the camp that the fifty general and field officers that had been sent in June to Charleston Harbor, S.C, had been exchanged, and that a general exchange of prisoners of war, which had been stopped, would now be resumed, and very soon we would all be back in Dixie. The Yankee sergeant who called the prison roll confirmed this "grape," but gave no time as to when the exchange would begin or where it would take place. After this confirmation by the Yankee sergeant the only topic of conversation amongst the prisoners was exchange. The man who did not believe this "grape" of exchange was looked upon by his fellow-prisoners as a man to be watched – a skeptic beyond reformation. After days of exchange talk, and the impossibility to clinch or give body to the rumor, interest died and we all resumed the quiet of our prison life. But a day or two of rest and there came another "grape." A ser-

geant of the guard told one of our officers that a new cartel of
exchange had been agreed upon and would surely take place just
as soon as the status of negro troops could be arranged. A few
days after this another "grape" was received, which said the question of exchanging negro troops was laid aside by both the Confederate and Federal governments, and now exchange was sure.
All this was taken as gospel truth by the prisoners in our camp,
but it all proved to be moonshine. But to revive all the "grape" of
the past and add new fuel to the exchange fire excitement, on the
17th day of August, 1864, the Irish sergeant. Murphy, who called
the prison roll, informed us before we broke ranks, after roll call,
that there would be an exchange of prisoners in a few days. The
rolls were being made out and in a few days the first batch would
be sent South. To disbelieve this was the rankest treason; so we
all accepted the story, yet we looked upon it as "grape." But
about 3 o'clock p. m., of August 17th, confirmation of the story
came, when an officer from the fort and Sergeant Murphy came
into the pen and ordered the prisoners to fall into line and answer
to their names, as they would be called, for exchange.

We soon fell into line, the roll call began and went on,
while the prisoners stood in death-like silence awaiting the call of
their names, each man showing on his face the hope of his heart;
each asking God, in silent, earnest prayer, that his name would be
called. I have looked into the faces of men in line before a battle,
when defeat seemed inevitable; I have seen the joy of victory take
the place of doubt; but never in all my life did I witness joy so
perfect as in the face of the man whose name was called, nor woe
so abject as on the face of the men whose names were passed
over. My agitation and suspense was just as great as that of my
comrades, and I did silently, away down in the depths of my
heart, beg God for deliverance from Fort Delaware prison. When
the M's were called on the roll I could hardly contain myself;
when my name was called I could have shouted for joy; and I
really felt sorry that all my comrades were not included in the list,
as we thought, for exchange. And yet the sequel proved that
those whose names were upon the list were the unfortunates, and

not those whose names had been passed over. Not dreaming of the terrible fate in store for us and the terrible ordeal we would be subjected to, we laid down that night upon our hard board bunks and dreamed sweet dreams of home and the welcome awaiting us from loved ones and comrades in Dixie.

Early on the morning of August 18th the whole camp was up and astir, impatient for the word to move. We were going home to Dixie, and I do believe each man had in his heart a resolve that he would never forget Fort Delaware and its cruelty. We whose names had been called for exchange were in a state of anxiety all day, awaiting the order to forward. The sun went down and our hope went with it. No order to move had come; we were still prisoners of war in terrible Fort Delaware prison. Speculation was rife. "Grape" after "grape," story after story came to us, running riot with our disappointment. Each story was given credence until finally, in the chaos, we came to the conclusion that exchange was but a dream, and the Yankees had perpetrated a cruel joke upon us and no exchange was to be made. Despair drove hope from our hearts and sleep from our eyes, and suspense held us in her ruthless grasp until the morning of August 20th, when the sergeant who called the prison roll came in to perform his duty and announced the order that the men whose names had been called for exchange should pack up their belongings and be ready to leave the prison pen on a moment's notice. This brought back hope and drove from our hearts despair; yet doubt still held on, and the high board fence about the prison pen shut us in from liberty and the world without. At 3 o'clock p.m., August 20th, the order came "Fall into line all you men whose names shall be called and be ready for exchange." The roll-call was made, five hundred and fifty sound, healthy men, and fifty wounded men fell into line and marched by fours out through the prison gate – not for exchange, as we fondly hoped, but to torture as brutal and wanton, as cowardly as was ever inflicted upon helpless prisoners of war by the most barbarous nations of savage man. While we stood in line in the prison yard awaiting the order to move there were some most pathetic as well as ridiculous scenes enacted between comrades who had stood in line of battle together, were captured together, and now one was going home, the other to remain a captive. We were saying good-bye, telling those we left behind to be of good heart, that it would be but a few days before they would join us in Dixie. We of that six hundred can now look back and laugh at the promises then made, some of them of the most impossible character. I recall one promise made in which we were all in accord. That was, just as soon as we put foot in Richmond we were all to go in a body to President Davis and Congress and demand that our comrades in Fort Delaware should be sent for at once. The fact that it would require the consent of the United States government to carry out this promise never entered our head. Some of the partings between mess-mates and friends, on that August day in the long ago, come back to me most vividly as I write. There were men who had stood together in the line of death, comrades in the army, companions in prison, but now to be separated, perchance forever. I remember now Capt. George W. Kurtz, Company K, 5th Va. Inf., Stonewall Brigade, one of the best and bravest men of that famous old command, coming down the line. As he reached me he said, "Ogden," and the great big tears began to run down his cheeks, "when you get back to the Valley I want you to get Harry Gilmore and a lot of the old brigade; get all you can, go down the Valley, capture Sheridan and hold him until you get me out of this place. If I stay here I will surely die." Of course I promised to comply with his request, and we sealed the compact with a kiss. It strikes me now that Lieutenants Bob Bowie and Pete both promised to join me in the matter. Poor Bowie has passed over the river; Kurtz and Akers are left with myself. During this scene my eyes were not dry nor was my heart joyous in leaving behind me in prison grand old comrades I had learned to love. Poor dear old Pete Akers said to one of his Lynchburg comrades, "You just wait until I get home. Blamed if I don't go out and catch old Grant and half of his army and hold them until you all get out of this place. Poor dear old Pete, his great heart was

Lieutenant P. B. Akers
11th Virginia

always in touch with those in trouble. The Morgan men, the For-
rest men, and Wheeler men all made their comrades most extrav-
agant promises. But our dreams of exchange were never to be
realized. It was the hope hidden by anticipation that was to make
our disappointment acute.

Finally the Yankee officer in charge gave the order to
march. We passed out through the prison gate to begin a siege of
torture. We marched down to the fort wharf and were packed on
board of the small gulf steamship *Crescent City* like cattle are
packed in railroad cars. The hold of the ship was fitted up with
rough pine bunks to hold eight men – four below, four above –
there was very little ventilation, and in this cramped apartment six
hundred human beings – prisoners of war – were shipped to Gen.
J.G. Foster, U.S.A., Hilton Head, S.C, to be inhumanly and bru-
tally treated. Our condition one can imagine; it can not be described. Six hundred prisoners of war, three hundred guards, the
boat's crew – all on board of a small gulf steamer built to accommodate not more than half our number. After the last prisoner
was packed below decks the steamer pulled out into the channel
of the Delaware River on the Jersey side. Here we laid until midnight tide, when we steamed away for Fortress Monroe, fully
convinced that we were to be exchanged, landed in Dixie to meet
our loved ones and comrades. Believing this, we suffered the
discomforts of the prison-ship without murmur. The hold – or
hole – of the *Crescent City*, in which we were packed, was below
the ship's water line, imperfectly ventilated, poorly lighted, and
vile in odor of tar and grease. Our guard – 110th Home Guards
of Ohio, hundred-day men who had never seen any field service
– were perfectly devoid of feeling, especially so for Confederate
soldiers, and made our condition much worse than those English
soldiers in the Black Hole of Calcutta. The guards were quartered
upon the upper deck of the ship; one sentinel was stationed on
deck at the hatchway and one below at foot of the ladder leading
on deck, and under no circumstances would these sentinels allow
more than two or three prisoners on deck at one time to catch a
breath of fresh air.

After a run of one day our ship came to anchor under the guns of Fortress Monroe and the ships of the fleet guarding that point. Here we laid at anchor some fifteen or more hours, suffering all the tortures of heat and seasickness; no rations, and the worst drinking water possible given us, and the stench from the hole we were confined in became almost stifling. Our men had been made seasick by motion of the boat, which made our quarters filthy. Beg as we might, we were not allowed to go on deck. After the long wait Captain Webster, who had charge of the guard and prisoners, came on board and informed us that the point of exchange, owing to the movements of Grant's and Lee's armies, had been changed from City Point, Va., to Charleston Harbor, S. C. Disappointment was visible on all faces. Here we were, in sight of the promised land, but not allowed to enter. Indigo was a bright color contrasted with our feelings and looks, yet we consoled ourselves with the hope and the fact that the delay would be but for a day or two longer, when we would be at home. Then, in our joy, we would forget the vile treatment given us on the Yankee prison-ship. All the men of our party save two or three had been made seasick on the run down from Fort Delaware, which, as I said before, made our close quarters below decks a veritable cesspool. We appealed to Captain Webster, in charge of the guard, but he gave no heed to our protest, and we were compelled to stand it as best we could. On the evening of August 22d the ship pulled up anchor and steamed out of Fortress Monroe Harbor, bound for Charleston Harbor, S. C, under escort of two United States gunboats. This looked strange, yet little attention was paid to it by our men. In fact, in rounding Cape Henry, all our men were seasick, and we did not take much heed if there was one or a hundred gunboats guarding us. The heat of the ship's boilers, the heat of the weather, and the seasickness made our condition a veritable orthodox hell, a regular sheol in miniature form. Notwithstanding all this torture, our men suffered in silence, and there was no complaining. We believed we were going back home, and we would not let the Yankees see that we suffered.

Late in the night I had pushed my way through the darkness to the stepladder that led up to the deck above, awaiting my turn to go on deck. In the dark some one spoke to me, and I recognized the voice of Col. Abe Fulkerson, 63d Tenn. Inf. I said, "Colonel, we have fallen into hard lines, but it will soon be over." "Yes," he said, "Murray, it will be over when they kill us, not before." Stepping back out of hearing of the sentinel, the Colonel said, "Murray, do you honestly believe we are to be exchanged?" "Why, most assuredly," I replied. "Why not? And when we get back to the army we will not forget this inhuman treatment." "Well, that's all right; but, Murray," said Fulkerson, "when you and I get back to Dixie the war will be done. If the Yankees intended to exchange us they would have paroled us at Fort Delaware and not sent this heavy guard with us. And now we have an additional guard in the gunboats. I tell you," he continued, "there is trouble ahead for us. Of what character I can not say, but bear in mind what I say to you: there will be no exchange of this six hundred men. I feel certain of what I say. Now, again," he said, "why are those two officers who took the oath at Fort Delaware on this boat? Why is it they are entertained in the cabin by the Yankee officers while we are kept below in this miserable hole? I tell you those fellows are birds of ill omen. These galvanized rascals mean trouble for some one."

This conversation with Fulkerson certainly put a damper on my hope, and the more I thought of the conversation the more depressed I became, until hope had almost fled. When we separated it was coming daylight. The ship was rolling badly, and there seemed to be much commotion on the upper deck. The guard at the hatchway was doubled and no one was allowed to go on deck. The engines had stopped working. By some means I got on deck, though how I got there I never could tell, and tried to ascertain the cause of the commotion. I heard one of the ship's officers say, "We are aground, sir, off Folly Island. Where should have been the Cape Romaine Light, we are stuck fast in the sand;" which later proved to be true. The night was very dark. The route was new the *Crescent's* officers, and they had run too close into shore and had run the ship aground and lost our escorts, the gunboats.

This accidental grounding of the ship sent my spirits away up, and the thought came to me, "Now we can certainly get back to Dixie without the formality of exchange." While I was thinking all this over, Col. Van Manning, 3d Ark. Inf., came on deck. I hastily told him the situation. He at once said, "Murray, we must take this ship." He went below, a hasty council was held with the prisoners, and it was determined that we should take the ship. It was arranged that Colonels Manning, DeGurney, Abe Fulkerson, and Maj. W. W. Goldsborough should make the demand for the surrender of the ship. If it was declined, those below were to rush the guard at foot of the ladder, get on deck, capture the guard, and go ashore on Folly Island. It was a desperate undertaking. It would have been certain death for some of us before we could have captured the guard; yet there was no thought of the consequences of failure, no hesitation as to who should lead. By consent, Col. Van Manning was the leader, and with him we were all ready to chance the fire of a thousand guns. Colonels Manning, Fulkerson, DeGurney, and Major Goldsborough went upon deck and demanded that Captain Webster, commanding the guard, should surrender the ship into our hands at once, otherwise we would take it. Our men below were all ready to obey the order to rush the guard. Hardly had Colonel Manning made the demand for the surrender of the ship when, to the surprise of all the committee, Captain Webster agreed to the surrender of the ship. My recollection is that he and his men were not to be put into prison, but taken to Charleston city and exchanged at once, or paroled and sent home; to which condition Colonel Manning agreed. We were to land our men on Folly Island, with assistance of the ship's lifeboats, and from there make our way to Charleston city. While the preliminaries of the surrender were being arranged a signal gun was heard out at sea and soon the gunboats hove in sight. Under the shadow of their frowning guns hope fled and black despair settled upon our hearts. The moment the gunboats came in sight the cowardly attitude of Captain Webster changed to that of impudent defiance. He forced some of our officers to go down in the coal bunkers of the ship and help to throw overboard coal to lighten us off the sand bar. The guard drove us all below, allowing no prisoners on deck until the ship was pulled off the bar.

There were two incidents which took place while our ship was aground worth recording. The first showed how deeply Webster and his guards hated everything Southern. The first mate of the *Crescent City* was an Irishman who had lived, before the war began, in New Orleans. He recognized, amongst the prisoners, several friends. Whenever the chance presented itself he would give our men tobacco, meat, bread, in fact anything he could get from the ship's stores. The Yankees saw this and reported it to Webster, their commander, who had the poor Irishman put in irons, transferred to the gunboats for court martial, charging the poor fellow with running the ship aground that we might escape. I have always believed and do still believe that Webster made the charge against the first mate of the *Crescent City* for the sole purpose of hiding his abject cowardice in agreeing to surrender the ship to unarmed men. We never learned what became of the mate. The other incident was the escape of Colonel Woolfolk from the ship. By some means, Colonel Woolfolk, a brave, honorable, and true Confederate officer, had permission to have a stateroom on the ship. Aboard the *Crescent City* was an old colored woman who had belonged to the Woolfolk family in South Carolina. She was the stewardess of the ship. She recognized Colonel Woolfolk, her young master, and determined to help him to escape. She took him into her linen room, hid him under the bed, and fed him. She hung out of the stern window of the ship a sheet to make the guard believe he had dropped by that means into the water and gone ashore in the darkness. She kept him concealed on board until after the ship had landed us on Morris Island. When the ship reached New York city the old woman smuggled him ashore and gave him money. He succeeded in getting to Canada, from there to England, and back to the South on a blockade runner; and the Yankees never learned how he made his escape until he published it after the war.

After some hours of delay, with the aid of the gunboats, we got off of the sand bar and proceeded on our way to Charleston Harbor. The atmosphere below deck had now become terrible, and Webster positively refused to allow the ship's crew to put the hose on the pumps and wash the filth out of our quarters. It was good enough for Rebels, he said. When we reached the blockading fleet off Charleston no one was allowed on deck from below. Again we were in sight of the promised land; would we enter? was the absorbing question we asked one another. The anxiety amongst the prisoners became intense. We all hoped for an exchange, yet there was a doubt.

After being kept a whole day below decks a request was made by Colonel Manning, of Captain Webster, that from fifteen to twenty of the prisoners should be allowed to go on deck at one time to get some fresh air. In his appeal to Webster, Colonel Manning said: "We are away out here in the ocean; we are surrounded by your gunboats, and no man can swim from here ashore; no man can escape; it's brutal to keep us down below in that pest hole." The only reply Webster made to this appeal was, "You must stay below decks." Colonel Manning then said, "Captain Webster, if you will not allow us on deck have the hose of the ship turned on and wash the filth out of our quarters." To this Webster again said no. We could obtain no information whatever about exchange from the guard, the sink of the ship was, we found out, on the upper deck near the wheel, so we kept a constant line of men going all the time that we might know if the flag of truce boats were together in the harbor, and when they separated. On the day after and for several days after our arrival in Charleston Harbor our hearts were gladdened by the reports from the upper deck that the flag of truce boats were together. At night they would separate, and we could judge, by the conduct of the Yankees towards us, that nothing had been accomplished in exchange. On the fifth day after our arrival off Charleston one of the Yankee guards told Lieut. Bob Bowie that the exchange of prisoners had all been fixed for next day, in Charleston Harbor.

We were all elated. To confirm this report our boat took up anchor and we steamed, as we thought, towards Charleston, but at daylight found ourselves far out at sea. During the day we steamed back to our old anchorage under the guns of the blockading fleet. No one seemed able to interpret this move. Late in the evening our scouts from the upper deck reported the flag of truce boats together, just off Fort Sumter. All night the excitement amongst the prisoners ran high. At night our ship again took up anchor and steamed out to sea, and next morning, when allowed to go on deck, we found ourselves in Hilton Head Harbor. Here we remained three days, daily begging Captain Webster to turn on the ship's hose and wash the filth out of our quarters, which he persistently refused to do. In fact, we could not get him to do the least thing to alleviate our suffering, although he was fully cognizant of the filthy condition of our prison quarters below decks. After our stay of three days at Hilton Head, at the mouth of Broad River, our ship again pulled anchor and we steamed back towards Charleston. In our close, hot quarters our suffering was the most intense. The Yankees knew it, yet they would do nothing to relieve us, but seemed to enjoy the torture they inflicted upon us. We arrived off Morris Island on the morning of September 7, 1864, and had now been eighteen days on this prison ship, suffering the tortures of the damned, and not the least effort was made by the brute who had charge of us to curtail our suffering. About 10 o'clock of this morning, September 7th, Captain Webster, who had charge of us, coolly informed us that it never had been the intention of the United States government to exchange us. That we would be placed on Morris Island under the fire of our own guns, in retaliation, he said, for the Union prisoners under fire in Charleston city of the guns of Morris Island and fleet shelling that city. After Webster had vouchsafed us this information, most forcibly came back to me Colonel Fulkerson's prophecy that the war would be over before we ever set foot in Dixie. On the afternoon of the 7th day of September we were landed on Morris Island. The day was hot, but we were once more in God's sunshine and out of the pest hole of the pris-

Lieutenant D. B. Merchant
4th Virginia Cavalry

on ship.

Two old dismantled schooner hulks, the *Jno. A. Genet* and the *Transit*, were utilized as our prison, and the 54th Mass. (negro) Regt., Col. E. N. Hallowell commanding, our guard. And now in truth began our torture. Every man seemed crushed. Not much talking was done by the prisoners, yet we all hoped that fate, in a relenting moment, would help us and drive away black despair.

After the first night on these old hulks, filled as they were with rats and vermin, that old courage that made the Confederate soldier a hero came back to us, and we determined to face the fate in store for us without flinching or whining. God had made us men; we could die like men, if need be, for the cause of right, even if death came to us in a Yankee prison. The charge that the Confederate government had six hundred Union officers under fire in Charleston city was as false as the brain that conceived the story; as false as the tongue that uttered it; and Secretary Stanton and Gen. J. G. Foster, U. S. A. knew there were no prisoners of war under fire in Charleston city. They had the testimony of their own officers, who had been prisoners of war in Charleston city, that the story was false. Yet the testimony and word of these gentlemen was ignored by Stanton and Foster, and the word of negroes and Confederate deserters taken as gospel truth. The officers who had been prisoners of war in Charleston city: Generals H. W. Wessells, Seymour, Scammon, et al, over their own signatures, say they were not under fire, but, on the contrary, in no danger; with good quarters and plenty to eat, kindly and courteously treated. Yet they were not listened to as reliable witnesses, but ignored because negroes and Confederate deserters said there were Union soldiers under fire in Charleston. General Wessells went so far in his letter to General Foster as to protest against putting officers under fire on Morris Island; yet General Foster paid no attention to the protest.

The life of a prisoner of war is at best hard and irksome; and it is extremely hard when he is restricted in all things necessary to the simplest comfort. He must suffer, he does suffer, and suffers more than tongue can describe or pen portray when his rations are curtailed to the point of barely keeping him from starvation. Time and time again the Confederate authorities protested against the inhuman treatment of our men in Northern prisons, and begged the Washington authorities, in humanity's name, to exchange prisoners of war. "Send your transports," said President Davis and General Lee, through Exchange Commissioner Ould, "and take your sick and wounded men. We can not feed them; we can not care for them." But Secretary Stanton said, "No, we will make no exchange; our men in your hands must suffer." The Union prisoners of war in all the Southern prisons were fed the same ration that was given the Confederate soldier in the field. What more could the Confederates do? General Lee, in an order, said, "All wounded on the field must be treated alike; all prisoners of war must be treated humanely"; and the Confederate Congress passed a law to this effect. Mr. Stanton and General Grant both said, "We can not, we will not, exchange prisoners of war. The South can not feed our men; we can not get any benefits from exchange, while the men we return to the South only help to swell Lee's army. Our men must suffer for the good of those who are now contending with the terrible Lee"; and these officials in Washington found it cheaper to starve Confederate soldiers in Northern prisons than fight them on the battlefield. The United States had the world from which to draw their army and their supplies; the Confederacy had but a small area, without the slightest chance of getting supplies from the outside world save when a blockade runner could slip through the fleets blockading our ports. Neither the men responsible for the wanton cruelty nor their apologists can give a valid reason for the inhuman treatment meted out to us on Morris Island, Hilton Head, and Fort Pulaski.

The following two letters – found in Vol. XXXV, *War Records* – show beyond question that the United States government officials at Washington, with Gen. J.G. Foster, made preparation for the infliction of their brutality upon us, and that Col. E.N. Hallowell, 54th Regt. Mass. Vols. (negroes), was chosen as commandant of our camp because of his brutal nature – just the man to carry out the beastly orders Gen. J. G. Foster, U. S. A., might issue by authority of Edwin M. Stanton, Secretary of War.

Headquarters Department of the South,
Charleston, S. C, August 23, 1864.

Brig.-Gen. A. Schimmelfennig,
Commanding Northern District,
Department South.

General:

I am directed by the major-general commanding to state he has ordered Captain Suter, Chief Engineer Department of South, to proceed to Morris Island for purpose of consulting with you in regard to the location of the camp for the prisoners of war daily expected in this department from the North. The major-general commanding desires that this camp be placed between Fort Strong and Battery Putnam. If this position is considered too dangerous you are authorized to locate the camp wherever yourself and Captain Suter shall deem the best and safest from attack of the enemy. Should it be necessary to have more troops to guard these six hundred, another regiment can be sent from this place. Still, it is desired that they may be guarded by the force at present in the Northern District if it is possible, as we want all the troops at this place that we now have.

I have the honor to be, General, very respectfully.
Your obedient servant,
W. L. M. Burger,
Assistant Adjutant-General

(*War Records*, Vol. XXXV, p. 256).

Headquarters Northern District, Department of the South,
Morris Island, September 8, 1864.

Gen. J. G. Foster,

General: – I have the honor to report that on yesterday the Rebel prisoners of war were safely landed and placed in the stockade in front of Fort Strong. I found on my arrival here that

General Schimmelfennig had already detailed the 54th Massachusetts Regiment (negroes), Colonel Hallowell, to guard the prisoners, and as I was expected as far as possible to carry out his plans, have not changed the detail. I believe no better officer than Colonel Hallowell can be found in whose hands to place the prisoners for their safe keeping, and thus far the duty has been well performed. Last night was so dark and the weather so stormy that the navy boats did not report for duty at Paine's Dock. My boat brigade was out but saw nothing unusual. The navy detail have reported this morning and no exertion will be spared to carry out successfully the object of the expedition.

   I am very respectfully,
       R. Saxton,
       Brig.-Gen. Commanding

(*War Records*, Vol. XXXV, pp. 275-276).

Lieutenant J. W. O. Funk
5th Virginia

CHAPTER THREE

March from old Schooner Hulk to Prison Stockade – Hot Sun – Sick Men Forced to Move On – Brutal White Officers and Negro Soldiers. Prison Stockade – Water, Rations, and Shelter.

After two days' confinement on the old schooner hulks, without much drinking water or rations, we were ordered, on the afternoon of the second day, to turn out and form in line on the beach. After forming and the counting of our number was finished the order was giving to march. We started up the beach in full view of Sumter's guns. The day was intensely hot; the sun shone down upon us in all its splendor. We had not gone over half a mile before some of our men, weakened from the eighteen days on the filthy prison ship, fell, from prostration, in the sand. I was of this unfortunate number. The brutal white officers of the 54th Massachusetts (negro) Regiment made the negro guards force us to get up and stagger on at the point of the bayonet in the hands of a negro soldier. When I had fallen in the sand an old man, wearing the badge of the Sanitary Commission, attempted to cross the guard line to help me. He was driven back by a burly Dutch lieutenant, with an oath, who ordered the negro guard to make me move on. I heard the old man protesting to the guard that we were human beings even if we were Rebels. When we reached the stockade prison-pen gate we were again halted, counted off by fours and sent inside the inclosure, where a negro sergeant assigned us to tents, putting four men in each small A-tent which would not comfortably hold more than two men. But what mattered this? We were prisoners of war, in the hands of a great and good government. Our camp was laid off between batteries Waggoner and Gregg: Waggoner in our rear, Gregg in our front. We were in exact line of the guns of Fort Sumter. To the left of Battery Gregg was a mortar battery; next to this was what the Yankees called an iron battery; further to our left, facing Charleston, was a large gun the Yanks called the "Swamp Angel"; and off to the right of our camp was the fleet of monitors with their guns all trained on our stockade prison, always ready shotted should we show the least sign of disobedience to the orders governing our prison. The guns on Battery Waggoner were arranged to sweep our camp from the rear, and the guns on Battery Gregg to rake our camp from the front. All these Federal batteries constantly drew the fire of our guns on Sumter, Johnson Island, Fort Moultrie and other forts guarding Charleston Harbor. The prison stockade was built of long pine poles driven in the sand and cleated together by pine boards. About the top of the high fence was a parapet, built that the negro guards might overlook our camp. This pen enclosed about two acres of sand. On the inside of the stockade fence, about ten feet from it, was stretched an inch rope, the rope being supported on pickets driven into the sand. This was designated the dead line. For a prisoner to approach this line, on any pretext, was sure death; the sentinels were ordered to shoot him without hesitation or challenge. The space between the dead line and fence curtailed the space in our stockade prison very much. At the head of the middle street was placed a Mitrailleuse Requa gun, loaded and ready to open upon our camp at a moment's notice. All this precaution was taken for fear we would overpower the negro guards and capture the island.

After we had been arranged in companies and assigned to tents Colonel Hallowell, commandant of the 54th Massachusetts Regiment, our guards, had read to each company of prisoners the rules for government of the stockade prison. One rule provided for the shooting of any prisoner that touched the dead line rope;

another rule was, that if ten or more prisoners were assembled together the sentinel was to order them to disperse, and if the order was not instantly obeyed by the prisoners the sentinel was instructed to fire into the crowd. This order kept us in constant fear of the ignorant negro guard shooting us. Owing to the crowded state of our prison boundary it was an utter impossibility for us to keep from forming crowds, and the negro guards had little consideration for the "Rebs," as they termed us. One day Colonels Van Manning, Fulkerson, and myself were standing at the end of the centre street of the stockade, talking; two other prisoners joined us, making the crowd just five. The negro sentinel on the parapet, in the most insolent manner, ordered us to "'sperse dat crowd." Conscious we were not violating any rule of the prison, we paid no heed to the negro. The second time he gave the order he bellowed out at the top of his voice: "'Sperse dat crowd, you damned Rebs; dar's ball in dis here gun, just melting to get into your body. Hear me, don't you?" Of course this last warning was sufficient to "'sperse de crowd." Another rule was, no lights or fires would be permitted in our camp at any time after taps were sounded; if a match was struck in our tents the negro sentinel was ordered to shoot into the tent where he saw the light. All the blankets given us at Fort Delaware were taken from us before we left the prison ship *Crescent City*, which left fully two-thirds of our number with only the clothes they stood in for covering. The following order for government of our prison is the most drastic ever made by men authorized by a government claiming civilization:

Headquarters United States Forces,
Morris Island, S.C., September 7, 1864.

The following rules and regulations are hereby announced for the government of the camp of the prisoners of war:

The prisoners will be divided into eight detachments, seventy-five in each, lettered A, B, C, etc., each prisoner numbered 1, 2, 3, 4, etc. Each detachment will be under the charge of a warden, who will be detailed from the guard for that duty. There will be three roll calls every day, the first at one hour after sunrise, the second at 12 m., the third at one half an hour before sunset, at which times the prisoners will be counted by the wardens, and the reports will be taken by the officer of the day at the company streets, before the ranks are broken. Each warden will see that the quarters of his detachment are properly policed, and will make the detail necessary for such duty (from the prisoners). Sick call will be at 9 o'clock a.m, each day. Each warden will make a morning report to the officers in charge, on blanks suitable for the purpose.

There will be two barrel sinks for each detachment, which will be placed on the flanks of the camp during the day, and at night in the company streets. They will be emptied after each roll call by detail from each detachment. No talking will be allowed after evening roll call, and no prisoner will leave his tent after that time except to obey the calls of nature. During the day the prisoners will be allowed the limits of the camp as marked by the rope running between the stockade and line of tents. Prisoners passing the line under any pretence whatever will be shot by the sentries. No persons, except the guard and officer being on duty at the camp, will be allowed to communicate with the prisoners without written permission from these, or superior headquarters. The sentries will always have their guns loaded and capped. If more than ten prisoners are seen together except at meal time they will be fired upon by the sentinels. If there is any disturbance whatever in the camp or any attempt made by the prisoners to escape, the camp will be opened upon with grape and canister musketry, and the Requa batteries. If a prisoner is sick he may purchase such luxuries as the surgeon in charge may direct. The prisoners will be allowed to purchase only the following named articles: Writing materials, pipes, tobacco, and necessary clothing. Everything bought by or sent them will be inspected by the provost marshal. The prisoners will be allowed to write letters once each week, not more than half sheet of paper to each letter. The letters will be open and pass through the hands of the provost-marshal before being mailed. No candles or lights of any kind will be allowed. The hours for meals will be as follows: Breakfast, 7 o'clock a.m.; dinner, 12 m.; supper, 5 o'clock p.m. The prisoners will be served under the direction of the provost marshal.

By order of Col. William Gurney, 127th N. Y. Vols., commanding post.

R.L. Jewett,
Captain 54th Mass. Vols.,
Acting Assistant Adjutant-General.

Official: G.W. Little,
1st Lieutenant 127th N. Y. Vols.,
Acting aide-de-camp.

Our rations, under this order, was a menu for wooden gods. It consisted of four hardtack army crackers, often rotten and green with mold, and one ounce of fat meat, issued to us at morning roll call; for dinner, we received one-half pint of bean or rice soup, made as the caprice of the cook suggested; for supper, we were allowed all the wind we could inhale. At sundown we were compelled to go into our tents and there remain until roll call in the early morning. The ration stated was all we received while on Morris Island. Our drinking water was obtained by digging holes in the sand, and then waiting until sufficient very insipid water would ooze out of the sand to quench thirst.

The second day of our confinement in the stockade will never be forgotten by the survivors of that six hundred. At early noon the Federal batteries on Morris Island, and all the guns of the Yankee fleet, opened on the Confederate forts and Charleston city. Our batteries all replied and for two or three hours the duel lasted. The shells from Sumter and our other batteries fell thick and fast upon the island, most of them uncomfortably close to our stockade. We began to think, for a time, our fellows in Sumter had forgotten we were prisoners on Morris Island; but before the duel was over we found our gunners were not directing their shells towards our pen. It was amusing to watch the negro guards on the parapet dodge and drop when a shell from Sumter went across our stockade, or burst over the pen; it was all Hallowell and his officers could do to keep the negro sentinels at their posts, the poor negroes were so frightened. Just as soon as they heard the report of a gun from Sumter they would drop down on the parapet in fear. Hallowell and his officers would beat them up with their swords. After this day there was only the general firing during the day, though at night our guns would be more rapidly fired, especially so our mortar guns.

After we had been on the luxurious diet of four hardtack army crackers, one ounce of fat meat, and half a pint of sandy bean soup (which often tasted like it had been seasoned with soap), and with the bad drinking water, our condition was pretty bad. Our cooking was done outside of the prison stockade by negroes detailed for the purpose. What filth these chefs put into the soup we could not see or know; it was brought into us – we could eat it or let it alone. We did not expect, as prisoners of war in Yankee hands, to have all the delicacies served by a Delmonico, but we did expect enough of food to sustain life. But Draco Stanton and his lieutenants, Gen. J. G. Foster and Colonel Hallowell, had different views of humanity. This menu of starvation, issued by the United States government, was good enough for helpless prisoners of war. Just think of this bill of fare:

Breakfast, four rotten hardtack crackers.

Dinner, one-half pint sandy soup.

Supper, all the wind one could inhale.

Our medical treatment was the acme of cruelty, rendered by a red-headed cow doctor, whose only remedy, no matter what your complaint, was an opium pill or dose of Jamaica ginger. This redheaded doctor always reminded me of a country cross-road cow doctor whose knowledge of medicine was culled from a patent medicine almanac, and his practice justified the conclusion.

The colonel of the 54th Massachusetts (negro) Regiment, his officers and negroes, were regular daisies. I recall one little sawed-off lieutenant who often called the prison roll; or rather took the report from the negroes who counted us three times each day. This little fellow had a sword about two feet longer than he was tall. The sword would get tangled up in his short legs, reminding one, as Pete Akers said, of a boy playing soldier. This fellow's dignity was huge – about on the order of a free negro parson before "de wah," at a lodge funeral.

Colonel Hallowell, with whom we were brought more in contact than any other officer – for the reason he had full control of our pen – was about the meanest fellow our misfortunes brought us in connection with; in fact, the negroes he commanded were Chesterfields in politeness in contrast with this fellow. After we had been some weeks in the stockade under fire of our own guns, and the starvation rations had begun to tell upon us, this doughty colonel one afternoon came into the stockade, had us drawn up in line, and made the following speech which I have never forgotten. He said:

> The fate of war has placed you prisoners in my hands, and I will treat you as prisoners. I feel it my bounded duty to fight men who have raised their unhallowed hands against their country's flag. But I will try and treat you as men, since you have fallen into my hands, and this will be my duty so long as you obey the rules and orders laid down for the government of this prison camp.

But he did not keep his word. He treated us like animals, and he did not intend to treat us like men when he said he would do so. He violated every promise he ever made us, both in the spirit and letter; there was nothing this fellow left undone to make us uncomfortable and annoy us; he never let one opportunity pass to show his hatred for the South and her soldiers. And yet in our six hundred prisoners were the sons and grandsons of ancestors who had helped to make American history and consecrate the American flag, when probably the ancestors of this fellow Hallowell were Massachusetts Tories, doing all they could to defeat the cause of the American Colonies, and possibly spies for the English crown. And yet the fate of war compelled us to listen to the impudence of this doughty hero – unable to resent his insults. How brave he was, backed as he was by the bayonets of his negro soldiers. One of his smart jokes was to come into our prison pen and say, in his arrogant drawl, "Gentlemen, to-morrow I will have some barrels placed in the streets of your inclosure into which you can throw your bones. Of course, I mean your meat bones." This was cruel; it was cowardly to make such jests of our starving condition. He could see daily how the treatment was breaking down and killing our men; he reveled in our terrible condition. Most of the prisoners were suffering with acute dysentery. From this terrible complaint not one escaped; but none of our men complained; none murmured against our government.

We knew the Richmond authorities were doing all they could for us, and, like the dying Cæsar, we were too proud to let our Yankee jailors see that we suffered. It seems like blasphemy to charge the creation of such a creature as this fellow to nature, and really an insult to his satanic majesty to say he created such a caricature on the human race as was Hallowell. As I stated before, acute dysentery, caused by the bad water we drank, and miserable rations of rotten, worm-filled hardtack crackers, put our men in very bad condition. On the night of September 28, 1864, Lieutenant Frank Peake, of Morgan's men, who was one of my tent mates, was taken very sick, with every symptom of cholera. We had nothing to relieve his pain, and did not dare go out to call for help. Had one of us left the tent or called for help, the negro guard would have fired on us and been glad of the opportunity to do so. Their orders were to shoot any man who left his tent after taps except to obey the calls of nature. Poor dear old Peake! He suffered, all the night through, the most intense pain. At roll call I told the negro sergeant that Lieutenant Peake was ill and needed the attention of the doctor at once; but the doctor never came in until 9 o'clock, the regular hour for sick call of the prison pen. When he did come in, Lieutenant Hudgins, C.S.N., and Lieutenant Hugh Dunlap, my other tent mates, requested me to see the doctor and ask him to come at once to see Lieutenant Peake. I went to the hospital tent, as it was called, approaching the doctor in the most polite manner and with the most polite language I could command, related to him Lieutenant Peake's condition, urging him to go over to see Peake, who, I thought, was in a dying condition, and would die unless he had immediate medical attention. Before this red-headed dispenser of pills replied to my urgent appeal for help, he looked me over from head to foot, then said, "Can't the man come to my tent?" "Why, of course not, doctor; he can not stand upon his feet; he is too ill to walk. Could he have come here I surely would not be so urgent in my appeal to you." "Well," he said, "if he is too bad to walk over here, he must wait until these other fellows here are served; they all need attention." "But, doctor," I said, "these gentlemen, in a manner, can help themselves. Lieutenant Peake is helpless, and I feel sure every gentlemen here will wait if you will go to see Lieutenant Peake." With this I turned upon my heel and left the doctor's presence in disgust. I could hardly believe there was a man living, wearing the badge of a fraternity whose aim was to save, not *destroy life*, who would refuse to relieve a dying fellow mortal, a helpless prisoner of war. I returned to my tent and reported my failure to get the doctor to respond. The boys could hardly credit it. Captain W.P. Crow, an old friend and companion of Lieutenant Peake, went over to see the dispenser of opium pills, but met with no more success than I did in inducing the doctor to see our patient. What can be said of such fellows as this doctor? Is nature responsible for their creation? Yes, but they sprang up from the foul growth of some Northern city during the war; they were the poison weeds in the garden of life, killing with their poison all that is good and beautiful. Late in the afternoon the doctor came to our tent, but poor Peake had passed beyond human skill. Death, with her cruel, cold hand, was reaching out for him. He lived during the night, suffering the pains of the damned. On the morning of September 29th Captain Crow and Lieutenant Dunlap succeeded in getting Colonel Hallowell to remove Lieutenant Peake from the prison pen to the hospital, just out of range of Sumter's guns. Poor, dear Peake! We who knew him loved him for his Christian virtues, manly courage, and gentleness of heart. When he was carried through the prison pen gate we all felt we had looked for the last time upon him alive. He lingered for a day or two and died on the afternoon of October 2, 1864, just four days after his removal from under fire. Far away from loved ones and home this grand hero closed his eyes, to open them again only when the Grand Commander of all armies shall announce the day of the great muster. There in the hospital tent on Morris Island, upon a pallet of straw, sleeping the sleep of the just, the true, and the brave, lay a Confederate soldier whose spirit had surrendered only to death. He laid down his life for the cause of the South, the land he loved. About him stood men in blue; they were enemies, they could not understand, they could not know, the great heart that had ceased to beat. In the twilight we dug him a grave in the sands of Morris Island, and laid him to rest, while the shot and the shells from Charleston and Sumter's batteries sang his funeral dirge. Peace to his ashes!

This is not the only case of heroism of the Confederate Army. The Confederate Army was composed of men like Lieutenant Peake. High upon the scroll of honor and fame their names are written in letters of gold. There they will ever remain, the brightest gems in the Southland's coronet. Story and song will tell their deeds of valor and courage; generations will sing their praise; they need no monuments of metal nor stone to perpetuate their memory and names. Their fortitude, courage, and fidelity to duty during four long, bloody years of war, such as the world never knew, is a monument that will outlast any that could be constructed by human hands. When the truthful history of the war is written, and the passion of men has cooled, that an authentic record may be made, upon that record will be found the names of every Confederate soldier who wore the gray and did his duty. It matters not if he came from the halls of wealth or the lowly cottage upon the mountain side, nor if he wore the stars of the general officer, or the gray blouse of the ranks. If he did his duty he was a patriot, a nobleman. His old gray jacket gave him a patent to nobility greater and grander than those conferred by mortal hands. God, Himself, gave to the Confederate soldier the right of nobility; the old gray jacket was his decoration and insignia of the cause we loved and lost – the nobility of manhood.

We had been now on Morris Island several weeks, suffering the pangs of starvation, and every man bearing himself with dignity and courage through the trying ordeal. One morning in October, to our surprise, the guns of old Sumter, Charleston,

Lieutenant-Colonel E. S. M. Le Broten
Louisiana

Moultrie, and Johnson were silent. We could not divine why, and began to make all kinds of surmises. The negro guards and their officers walked leisurely about, without the fearful look they generally bore. After a long time we ascertained, from one of the negro sergeants in charge of our camp, that the Confederate government had demanded our removal from under fire and off of Morris Island, or they were going to place six hundred officers (Federal prisoners of war) on the ramparts of Fort Sumter. He also stated that General Foster, commanding United States forces, had asked for a flag of truce conference, which was then in session. We could see the men on Fort Sumter's ramparts. All was as serene as a church picnic. Later on, this negro sergeant informed us that the Secretary of War, himself, from Washington, was on the flag of truce boat with his cabinet, and was making arrangements to exchange all the prisoners of war, colored troops included. We were, of course, elated at this information, and speculation, rumors and "grape" filled the camp. At sundown the guns of Charleston, Sumter, and the Yankee guns on Morris Island began booming; then we knew there was to be no exchange; but next morning the guns were again silent, the flag of truce boats were again together. At evening roll call the negro sergeant informed us exchange had been accomplished. To confirm this Colonel Hallowell informed us he was going to be rid of us at last, and ordered us to be ready at daylight the next morning to move out of the stockade and off the island, for exchange. At daylight we were ordered to fall into line; out of the prison stockade we marched, down the beach to the old schooner hulks, which were utilized as our prison when we first landed on the island. We were packed on board of these old schooner hulks, the *Transit* and *J. A. Genet*, where we remained thirty-six hours while the flag of truce boats were together off Fort Sumter. The conference failed to agree upon an exchange and we were marched back into the stockade prison pen in the afternoon, to again face the rigors of retaliation and brutality; and it can be said the Immortal Six Hundred faced the music like men. Why the exchange had failed of accomplishment we could never learn. On our return to the prison pen, from our march down the beach, our hearts were made glad by a lot of boxes of tobacco, sweet potatoes, and peanuts our government had sent us under flag of truce. This renewed our strength, and we were all grateful. It was all our government had to send, and it told us the story of want at home, and gave us the cheering, silent news that we were not forgotten by our government and people in our trials and tribulations. For several days we just reveled in good old Rebel sweet potatoes and peanuts, and blew off our misfortunes in the smoke of good old Dixie tobacco. Our cares for the time vanished, and we slept like princes after a banquet. In the early morning the shelling of the island awoke us, the same old monotony settled upon the camp, the negro sentinels surrounded our camp, and the daily roll calls of the Yanks kept us from forgetting we were still prisoners of war on Morris Island, under fire of our own guns, suffering all the torments of retaliation, as unjust as it was cowardly and cruel.

After several days we were again ordered to pack up and be ready to move at daylight from the prison pen. Colonel Hallowell, who gave the order, said, "In view of the fact that you are to move early in the morning, you can all leave your tents earlier than usual to prepare for the march." Thinking, of course, he would give orders to the sentinels to allow us to leave our tents (and he said he would give the order), some of our fellows, prisoners, got up very early and built a small fire in the rear of their tents to boil some sweet potatoes. The negro sentinel ordered them to put out that fire, and followed his order with a shot from his musket, seriously but not dangerously wounding Captain Blair, of North Carolina, and Lieutenant Harris, of Virginia. The matter was reported to Colonel Hallowell, but no punishment or reprimand was inflicted upon the negro sentinel who had so flagrantly violated Colonel Hallowell's order; and I right here want to say that it was the general belief of our men that Hallowell never gave the order to his negro sentinels. Most likely the negro was complimented for shooting Rebel prisoners of war.

Here is an order that Colonel Hallowell most openly violated. On page 312, Volume XXXV, *War Records*, Stewart M. Taylor, Assistant Adjutant-General, Department of South, in a letter to Colonel Hallowell, says:

> * * * I am directed to inform you that the brigadier-general commanding is not desirous that the Rebel prisoners should be employed to empty their sink tubs. Our officers in the hands of the Rebel authorities are not subjected to this indignity. * * *

The letter is dated October 6, 1864, and addressed to Colonel Hallowell, in command of prison camp, Morris Island, S.C. Yet Colonel Hallowell never gave the least attention to the order, and compelled us to do this menial thing, although they admit that our people did not subject the Federal prisoners of war to such indignities.

On pages 284-285, General Foster, in a letter to General Saxton, commanding Morris Island, says:

> * * * The rations of our officers (prisoners of war) in Charleston have been ascertained to be as follows: Fresh meat, three fourths pound, or one-half pound salt meat; one-fifth pint of rice; one-half pound of hard bread or one-half pint of meal; one-fifth pint of beans. I desire, in rationing the prisoners of war now in your hands, that you should be governed accordingly, making sure that they receive no more than the above, except what salt or vinegar may be necessary for them. Our prisoners confined in Charleston do their own cooking, and I desire that the prisoners in your hands be made to do the same. The cooking must be done within the limits of the prison camp, and the printed orders of Colonel Gurney modified accordingly. * * *

Now here is an admission from the major-general commanding the Department of the South that it had been ascertained that the Confederate government was feeding the prisoners of war good rations in Charleston, yet we prisoners of war in General Foster's hands, under fire on Morris Island, were fed four rotten hardtack crackers, with half a pint of soup each day. Was, we ask, this cruelty wanton? If these Yanks had treated us half as well as our government treated Federal prisoners of war we would have made no protest. On the word of a deserter (Charles Harris) from Charleston, who said there were 600 or 700 Federal prisoners of war under fire in Charleston, was this cruel, cowardly retaliation *inflicted upon us Confederate soldiers*. Further on in the same letter General Foster calls Saxton's attention to the possible attempt that might be made by our forces to release us. He says, "In case of an attack, shoot down any Rebel prisoners found out of the stockade." What humanity General Foster displays in this order; what a contrast between the treatment of the Union prisoners of war in our hands and the Confederate prisoners of war in the Federal prisons of the North.

When the order came to move out of the stockade pen we thanked God exchange had come at last. We would soon be free men, back in Dixie, away from Hallowell, Foster, and their brutal negroes. But, alas, disappointment awaited us; hope was to be ousted from our hearts by despair, and fate had in store for us a harder ordeal. As we marched down the beach to once more board the old schooner hulks our hearts were glad, but before the sun set we knew exchange was not for us. Before leaving Morris Island all blankets marked U.S. were taken from those who had them. This was done by order, we were told, of General Foster. After being packed on the old schooner hulks the 127th New York Volunteers took charge of us. White troops, at last! This was at least a betterment of our condition. After a short delay at the Morris Island wharf, a gunboat took us in tow for Fort Pulaski, on Cock-Spur Island, at the mouth of the Savannah River.

Before leaving Morris Island some of our number, through influence at home, succeeded in being exchanged specially. All the wounded of our party (fifty or more) were exchanged at Hilton Head.

There was nothing of great moment occurred on the trip from Morris Island to Fort Pulaski. The white troops gave us of their rations, and made our condition as comfortable as they could.

There was an incident occurred, just as we were leaving the stockade pen on Morris Island, that made me regret very much my hasty action. As I said before, it was the general impression, as we marched out of the pen, that we were to be exchanged; and this fact made me feel like telling Colonel Hallowell my opinion of him. He was standing at the prison gate, glaring at us as we passed out. We were marching by fours; in the fours just ahead of me was Capt. Bruce Gibson, Major W. W. Goldsborough, and two other officers whose identity I now forget. When I reached Hallowell I halted and said, "You yellow-faced scoundrel, we are going back home now, and I hope and pray to God that it may be my fortune to get my hands on you, that the world may be rid of such a brute." His face turned livid with rage. He shouted out to one of the negro guards to shoot that man, meaning me; but the guard pointed his gun direct at Capt. Bruce Gibson, and would have killed him but for the order of one of the negro sergeants to put down his gun. By this time the line had passed Hallowell, and Captain Gibson was saved. I never in all my life was so unstrung; my foolish temper had almost cost an innocent life – the life of my dearest friend. After this incident my temper was kept under control. This was the only conversation I ever had with Hallowell. When he came into our prison pen I got out of his way. I hated the man with an insane hate for his treatment of Lieutenant Peake. After we learned that we were not to be exchanged we began to speculate as to what the Yanks would do to us, now they had taken us from under fire. The wildest talk that was ever heard was listened to on the transport that night. Lieut. Pete Akers said he was sure we were all to be slaughtered, and boots for General Foster and his staff made of our hides. Others said we were to be put to work on river and harbor fortifications; but Captain Hammack, of Kentucky, said a sentinel told him, confidentially, that we were to be slaughtered at Fort Pulaski, packed in salt, and fed to Foster's negroes to make them fight. At daylight on the morning after leaving Morris Island we arrived at Fort Pulaski's wharf. About 9 o'clock we were ordered to fall into line on deck. Then we were marched onto the fort wharf, lined up and searched. What few U.S. blankets our men had hid from the Morris Island search were taken from us, leaving a large majority of us with only the clothes we stood in. After this exercise we were marched into the fort casemates, on the north side of the fort. Here we found luxurious quarters, consisting of rough pine board bunks to hold four people – two on top, two below – no stoves, no blankets, no comforts, but the hard, rough pine board bunks; no downy pillows; no good, thick, warm comforts; no washstands, no easy rockers. All was hard, rough pine board bunks, and some of our fellows had the temerity to openly complain of such winter quarters, and say ugly things of the best government, etc., etc., while others of us thanked God we had white troops as guards. Our first meal in Fort Pulaski was a feast fit for the gods. It consisted of excellent white bread, good fat meat, and a great big tin cup of delicious vegetable soup, with lots of grease in it. After getting settled in the fort, with splendid cisterns of good drinking water, we began to think our troubles and woes had ended. On the day after our arrival, Col. P. P. Brown, commandant of Fort Pulaski, colonel 127th New York Volunteers, came into our prison quarters. We were drawn up in line, and he made a short speech. He said: "Gentlemen, you shall be treated, while in my custody, humanely. You who have friends within our lines with whom you can correspond may write them at once for money, clothing, and such other articles that will add to your comfort. I will do all for you I can do, consistent with my duty, to make you as comfortable as possible. Myself and my regiment have seen service in the field and know what is due a brave foe. I will make this the model military prison of the United States. I have already made requisition on headquarters for blankets and clothing for you, and full army rations, together with plenty of fuel. All I shall ask is that you obey orders for government of the prison, and such sanitary rules as shall be issued by me."

We began to believe this was a dream. For a few days we had good white bread and plenty of it – full army rations for a fact. But, alas, we were to be rudely awakened from this happy

dream. Colonel Brown informed us his requisition had been ignored by Gen. J. G. Foster, commandant of the department, and
he (Brown) was ordered to issue to us ten ounces of corn meal
and one-half pint of onion pickle each twenty-four hours, as a
ration, without salt, meat, grease, or vegetables. Ten ounces of
corn meal, one-half pint of pickle – nothing more. No fuel but
twelve sticks of pine cord wood for each division of twenty-eight
men. The order, he said, was peremptory, leaving him no discre-
tion whatever, and he was powerless in the matter. It must be
said of Colonel Brown and his officers that they were gentlemen,
and when he made the promise to treat us humanely and kindly
he intended to keep his promise to the letter. The officers and
men of the 127th New York (our guards) never failed to show
their disgust for General Foster and his brutal corn meal order.
No one but a brute like Foster could have conceived such a ration
to starve men. If the corn meal had been good we might have
managed to live upon it and kept off the scurvy; but the meal was
rotten – filled with black weevil bugs and worms. The barrels
were branded, "Corn meal, kiln dried from — Mills, 1861,"
showing by the brand and date on the barrels that it was four
years old; condemned by the quartermaster as unfit food for
negro troops, but excellent diet for helpless Confederate prisoners
of war. The acid onion and cucumber pickle was given us, it was
said, to prevent scurvy; but the fact is this: it was issued to create
appetite and add misery to our hunger. To fully understand this
ten-ounces-of-rotten-corn-meal-and-pickle order one must com-
pare it with the United States Army regulation ration, which is
one and one quarter pounds ground corn – ground with peas –
besides coffee, tea, sugar, bread, and meat. But our ration was
simply ten ounces of rotten corn meal and one-half pint of acid
onion and cucumber pickle, without salt or meat or grease – save
the worms and bugs in the meal – and this was to sustain life.
After picking out the lumps, bugs, and worms in this rotten corn
meal there was not more than seven ounces of meal left fit for
use. And here I claim Gen. J. G. Foster, by issuing us unsound
corn meal, robbed us of what his humane government intended

we should have. Some of my comrades say that about the 1st of March, 1865, this corn meal ration was supplemented by four ounces of white bread. This may have been so, but this I do know: that six of us were not in the least benefitted by the bread addition. We were locked up in a damp, cold cell in another part of the prison. Why, I will tell further on. Upon the corn-meal-pickle ration we lived for sixty-three days, our men suffering the torments of the lost. After we had been a few weeks at Fort Pulaski General Foster ordered that, for sanitary reasons, our number should be divided and part sent to him at Hilton Head. I have always, and do now, believe that General Foster ordered part of our men sent to him at Hilton Head, his headquarters, that, like Nero, he could look on and enjoy the sufferings of his helpless victims starving to death. About December 10th scurvy made its appearance in our prison amongst the weakest of the prisoners. Most every man in the prison was suffering more or less with dysentery, and a large majority were, from the starvation diet, unable to leave their bunks. It was a pitiable sight to see human beings being starved to death by a government claiming to be civilized, humane, and religious.

Each man was his own cook. In the casemate of each division of prisoners there was a very large cook stove; each twenty-four hours twelve cord sticks of wood – pine – was issued to each twenty-eight men or division, as they were designated. Every morning the corn meal was issued. The fires were started in the cook stoves but once each day – at noon – so that the prisoner who was not ready to cook his meal when the fire was started, ate it raw or let it alone until noon next day, when the fire would be again started. And bear in mind, my readers, it was rotten corn meal, without salt, meat, or grease to flavor it with.

The drinking water was excellent, obtained from the fort cisterns. There was no fuel allowed us for fires during the day, yet some of our men would manage to get hold of a chunk of coal, and, with an old camp kettle, they constructed stoves, and kept the atmosphere just above the freezing point. We had no blankets to keep us warm at night, and our beds were hard pine

Colonel J. E. Cantwell
North Carolina

boards with no soft sides. No idea can be formed of our condition while we remained at Fort Pulaski. On Christmas day, 1864, the snow on the fort parade ground was four inches deep, and we prisoners of war had neither fire, blankets, nor clothing to shield us from the rigors of the winter weather.

Really, it seemed like the elements had joined hands with Stanton and Foster to destroy us. There can be no claim set up by the Federal authorities and General Foster, commanding Department of the South, that the ration given us was the best that could be done for us. If such claim is made, it is false, for I do know that the storehouse of the fort contained commissary stores going to waste, while we human beings were being starved to death. The treatment of our prisoners of war by General Foster, U. S. A., was the refinement of cruelty. God grant I may never be again subjected to such cruelty, nor witness such infamous barbarity, as that inflicted upon the six hundred Confederate officers at Fort Pulaski. It was shocking to look upon these poor helpless prisoners of war, starved until they became walking skeletons; and some of the six hundred were wounded men, whose wounds had not yet healed over. Why they were not exchanged with those at Hilton Head I do not know. Hunger drove our men to catching and eating dogs, cats, and rats. Now, when I can calmly think over the terrible ordeal, I wonder why we did not eat each other. How one man of the Immortal Six Hundred came out of Fort Pulaski and Hilton Head prisons alive is beyond the ken of man. God only knows. Our men became as expert as cats at catching rats. If a rodent poked his nose out of his hole some fellow would nab him like a cat. We had cleaned out all the cats about the fort but one. He was a pet of Colonel Brown's wife; she begged us not to disturb him, so Tom came in our prison perfectly free from danger, although I must say that about Christmas day the temptation was very great to make a Christmas roast of Tom. We went through Christmas week dreaming and talking of the good things our people must have at home in Dixie, and we would wonder if our loved ones and comrades had anything to eat beyond their army rations.

On the first day of January, 1865, the scurvy became prevalent in our prison. The doctor, whose name I can not remember, did the best he could for us with the medicine General Foster's order allowed him to use in practice amongst the prisoners. He would often say, "Men, the medicines allowed me are not the proper remedies for scurvy, but I can get no other for you. I am doing all I can for you. On or about the 15th of January, 1865, our condition became so serious that Capt. J. Lewis Cantwell, of North Carolina, wrote a letter to some friends in relation to our treatment. If the letter ever reached Richmond I do not know. Below is a copy of the letter sent by Captain Cantwell:

Fort Pulaski, Ga., February 6, 1865.

Hon. George Davis,
    Attorney-General C.S.A.,
      Richmond, Va.

My Dear Sir:
    Believing that it is not contraband and that the Federal authorities do not desire to conceal the facts, I write to you to state briefly the suffering and privation to which we are subjected, and I challenge a denial. Since the 1st day of January last our ration has been per day ten ounces of corn meal, about four ounces of wheat bread, salt, etc, and more pickles than we can eat! And until very recently this, too, was the only diet for those of us who were sick. Three-fourths of our number are in consequence sick with scurvy, diarrhœa, and coughs, and supplies have not been allowed to reach such of us as had friends to send them, but were returned; and we are directed to apply to General Wessel at Washington, D.C, for permits to receive them. A number of applications have been made, but as yet no reply has been received. I write requesting that these facts be made known in the proper quarter. To our enemies I have no complaint to make.
    Very truly your friend,

John S. Cantwell,
    Captain 3d N.C Inf.,
      Prisoner of War.

Our condition was almost beyond endurance during the last days of January. Colonels De Gurney, Le Breton, Captain Cantwell, and others wrote Colonel Brown, commandant of the prison, a letter, which must have been sent to General Grover, commanding Savannah District, who sent his medical director to inspect our prison and report our condition. Here is General Grover's letter to superior headquarters:

Headquarters District of Savannah,
Savannah, Ga., February 7, 1865.

Assistant Adjutant-General,
Headquarters Department of the South.

My medical director yesterday inspected the condition of the Rebel prisoners confined at Fort Pulaski, and represents that they are in a condition of great suffering and exhaustion for want of sufficient food and clothing; also, that they have scurvy to considerable extent. He recommends, as a necessary sanitary measure, that they be at once put on full prison rations and, also, that they be allowed to receive necessary articles of clothing from friends. I would respectfully endorse the surgeon's recommendations, and ask authority to take such steps as may be necessary to relieve actual sickness and suffering.

C. Grover,
Brev. Maj.-Gen. Commanding.

(*War Records*, Vol. VIII, Series II, Serial 121, p. 163).

No attention was paid by headquarters to this request of General Grover. The corn-meal-pickle diet went on, and we suffered. No blankets, no clothing was ever given us – and I have been informed by Dr. Cherry, now of Virginia, that he was one of a committee who delivered to Gen. J. G. Foster, under flag of truce, clothing and other articles for our comfort, which General Foster's flag of truce officers received and promised should be delivered to the prisoners at Fort Pulaski and Hilton Head, but which never were given us, but stolen by the men, I suppose, who received them for us under a flag of truce. General Foster, U.S.A., has much to be proud of in this transaction. I shall pass it without further comment.

About the last days of January and during the month of February our suffering was most intense. Scurvy had strong hold on our men, and the doctor in charge of the prison was not allowed the proper medicine to combat the dread disease. I say again, it is strange that we did not eat each other. Nothing but the bayonets of the guards prevented it. The first dog meat used in our prison was the suggestion of Lieut. Dave N. Prewett, one of Morgan's famous cavalry, who by his persuasive manner, decoyed inside of the dead line a beautiful setter dog, property of one of the fort officers. When the dog crossed the dead line it was but a few moments before Prewitt had him inside the prison. In very short order the carcass of the dog was ready for the pan, in the shape of chops, roasts, and fries. After cooking the dog meat Prewitt invited some of his friends to the feast, I amongst them. The meat, to us starving men, was delicious. The next feast of dog meat was served by Lieut. Matt Hixon, Arkansas. There was a fine, large, fat pointer that often came into our prison, and Hixon concluded one day to slaughter this dog, which he did; and again we reveled in dog meat. We had steaks, roasts, and soup. The meat was tender and white; but, reader, I do not commend dog meat as a daily food, but if you ever are so unfortunate as to be a prisoner of war in the hands of a Gen. J. G. Foster, living on retaliation rations, you will find in your hunger that dog meat is most excellent, indeed.

It is impossible to explain how we lived through the terrible ordeal of fire and starvation. Those were horrible days – days which most thoroughly convinced me that nothing but actual experiment can determine how much starvation, hunger, and bad treatment a human being can stand, especially if he was a prisoner of war in the hands of the Federal government during the years 1861-65. When the wolf, hunger, takes hold of a man, all that is human in the man disappears. He will, in his hunger, eat anything. I most fully understand, after my personal experience, why those poor fellows on the late expedition to the North Pole did eat each other, and thought it no crime. No person knows what hunger is, what it really means, unless they have had an experience in starvation's grasp. The torture of starvation exceeds all other torture in intensity; it beats sheol itself. What can be greater torture to a man with the least heart than to suffer himself and see those he loves suffering about him, and he powerless to help them? It was sad, it was heart-breaking, to see the suffering of our men in the Fort Pulaski prison; suffering because Gen. J.G. Foster preferred to take the word of Confederate deserters to the word of his own officers and men who, over their own signatures, wrote him they were not under fire, not in danger, but kindly and fairly treated by the Confederate authorities, both officers and men, who guarded them.

One of the very sad cases of the regime at Fort Pulaski prison comes vividly back to me now. Lieut. Billy Funk, 5th Regt., Stonewall Brigade, one of our number, was little more than a boy in years when he joined the Confederate Army in 1861. A gallant, brave boy, he was captured May 12, 1864, at the battle of Spottsylvania Court House, reaching Fort Delaware prison just in time to be selected as one of the six hundred to be turned over to the tender care of humane Gen. J.G. Foster, U.S.A. Upon Lieutenant Funk the rigors of retaliation worked very hard, and soon completely broke him down. But never a complaint escaped his lips, and he bore his suffering like a hero. Lieut. Tom S. Doyle, a noble fellow, Funk's messmate and regimental comrade, with us all, did all we could do to help him and keep him alive, giving him part of our scanty corn meal ration and all the white bread given us, which was just two ounces. (This white bread was not added to our corn-meal pickle ration until late in February.) In his suffering with dysentery and scurvy Funk lost heart and nerve, slowly starving to death. One day I had the good fortune to catch a big fat cat. Capt. Thornton Hammack, 49th Ky. Regt., skinned the animal for me, and dressed it for the pan. In an old tin can I made soup of part of the cat for Funk, and, after threats and coaxing, I prevailed upon him to drink some of the soup. The effect upon him was magical. It revived him in spirits and for a time counteracted the effects of the scurvy. As long as I could get him rat and cat meat he showed signs of improvement; but the cats gave out, and the rats I could not catch. I had not the wealth to purchase them from the fellows who could, so poor Billy Funk relapsed back into his former condition. He never rallied, and died, shortly after our return to Fort Delaware prison, in the arms of his mother who was allowed to see him an hour or two before his death. Poor, dear Billy Funk! Methinks I can see your sad face now, and hear your gentle voice in prayer to God for relief denied you by your fellow man. Lieutenant Funk's remains now rest in Mount Hebron Cemetery – hallowed grounds – in Winchester, Va., beside the remains of his gallant brother, Col. Stover Funk, commanding the old Stonewall Brigade, who was mortally wounded, almost in sight of his home, near the close of the war. Billy Funk was a good Christian man. God bless the mothers of the South who gave such boys to the cause of right.

We had not less than two hundred of our number at Fort Pulaski suffering with dysentery and scurvy. At one time many died and were buried in the graveyard of the fort.

The officers and men of the 127th New York Volunteers were, from Colonel Brown down the line, clever, humane men. They felt our condition and did whatever they dared to alleviate our suffering. The doctor in charge of our prison medical department was a kindhearted man; I regret his name has gone from me, but his kindness to our suffering men will never be forgotten. Often, in these days of peace and plenty, the days of the ordeal of 1864-5 at Pulaski, comes back to me, and the kind face of that doctor, who did all that man could do for us with the medicines allowed for our use by that Christian soldier, Gen. J. G. Foster, U.S.A. All the doctor had in his medicine chest for use in the prison was calomel pills, opium pills, salts, and Jamaica ginger, with a few other medicines the doctor would smuggle into the prison for the very sick. Had he been detected by Foster's spies in this act of humanity, he would have lost his commission, and possibly his liberty, for disobedience of orders. Language can not describe our condition during the last days at Fort Pulaski, on the corn meal and pickle diet. Words are inadequate to make the picture. No pen can draw the ghastly picture and horrors of those days and nights, when the United States government permitted Gen. J. G. Foster, U. S. A., to starve six hundred helpless Confederate prisoners of war, at Fort Pulaski and Hilton Head. Edwin M. Stanton, Federal Secretary of War, gave the orders; Gen. J. G. Foster executed them.

The very idea of feeding human beings on ten ounces of corn meal and half a pint of acid pickles is revolting in itself. But couple it with the fact that the meal was rotten, filled with worms, without salt, meat, or grease to flavor it, is almost beyond belief. Yet the proof is beyond question that this rotten corn meal and pickle was all the ration Gen. J. G. Foster, the humane modern Nero, gave us while held at Hilton Head and Fort Pulaski as prisoners of war.

What was the result from this cruel order of retaliation? Under the sands of Morris Island, Hilton Head, S. C., and in the swamp graveyard of Fort Pulaski, and buried under the swamp, are Confederate soldiers – prisoners of war – murdered by the cruel retaliation orders of Edwin M. Stanton, Secretary of War, and his chief executioner, Gen. J. G. Foster, U. S. A.

Over the graves of these grand Confederate braves the bright stars of heaven keep vigil; the wild sea birds sing requiems to their rest, far away from their loved dead the hearts of many mothers mourn their boys, many a poor wife her husband, many a noble and sweet woman her soldier lover, who had left her and marched away to battle for the land he loved with her prayer – "God keep you and bless you, my darling" – ringing in his ear, who found an unmarked but honored grave under the sands of Morris Island, Hilton Head, and in the swamps about Fort Pulaski; and these graves point heavenward, monuments to the vindictive and wanton cruelty of Stanton and Foster to the six hundred Confederate officers, victims of their hate.

Col. P. P. Brown, I repeat, was a humane man. His soul revolted at the cruelty inflicted upon us by order of his superior

Major L. Clarke Leftwitch
Virginia

officer, General Foster. Colonel Brown, we were informed by his officers, had asked General Foster, time and time again, to send him and his regiment to the front; that they loathed their positions as jailors over helpless, starving men, over whose treatment they had no control. We wrote Colonel Brown a petition on one occasion, asking him to come into our prison and see our actual condition. His reply was, "I can not come and see the suffering of my fellow man which I am completely powerless to modify or prevent. My requests for you have all been ignored by headquarters; I can do nothing to alleviate your condition." On Sunday inspection Colonel Brown and his staff would rush through our prison like they were glad to get away from the sight of cruelty presented to them.

I want to say a few words for Colonel Brown's wife. One day, in a fit of desperation, I wrote Colonel Brown a note, asking him to grant me an interview. To my surprise, on the following day he granted it. A sergeant conducted me to his office quarters. The Colonel received me politely. I told him I had an uncle in St. Louis, St. Andrew Murray, who would gladly aid me with money if I were allowed to communicate with him. His reply was, "Sir, I, personally, would be glad to grant your request; but I am sorry indeed I can not, under my orders, do so. I am powerless." For a few moments he left the office. The lady who had been present during the interview was Colonel Brown's wife. Turning to me she said, "Write your draft on your uncle; you shall have the money." I made the draft as she directed, and in due time received the money. This kind, noble lady, God bless her, gave me, as I left the office, a paper containing two large slices of bread, butter, and ham. I took them to my sick comrade, Billy Funk. I say again, God bless that noble woman! May the Grand Master who implanted the Christian heart in her breast give her a crown in that better world of love and peace.

There were lots of good fellows in the 127th New York Volunteers. They had been often under fire, and could appreciate the condition and feel for the prisoners of war. Often, when they were on duty about the prison some of them would put a loaf of bread or piece of meat on the end of their bayonets and dare any Rebel to take it off, always holding their guns in such position that the meat or bread could be taken off by the prisoners. These men took this method of helping us and getting around the orders. They dared not openly disobey. There was one officer in this regiment who deserves well of every Fort Pulaski prisoner. He was Major Place, quartermaster of post. His kindness to the prisoners will ever be remembered by us all of the Fort Pulaski detachment. On one occasion this kind hearted fellow took a lot of his men fishing with seines in the Savannah River about the fort. At night, after their return, Major Place gave Capt. Ed. Chambers, of Alabama, one of the prisoners, a barrel of the fish he and his men had caught during the day. "These," he said, "Captain Chambers, distribute to your sick men who at another time he gave Captain Chambers a half-barrel of damaged coffee, which had been condemned by the quartermaster department, and would have been thrown out. Some spy about the fort reported this matter to Major-General Foster, commanding department; an investigation was made, but nothing resulted from it to Major Place. No doubt had General Foster's investigation proved the giving of the coffee to the prisoners, Major Place would have lost his commission for his humanity to starving men. God bless you. Major Place! May you prosper in this world, and the world to come, for your goodness and humanity to our starving men. Yours was the true Christian charity the Master taught.

These six hundred Confederate officers – prisoners of war – who went through the fearful ordeal of fire and starvation were a noble body of men. There were a few scallawags in our number, which is always the case in large or small bodies of men; but it is a proud record to present to the world, that, notwithstanding the ordeal of fire, starvation, and disease, there were but eighteen of the six hundred who faltered and took the oath of allegiance to the United States government, disgracing themselves, dishonoring their uniforms, leaving their comrades to suffer. What nation of the world can present a better record than this? And does it not prove the oft-repeated claim that the Confederate army was an army of heroes, whose hearts were as true and brave as ever beat in the breast of an Alexander, or a Ney? What could be said that would be flattery of the five hundred and eighty-three men who kept the faith throughout the terrible ordeal? No torture could wring from these men one whimper of pain, nor one regret that they had linked their fortunes with the cause of the South and followed her flag whither it led. These men were heroes by nature's gift; they were Southern men by birth, noblemen whose right to nobility came from God.

There is no place where the virtues and the vices, the true character of men, will so soon show itself, and so prominently, as it will when men are placed in the position as were these six hundred Confederate officers; the good or bad in a man's nature will rise to the surface like oil on water, do what he may to keep it down. And what a consolation it is to those who kept the faith, who now in the evening of life can recall that bitter past. They can tell it to their children without shame or regret, and thank God for the strength given them to bear the ordeal they were forced to undergo. Col. Abe Fulkerson, brave, generous, true, noble fellow, wrote me, just before his death: "Murray, I always thank God, and I have never forgotten to do this, for His goodness and mercy in allowing me to be one of the Immortal Six Hundred who kept the faith unto the end." Shortly after receipt of this letter Colonel Fulkerson was summoned to answer the roll call over the river. He is now resting under the trees in the camp of God's love. A braver or truer man never lived.

Charles F. Crisp, Lieutenant 10th Va. Regt. Inf., was one of the six hundred. After the war closed he became speaker of the United States Congress. Lieut. J. E. Cobb, 5th Texas, also became a member of Congress. Capt. Bruce Gibson, 6th Va. Cav., a true, generous soul, whose ministration to his sick comrades of the six hundred made him loved and honored – he, too, has gone to rest. I recall, as I sit and write, the dreadful sights of misery in that Fort Pulaski prison – loved comrades starving to death, dying with that terrible disease scurvy, and the great government of the United States responsible for all this wanton cruelty; and yet no effort was made to alleviate or curtail it. Who of the six hundred will ever forget grand old Capt. John Lucas Cantwell, N.C.? Gentle, kind, true; never tiring of helping his sick comrades. Grand old hero, your name is engraved upon our hearts; we can bear testimony for you before the bar of God. Dear old Capt. Ed Chambers, have you passed to your reward? You carried out the command of the divine Master, "love thy neighbor as thyself." Capt. Lewis Harman, 12th Va. Cav., generous with whatever he had. Lieut. Tom S. Doyle and Capt. J.L. Hempstead, doing all that men could do to better the condition of their sick comrades. And Lieut. Peter B. Akers – dear old Pete, the soul of generosity, the most unselfish man I ever knew in all my life; never thinking of himself, always doing for others. When it is God's pleasure to call dear old Pete over the line, I feel sure no crown in the kingdom of God's love will be brighter than that which will be given to P.B. Akers. All these dear old comrades were nature's noblemen; the leaven which God in His goodness gave to man, to lead him up to the higher life. As I gaze at the photographs that hang upon my room walls I see that one of dear comrade Le Broten, of Louisiana, gentle, kind, suffering without a murmur. A soldier of the Confederacy, he could die for principle; he would not surrender it. Then comes Capt. J.L. Hempstead, once during the war drill master of the 5th Va. Inft., Stonewall's Brigade; gentle as a woman, brave as the lion, a courtly knight of the old school, his heart went out in sympathy to his suffering comrades, his generous hand relieved their wants from his scanty ration. Captain Hempstead was born in Iowa, of Virginian parentage. When the war tocsin sounded he gave up home, loved ones, and comfort to help in the defense of Virginia's honor. Capt. Will Page Carter, Page's Battery, a lovable comrade, kind and generous, a dignified gentleman. "We can suffer, men, for principle; we can not surrender without dishonor," I heard him say to those comrades about him who were not able to leave their bunks. I wish it were possible for me to recall all the noble spirits of that Immortal Six Hundred. Their names are written on Fame's scroll. God knows them; the world will honor them. Many of those dear comrades have joined the silent army. Their memory shall always have the warmest spot in my heart; my prayer is for God's choicest blessings upon them all who were true unto the end of the inhuman ordeal of retaliation inflicted upon us by Stanton and Foster, backed by the United States government. We who were true can speak of the comradeship of love to each other. It was born in suffering, cemented by the brutality of a civilized government controlled by brutes. Men, as a rule, when suffering, become selfish; but this was not true of the majority of the six hundred. Of course, there were some selfish men in our number, but it can be truthfully said, take out from our number the seventeen scallawags who took the oath of allegiance, surrendering their manhood, and there never was a grander lot of men brought together than the Immortal Six Hundred. The efforts of one prisoner to relieve the other were sublime; it was grand. Captain Cantwell's conception of a prison aid society was a true index of the man's heart. Below is a copy of the intention of the society, its constitution and membership:

Relief Association of Fort Pulaski, 1864.

Confederate States Officers' Prison Barracks,
Fort Pulaski, Ga., December 13, 1864.

At a called meeting of the Confederate States officers confined in these quarters, held at the quarters of Major Jones, Col. A. Fulkerson was called to the chair and Capt. Jno. L. Cantwell requested to act as secretary. At the request of the chairman, Capt. H. C. Dickinson explained the objects of the meeting, to wit, to be the formation of an association for the relief, etc., of the sick of our number, etc., and submitted the following preamble and constitution, which were, on motion, adopted:

Whereas, It has been suggested that a number of our brother officers, confined with us as prisoners of war at Fort Pulaski, are deprived of some absolute necessaries of life, by reason of their inability to communicate with their homes and friends; and

Whereas, Some of such officers, by reason of the dis-

Captain J. L. Hempstead
5th Virginia

eases incident to prison life, are exposed to much suffering and in danger of neglect if left to the care of individuals, and

Whereas, We recognize the binding obligation on us, as Confederate officers, to search for and relieve the distress of all worthy officers and soldiers of our common country; now the more effectually to carry out our purpose we, whose names are signed to this paper,

Do Hereby Organize "The Confederate Relief Association," adopt the following constitution and by-laws for our government, and pledge ourselves, as individuals, from time to time, when called on by the proper officers of the "Association," to aid in sustaining it to the extent of our ability.

Constitution.

First Article. The officers of the Confederate Relief Association shall consist of a president, a vice-president, a treasurer, a secretary, and an executive committee of one man from each of the five divisions into which we are at present formed. Each of these officers shall be elected *viva voce*, and shall continue in office till a change in our situation or condition renders a new election necessary.

Second Article. It shall be the duty of the president to convene this Association when in his opinion it may be necessary. He shall preside at all the meetings, shall call on the Association for contributions to the treasurer, and shall detail, upon the suggestion of either member of the executive committee, nurses for the sick, and where practicable may command the medical services of any member of the society who may have been a physician.

Third Article. The vice-president shall preside during the absence or sickness of the president and is charged with the duty of assisting the president, as far as necessary, in all his duties.

Fourth Article. The secretary shall keep a record of all the proceedings, including a balance sheet of weekly receipts and expenditures, and shall countersign all orders for the expenditure of money.

Fifth Article. The treasurer shall receive and keep all moneys of the Association with an account of the same, and shall pay such moneys upon the orders of either member of the executive committee countersigned by the secretary.

Sixth Article. The executive committee shall be the active body of this Association, it being expected that they will search out all cases of sickness or suffering in this prison or any Confederate hospital connected with it, and report the same to the president; that they shall frequently meet on the call of the ranking officer of the committee to devise means for the aid and comfort of sick or suffering officers, and that when relief is necessary for any man in the division of either member of the said committee, he shall procure the same by a requisition upon the treasurer countersigned by the secretary.

The Association organized by electing the following officers:

Col. A. Fulkerson, president; Major Mac-Creary, vice-president; Capt. H.C. Dickinson, treasurer; Capt. J.L. Cantwell, secretary; and Capt. J.G. Knox, Major Jones, Captain Ake, Captain Campbell, and Major Zeigler, as members of the executive committee from Divisions No. 1, 2, 3, 4, and 5 respectively.

On motion adjourned.

John L. Cantwell, Secretary.

A List of Members of Confederate Relief Association.

A. Fulkerson	W.F. Leathers	H.T. Coalter
H.C. Dickinson	A. Dobyns	S. Lowe
P.V. Batte	J.W.A. Ford	C.S. Lewis
M.R. Wilson	T.M. Hammack	T.H. Harris
S.P. Allensworth	J. Ogden Murray	G.C. Nast
A.M. King	F. Foussia	T.J. Doyle
Rodes Massie	M.G. Zeigler	J.G. Brown
J.M. Surges	Wm. Barries	Dr. F. Booton
H.S. Handerson	D.A. Imes	H.M. Dixon
W.J. Dumas	J.B. McCreary	John L. Lemon
T.H. Board	J.N. Chisholm	Jno. B. Fitzpatrick
John L. Cantwell	R.L. Miller	
John D. Ashton	W.A. Martin	

December 28th.

The executive committee met and reported progress. The president reported collections made to amount of $11.00 and expenditures to amount of $11.00. The secretary was instructed to prepare an appeal to the prisoners for contributions to be placed in the hands of the executive committee.

Adjourned.

J.L. Cantwell, Secretary.

Hilton Head, S.C, November 24, 1864.

Capt. John L. Cantwell,

Dear Sir: – Agreeable to promise, I embrace this opportunity of writing you a few lines to inform you of our safe arrival at this place, all well. We arrived about seven o'clock the evening of the day we left Fort Pulaski. We are camped about one mile from the town, three in a tent – the same tents we lived in at Morris Island. Lieutenants Henderson, Merchant, and myself are together. Since we have been here we have had a very disagreeable time. The weather has been quite cold – we had ice last night and night before from a half to one inch thick. You would be amused to see our chimney which we have erected to our tent. The material is sand and grass. We had a fire in it last night for the first time, and made our tent comfortable, notwithstanding it smoked some. Built it higher this morning and hope it will draw better. No news of interest. Give my very best respects to Captains MacRae and Cowan, Lieutenants Gurganus, Henderson, and Childs and all enquiring friends. My address is Hilton Head, S. C. 3d Division. Hoping this may reach you safe and find you in good health, I remain

Yours very respectfully,

George M. Crasson,
Prisoner of War.

This was one of the letters that came to Fort Pulaski from Hilton Head after part of our number had been sent to that place. The incidents of the Fort Pulaski prison are written from memory; many have been forgotten. One thing that often impressed me was the heroic conduct of our men under the ordeal. Before taps, every night, some of our comrades would get together in one of the casemates of the prison and sing the old familiar songs of the South, seeming for the time to forget the pains of retaliation and their hunger. Some day I hope some of the noble six hundred will group together the incidents as they come to them, and put them in shape for preservation – the amusing with the pathetic, for they are all worth the keeping, and help to tell the story of those brave and true men.

One incident comes to me just now. One very cold day while standing by the cooking stove awaiting the building of the fire, I noticed a Georgia captain, of our party, picking from his ration of meal the lumps, bugs, and worms. I said, "Captain, why do you throw your corn meal away?" "I am not throwing it away," he replied, "I am picking out the bugs, worms, and filth." "Why, man," I said, "the bugs and worms are the meat intended for you, and will help to give taste to the meal." "That's so," he said, and quit the work. We had one or two opium eaters in our party, made so by the medicine furnished by order of General Foster. It was heartrending to see these poor, dear fellows begging for opium pills from the doctor, when sick call was made. It may have been wrong in me to do so, yet, when I saw their suffering for the drug, I would go to the doctor and get him to give me pills, which I would give to these grand men, made beasts by the cruelty of the United States government. One of the poor fellows died and was buried – Lieutenant Fitzgerald, C. S. N.

All matter personal to myself, so far as possible, has been left out of this history with the narration of the attempt of some of us to escape from Fort Pulaski, and letters from comrades. The story of Hilton Head prison is told with this story of those who did escape.

Christmas eve night, December 24, 1864, was one of the coldest nights, I think, we had to endure while at Fort Pulaski prison. I was lying in my bunk, praying that God would let me go to sleep and never awake in life. Yes, I was begging God to let me die and end my torture. I was cold and hungry, no blanket to cover me, no fire to warm me. As I turned over in my bunk, to warm the side of my body exposed to the cold, one of the boards fell from the bunk, and I got out to replace it, that I might lie down. In fixing the board in its place, by the dim light of the prison lamp, I saw beneath my bunk a trap door. For a few moments I felt dazed and really believed I was but dreaming. After a little while I gathered my wits, and this thought came to me: "Providence has answered your prayer; through this door you can reach liberty." Little sleep came to me after this discovery. I laid all sorts of plans, only to brush them aside. At daylight I awoke my comrade, Dave Prewitt, of Kentucky, and communicated to him my discovery. I can, in my mind, recall the look of pity Prewitt gave me after he had heard my story. It was a look that plainly said, "Poor Murray, he's gone; the cruelty was too much for him." But when he saw the door, like myself he concluded Providence made it especially for our escape. We sat on the side of my bunk guarding our secret as though it was a gem. We made plans, we rejected them, and we finally concluded to find out the construction plan of the fort before we moved. Capt. Ed. Chambers, of Alabama, one of our number, had some experience in building forts. After pledging him to secrecy, we unfolded to him our find, and the first reply he made to our inquiry threw upon us hogsheads of cold water. "Why, boys," he said, "this fort's foundation is no doubt a lot of large blocks of granite which you could not cut through in forty years if you had all the improved tools necessary for the purpose. And yet, it may be," he added, "the foundation is built of hard brick, set in cement. The door under your bunk goes down into an air chamber built for the purpose of keeping these casemate floors dry. One chamber does not connect with the other by any opening. These chambers are fifteen or twenty feet square and are built all under this fort. If you boys go down you will find yourselves in ten feet of water and mud that has oozed in from the moat; so take my advice and give up the project. It will not work."

When we finished this interview with Captain Chambers

our hearts were way down below zero. For a few hours we brooded over the matter saying very little of it to each other. December 25th, Prewitt and myself sat on the side of my bunk, talking of the good fat turkeys and luscious hams they were eating at his home in Kentucky, and how we could enjoy just the turkey bones, if we had them, when suddenly Prewitt turned to me and said, "Ogden, let's try and get to where those turkeys and good things are; let's go down through that trapdoor and find a way out of this hole." It was all done in a moment. Down in that hole we went, up to our armpits in water and mud; and the coldest water I ever dropped into. We groped about in the dark, feeling our way around the wall, but could find no opening. We did, however, find out that the foundation was brick, set in cement good and hard. After this discovery we found also that the wall at the water line was much wider than it was next to the floor. We got out by Prewitt getting on my shoulders and pulling himself out by the floor; then he pulled me out. Prewitt had two pair of pants, and part of an old blanket. He put on the pants and loaned me the blanket to keep me from freezing while my pants dried. I do positively believe I had to tell my comrades six million lies about how I fell down in one of the cisterns that some one left open. We gave Captain Chambers full details of our exploration below, but his advice was to stop our foolishness before we took cold and died. While talking to Chambers, he said: "If you had a good hard saw to cut out the cement, and a bar to pry out the bricks you might, in months of hard work, cut from one air chamber to the other until you cut outside of the guard line" – but this was doubtful. Well, this settled it, and we determined to cut that wall. We got hold of an eighteen-inch stove poker; Prewitt had an old dinner knife of which we made a saw; Billy Funk agreed to watch for the coming of the guard or officer of the day, and that night, December 25, 1864, we began what seemed to be a hopeless task. After taps, every night for a week, Lieutenant Funk would take up his position on my bunk, and if anything moved he notified us by knocking on the floor with his heels. We would then stop work until he gave the signal all was well. We worked on for one week, getting out but few bricks. We finally concluded to take into our confidence some help, so we organized a working party of Capt. W. W. Griffin, 1st Maryland Battery, C. S. A.; Captain Kent, Georgia; Lieutenant W. H. Chew, Georgia; Lieut. Hugh Dunlap, Tennessee; and Capt. Ed. Chambers, Alabama, with Prewitt and myself. One night a fellow named Gillespie caught Prewitt coming out of the trapdoor, so we took him in with us to keep him quiet. Every night we would go down in pairs to work on the wall. Our only tools were the case knife, made into a saw, and the eighteen-inch fire poker. We worked waist deep in water from the 25th of December, 1864, to February 28, 1865. We never missed one night, and our efforts were finally rewarded. We had cut through forty-two brick walls that were eight feet thick, making a cut through just 336 feet of solid brick walls, with that old case knife and poker. At last we were done and fixed upon the night of February 28, 1865 (which was Saturday night), to say good bye to our Yankee captors. So silently had we worked, so guarded was our secret, that not one of the prisoners outside of Lieut. Billy Funk knew we were at work on the tunnel of escape. By saving an ounce or two of corn meal each day, from our rations, we had considerable pone to sustain us until we could cross over the Savannah River and find friends from whom we could obtain food. At 11 p. m., February 28, 1865, we began our exit. Captain Griffin was the first man below. Lieutenant Chew followed, then Captain Kent, then Dunlap, Gillespie, Prewitt, then myself. When we had all gotten below, Captain Chambers could not, he said, get through the trap door, so we left him. Poor Lieut. Billy Funk cried and pleaded to be taken with us, but the poor fellow was unable to get out of the bunk, practically dead with scurvy. We chose the night of February 28th to make the move to escape, first, because the tunnel in the walls was finished; second, because General Mollineux, 157th N. Y. Vols., came this night with his command, to relieve the 127th New York and, in the confusion of transfer, we thought our chances would be better for success. The night was dark, and a drizzling rain was falling. All went well with us through the tun-

Lieutenant Pat Hogan
27th Virginia

nel until we reached the trapdoor in the casemate at the end of our tunnel, which we were to ascend through to the casemate above. When we attempted to remove the door we found, to our consternation, that it was weighted down by some very heavy weight. It was a dilemma we had not counted on. We knew we could not cut through another wall by daylight, so we concluded to force up that door at all risks. Four or five of us got under it, pushing with our hands and heads until Dave Prewitt could get the poker under the edge of the door. When he pried down on the poker he started the heavy body on the door to moving. Well, I have heard the artillery of Jackson in the Valley; I heard the roar of the guns at Gettysburg; I have heard the heavenly thunders of the Rocky Mountains; but I say to you, all these sounds combined were but pop-gun reports when compared to the noise those barrels made above our heads rolling over the casemate floor; and yet, strange as it may be, the noise did not disturb the slumbers of a whole company of the 157th New York Volunteers, asleep in the very next casemate. After waiting for a time, to hear if the noise alarmed the sentinels about the fort, we began to ask each other, "Shall we go back or go on?" (We could not see each other's faces in the darkness, yet I feel confident they would have been a study for an artist's pencil.) The question was put to vote – majority said, "Let's go on." Hearing no one moving above, we pushed up the trapdoor and began the ascent to the casemate above. Lieut. W. H. Chew, of Georgia, being the smallest man in our party, we raised him upon our shoulders to the floor. He, with the help of our rope, made of old pieces of clothing, blankets, and such material as we could from time to time get, pulled us up one by one. When we had all reached the casemate we had no trouble in getting out of the casemate window. Groping about the casemate in the darkness, we found an old army blanket. This, cut into strips, materially strengthened our rope. All being ready, we threw out our rope and began our exit from the fort porthole. I was delegated to remain and get rid of the rope. While the others were going down the rope I found an open barrel of brown sugar, ate bountifully of it, and filled my coat and pants pockets.

I forgot, in my hungry greediness, that I would be compelled to swim through the waters of the moat to reach the bank. When Gillespie, the last man to leave the fort before me, slid down the rope into the water he made as much noise as a whale, and I believe now he was then doing his best to attract the attention of the sentinel. I saw him finally go over the moat bank. I then followed down the rope, landed safely in the water, and had reached the moat bank when, just as I started to climb up the bank, the midnight relief came in sight. I was compelled to roll back into the water and remain until the guard passed on. After getting over the bank into the swamp I found the boys awaiting my coming. But I want to relate that the moat water dissolved all my sugar and left me in a sticky condition. I had tugged at the rope, but could not get it to budge, so left it hanging out of the casemate window. As the night was dark and rainy the guards did not see it as they passed.

Now that we were in the swamp, free from the prison, the problem presented itself, how to get a boat to leave the island. Then came the question, who should go forward and overpower the sentinel over the boats at the wharf, where they were kept moored, constantly guarded. Lieutenant Chew suggested that we draw cattails. This was adopted. Chew held the cuts, and the choice fell on Gillespie. He at once objected to going, on the ground that a smaller man could get through the swamp better than he. Not having time to discuss the philosophy of his objection, Prewitt said, "Come on, Murray. You and I will go ahead." Off we started, Prewitt in the lead, I next, and Captain Kent, of Georgia, close behind me, with Captain Griffin, Chew, and others following in our wake, some fifty feet behind, so as not to attract the sentinel. We came in sight of the wharf; against the horizon we could see the sentinel walking his beat. We stopped to arrange a plan of attack upon him. Prewitt was to move down on the right of the boats, I on the left, and Kent, direct from the point we halted. We started; everything was going nicely, and in a very few minutes we would have had the sentinel, and the boats would have been ours. We were slowly getting nearer and nearer to the bridge upon which the sentinel walked, which was built upon piles about two feet above the water. Just as we were ready for the final move, out on the night air rang the voice of Gillespie, howling, "don't shoot! don't shoot!" This, of course, alarmed the sentinel on the bridge; he fired his gun and called lustily for the sergeant of the guard; the fort was alarmed, the guards turned out, and our liberty was gone. In a few moments more we would have been sailing across the mouth of the Savannah River, free men, had not Gillespie howled out like a wolf.

Prewitt and myself pulled ourselves under the bridge, and Kent was taken in by the guard, who came flocking to the relief of the sentinel at the boat wharf. All were captured but Prewitt and myself. We remained in the water under the bridge, and were not recaptured until daylight. The whole garrison of the fort was under arms; there was no possible way for us now to escape.

While we laid under the bridge we could hear the sentinel telling the sergeant, "Why, I could have killed those fellows. I saw one on my right and one on my left, in the swamp, but thought they were alligators." Poor old fellow, whoever you were, on guard that night, walking your beat, you did not dream that there were three Rebels creeping towards you, determined on your capture. They were determined upon gaining their liberty. You stood between them and home.

When we were taken into the fort this man Gillespie took the oath of allegiance. Chew, Griffin, Kent, Dunlap, Prewitt, and myself were put in a dark cell; no dry clothing given us, and no fire allowed us, nor would Captain Sexton, the provost-marshal, allow us to have fire to dry our wet clothing.

Why Gillespie betrayed us has always been a mystery to me. He worked just as hard as any one of our party to cut the tunnel through the walls, and ate his corn meal and pickle with us. I can only account for his conduct on the ground that when it came to killing the sentinel over the boats he thought, if the escape failed, we would all be shot; and this broke his nerve and made him shout as he did. Afterward, shame of his conduct made him take the oath, that he would not be put in the cell with us. I never liked Gillespie. He was at heart a coward. I heard Lieut. Hugh Dunlap, of Tennessee, one of the most generous and kind men of our party, in a very gentle manner correct some statement Gillespie made about the Western army. Gillespie persisted in his statement. Lieutenant Dunlap arose from my bunk, where he was sitting, walked over to the fellow, shook his fist in his face, and said, "Gillespie, you are a liar, and you knowingly utter your slander." Gillespie dared not resent this, and I never liked him after the incident. Some years ago I heard Gillespie was alive and lived in Texas. If he be dead or alive I do not care; in his going or coming I have no concern. I do know he betrayed us and increased our sufferings. If he can hide his treachery from the world, he can not hide it from his God. His sin will find him out.

We were recaptured March 1, 1865, and we remained in the dark cell, without fire or dry clothing, until the 4th day of March, when we were started on our way back to Fort Delaware.

While we were confined in the dark cell we had a good deal of fun with Captain Sexton, the provost-marshal. He had a lot of balls with chains brought up to the cell door, rattling them around, and saying in a loud tone of voice, "I guess these will keep those Rebels from cutting walls. Sentinel, if you hear the least movement on the part of those fellows to break out of that cell, shoot them, and shoot to kill." He would come into our cell three and four times during the days we were confined, and volunteer the information that our case had been telegraphed to Washington city for advice; that in a few days we would all be tried and shot for destroying government property. He was always full of just such stuff as this. We would poke fun at him, telling him to hurry up the shooting. The day before we were put on the steamer to be sent back to Fort Delaware this man Sexton came into our cell and offered, if we would tell him who cut the walls first, who organized the party and plan to escape, he would let us go back into the regular prison and give us dry clothing. We told him if he would go and bring us in a good drink of whisky for each man, as we would not try the same plan again, we would tell him all about it. To our surprise, he brought in the whisky. We told him all about the scheme and plan, but he did not give us the dry clothing nor put us back in the regular prison. The irons that had been put on Prewitt and myself were taken off our hands and legs.

Early on the morning of March 4, 1865, Captain Sexton, with a guard, came to our cell, opened the door, and ordered us to fall into line. We marched down to the fort wharf, where we found the small steamer *Ashland* with the other prisoners (our comrades) on board. We were placed in the forward part of the ship's deck, and I heard Sexton tell the captain of the guard, "I hardly think it necessary to iron these fellows. They won't jump overboard, but they need close watching." Late in the afternoon, on March 4th, we steamed away from Fort Pulaski for Hilton Head, S. C. After some delay and protest by the officers of the guard (157th New York Volunteers) to going to sea in such a small steamer as the *Ashland*, overcrowded, we were transferred to the large ocean steamer *Illinois*, and put out to sea. "Grape" was rife amongst the prisoners. The Yankees said we were to be exchanged at Fortress Monroe, and sent from there up the river to Richmond. I do not think our fellows took any stock in the "grape" of exchange. Most of them were in such physical condition that they did not care what became of them.

On the sail back to Fort Delaware the officers and men of the 157th New York Volunteers gave us all the liberty of the ship we wanted; allowed us on deck, and to have staterooms if we could pay for them; and gave us good rations. They were soldiers, not brutes like Stanton and Foster. These men had been in the field. After a sail of several days we anchored in the harbor of Norfolk. Here Captains Leon Jestremeska, of Louisiana, and Du Preist, of Virginia, made their escape, account of which will be found in this work. While we lay in the James River the Norfolk people learned of it. They flocked down on the wharf, waving handkerchiefs and cheering us. While we were in Norfolk Harbor one of the officers of the 157th New York Volunteers told us we would not be exchanged. "Just what is to be done with you I do not know," he said, "but I do not think you will be exchanged.

You may all be placed in the hospital."

Later on, another one of the 157th New York officers said, positively, we were to be exchanged and would be home in a day or two. Believing this story to be true, I really did not think it worth while to escape from the boat, and Prewitt and myself abandoned a plan we had made to leave the ship.

After laying in the harbor for some time, our ship steamed out to sea. Nobody was allowed on deck; all must go below and stay there. This order was strictly enforced by the guard until we were well out at sea.

It soon became the general belief amongst the prisoners that we were going back to corn meal and pickle retaliation on Morris Island. Lieutenant Maury, one of our number, an old naval officer and familiar with the ocean, gave it as his opinion, from what he could see of the stars, that the ship was steaming south. This helped to confirm our belief that we were not done with the retaliation measures of Stanton. The anxiety and suspense became so intense amongst the prisoners that Col. Van Manning called the captain in charge of our guard and asked him to tell him candidly where we were going. The captain said very frankly that General Lee had begun an attack on Fort Steadman, in General Grant's front, the morning of our arrival at Fortress Monroe, and he (the captain of the guard) had orders to deliver us at Fort Delaware; that no more exchange of prisoners would be made.

It was the most dejected and broken lot of men on earth when this news came to us, yet we said one to the other, "Fort Delaware is far better than Fort Pulaski and its corn-meal-and-pickle ration." At night we pulled out of Norfolk Harbor; on the morning of the following day we were landed on the wharf of Fort Delaware, and turned again into the old prison pen from which we had been taken eight months before. On the voyage from Fortress Monroe to Fort Delaware two of our number died and were buried in the ocean – dumped overboard, their bodies sewed in canvas bags. These poor fellows could have been kept until we landed, as we were but an hour or two's sail from Fort Delaware.

We had not been in our old quarters one moment before we were compelled to relate to our comrades the story of our hardships and the inhuman cruelty inflicted upon us at Morris Island and the other points of our imprisonment. Our comrades at Fort Delaware had greatly increased in numbers during our absence; they all seemed to be in good health, and had good clothes, which made the contrast between our haggard, ragged, emaciated crowd very perceptible. Our comrades brought out their stores of provisions and extra clothing, giving us freely all they could spare. What a grand chance the United States Sanitary Commission missed in not having a photograph made of the survivors of Secretary Stanton's brutality. What a grand contrast our photo would have made with those photos alleged to have been made at Andersonville and other Southern prisons after the surrender. It is a pity, indeed, those loyal souls who were ever anxious to stir the Northern heart did not have taken, for distribution in the North, our photos. Our condition would have brought the blush of shame to every Northern cheek, and made even Edwin M. Stanton turn pale at the sight of the victims of his brutality. We enjoyed the limited freedom of Fort Delaware. We were away from Colonel Hallowell and his negro guards; free now from their insolence. The prison life at Fort Delaware was broken in numerous ways by the diversity of the "law schools," "medical schools," and "divinity schools." Lieut. George W. Finley, now the reverend and eloquent D. D. of the Presbyterian Church of Virginia, began his study for the ministry in the prison of Fort Delaware, under Rev. Dr. Handy.

There were in our prison gamblers, barbers, tailors, laundrymen, workers in rubber, and a minstrel troop, which gave performances in the mess hall of the prison when the commandant gave the permission. The proceeds from these shows went to relieve our sick comrades in the prison hospital. Sutler's checks was the currency of the prison, and these checks were taken at the mess house door for admission to the show. General Schoepf and his staff often attended these shows. Peter B. Aker as the tambourine, and J. Ogden Murray as bones, were the star performers of the show, with Capt. Ed. Chambers as the manager.

Now spring had come and the fatal 9th day of April had brought to us the news of the surrender of Gen. Robert E. Lee, at Appomattox. President Lincoln was assassinated. The end had come, and we were men without a country – soldiers without a flag. We were broken indeed. Some days after General Lee's surrender the authorities at Washington ordered General Schoepf to ascertain how many of the prisoners at Fort Delaware prison would take the oath of allegiance to the United States government. On first roll call about seven hundred of the fifteen hundred officers – prisoners of war – gave their assent to "swallow the yaller dorg" as we called taking the oath. We who refused to take the oath held an indignation meeting, protesting against the insult offered us by asking us to take the oath. Col. Van Manning, Maj. P. J. Otey, Colonel Fellows, and others spoke at this meeting against our comrades taking the oath, but it did no good in stemming the desire of our men to get home. They were worn out by prison cruelty, and General Lee had no army. The men pined for home and liberty. In a few days the roll was again called. At this call but two hundred of us were left who refused to take the oath, and at the third call there were but three of us left, out of the whole number, who declined to take the oath upon any condition. Shortly after these roll calls Gen. Joseph E. Johnston surrendered his army. The Confederacy had now but Gen. Dick Taylor's army in the field, and he at last surrendered. About July 25, 1865, most of the prisoners except the three who declined to take the oath, and the field officer prisoners, were released and sent to their homes in the different States of the South. Finally all were released and sent home.

We left sleeping in death at Fort Delaware some grand men – murdered by the cruelty of prison life. Those who lived through the ordeal returned to their homes to find them in ruins. Desolation had spread its black wings over our beloved South. The blue uniform of the Yankee soldier was to be seen everywhere. Yet, at the sight of all this ruin and desolation, the men who followed Lee did not falter. They went to work to rebuild, upon the ruins of the old, new homes. They soon convinced the world that they were as good builders as they were fighters. The same old courage, obedience, and fortitude that made them the ideal soldiers of the world came to their aid. From the wreck and the ruin of war was built the Southland of today; and built upon the only capital the Confederate soldier had after the war was done – his honor and courage. Indeed was our land the land described by the poet priest of the South in his beautiful poem:

> Yes, give me the land that the battle's red blast
> Has flashed to the future the fame of the past;
> Yes, give me the land that hath legend and lay
> That tells of the memories of long vanished days;
> Yes, give me the land that hath story and song,
> Enshrining the strife of the right with the wrong.
> Yes, give me the land with a grave in each spot,
> And names in the graves that shall not be forgot,
> And the graves of the dead with the grass overgrown
> Will yet be the footstool in liberty's throne.

———————————

Morristown, Tenn., April 25, 1898.

My Dear Old Murray: – Your letter came to me safely, am delighted to hear from you again, and pleased beyond measure that you are getting ready to put in print the story of the Immortal Six Hundred. I can not, in my condition, help you much with the work. You know all the details of the trip much better than I. As you say, the story can only be told from a personal experience of that which came under your observation. Write, Ogden, as you know it. If the story is not full in all details it will convey to the world an idea of the wanton cruelty inflicted upon us in that stockade pen on Morris Island, while under the fire of our own guns, and while we were on those starvation rations following our removal from Morris Island to Fort Pulaski and Hilton Head. I will aid you all I can.

How I would love to see you, dear old Murray. You were always bright, never faltering, never bemoaning that the fates had cast us into that hell on earth. As I write I am wondering if time has made much change in you. Have the fates dealt out to you much sorrow, or given you much pleasure? You deserve well of the fates, and the love of your comrades of the Six Hundred. Generous, dear old fellow, come and see me here on the old farm (I call it the Rabbit Patch); come, that we may once more meet, that I can shake your hand and tell you my love for you has not grown less.

I can see you, dear old fellow, sitting on that stage in the mess hall at Fort Delaware. I can hear your voice as you sing "The Little Groceryman"; I see you dancing and singing "Old Bob Ridley," to help your sick comrades in the prison hospital.

My physical condition is not much, but my heart is as true, and my love as intense as ever for each one of that dear old Six Hundred who kept the faith unto the end, as they did in those days of corn meal and pickle rations. We can never forget the dog meat, the cat and rat meat – the luxury of our starving men. Print, in large black letters, the names of those fellows who took the oath. They made this roll of dishonor themselves; they elected to wear the badge of dishonor; why should we shield them now?

Your letters are always welcome. They bring me sunshine. I have written my brother, Maj. Albert Akers, who lives in Washington city, to hunt you up and meet you when he goes to Winchester. God bless you and bless yours. May He, in His mercy, permit us to meet once more on this side of the picket line of life.

Affectionately your comrade,
P.B. Akers.

CHAPTER FOUR

Accounts of Hilton Head Prison and Escape
by Lieutenant Peter B. Akers of Lynchburg, Virginia,
Capt. Leon Jestremeska of Alberville, Louisiana,
and Capt. W.D. Ballantine of Pensacola, Florida

On the 27th day of October, 1864, when we had been but a few days at Fort Pulaski prison, Gen. J. G. Foster, commanding Department of the South, headquarters at Hilton Head, S.C., sent an order to send him two hundred of the prisoners of war confined at Fort Pulaski, Ga., this being necessary, said the surgeon's report of the fort, to preserve our health and better our condition.

On the afternoon of October 21, 1864, two hundred and twenty of the six hundred were picked out of the number at Fort Pulaski, put on board of the steamer *Cannonicus*, under guard of the 144th New York Volunteers, and sailed away to be the special guests of Gen. J.G. Foster, U.S.A., commanding Department of the South. We were his guests for torture. He was the modern Nero, we his victims. We reached Hilton Head on Saturday afternoon and remained on the steamer until Sunday morning, when we were unloaded on the wharf, at Hilton Head, and marched under guard to a camp a mile in rear of Hilton Head village. The same old A-tents we used on Morris Island had been put up for our shelter. The first night in camp was very uncomfortable. The air was cold and crisp, we were not allowed fire, many of us were without blankets and had very light clothing, our beds was the bare sand, our discomforts more than tongue can tell. Monday morning came clear and cold. To keep ourselves warm we ran and jumped about inside of the dead line. We made no complaints. It was useless to complain to Nero Foster. With stolid indifference we took whatever came. We remained one week in this camp, suffering from cold and hunger. At the end of the week we were removed from the canvas city into a large log building in the town of Hilton Head. This log house was built and used by the United States government as a military prison for the Department of the South, to confine the white and negro Yankee deserters, oath-takers, murderers, thieves, and all the camp-following villains of the United States army.

The rations for the first week of our sojourn at Hilton Head were first class. But after that week it was followed by the delicious, the palatable, and strength destroying ration of ten ounces of rotten corn meal and one-half pint of cucumber and onion pickle, without salt or grease of any kind – all we got was rotten corn meal and pickle. It now began to dawn upon our minds that we were, sure enough, General Foster's victims. After ten days on the corn meal diet, our condition was horrible. Col. Van Manning made a personal protest, against this cruelty and rations, to Colonel Gurney, the provost-marshal in charge of our prison, and made a written protest to General Foster; but the ration of corn meal was not changed, nor the cruelty of Foster in the least abated. If the Confederate government had been feeding prisoners of war in their prisons a corn meal and pickle diet there would have been no complaint from us. We knew our government was feeding Federal prisoners better rations than corn meal and acid pickle. We knew all prisoners of war in Confederate prisons were getting the same ration as the Confederate soldiers in the field received. It is a great pity that those artists of the North, who from their fertile brains created the pictures of the woe and suffering of the Yankee prisoners of war in the prisons of the South, let our Hilton Head prison escape their lurid pencils. What grand subjects of suffering they could have drawn from our condition in that prison. Yea, they would have found much to depict to their readers in the North, and much, indeed, to make

Captain W. D. Ballantine
5th Florida

them hide their heads in shame at the slanders they wrote against the South and our people. To misstate the facts, to slander the South, and vilify President Davis, seemed to be, during the war of 1861-65, the only mission of the Yankee artist. It fired the Northern heart; it brought new recruits to the army of coercion. Those correspondents and artists did their work well. It was cruel work, but it brought them the blood money. What cared they for the truth? It would not pay them to tell it.

It was a brutal mind that conceived the corn meal and pickle diet. It was the brutal hand of Foster that executed it upon helpless prisoners of war. On this diet of corn meal, with no meat or vegetables, scurvy soon came to add to our suffering, and acute dysentery was prevalent among our men. It took stout hearts to bear the burden put upon us. Many of our number physically gave way under the cruelty, but, in spite of it all, our men bore it with dignity and courage.

We expected no favors – we asked none – of a government so cruel as was the United States government in 1861-65. The pangs of starvation became terrible; hunger drove our men to catching and eating dogs, cats, and rats. It was dainty food to starving men. When history records the true story of the great conflict of 1861-65, I wonder what the verdict of those who will read of the wanton cruelty of the United States government – inflicted upon its prisoners of war – will be. It was cowardly, it was cruel, it was brutal, and unjust before God and man. The official records show that Gen. J. G. Foster, U. S. A., commanding Department of the South, was the executioner for Secretary Stanton's cruel orders of retaliation, and these same records do not, and dare not, publish the corn-meal ration order. During those days of our torture a petition from the citizens of Indiana was presented in the United States Congress, by Senator Lane, asking the United States government to retaliate upon all Confederate prisoners of war in the Federal prisons of the North; for the reason, the petition set forth, that the Confederate government was inhumanely treating Federal prisoners of war confined in Southern prisons. This whole petition recited a bold, broad lie; a mean, deliberate, malicious slander on the brave people and government of the South. It was then a well known fact, and at this day proven beyond question, that the Confederate government was willing and anxious to exchange prisoners of war, but the powers at Washington, and General U.S. Grant, refused to make exchange, and rejected all offers for exchange made to them by the Confederate authorities. In fact, the United States authorities even refused to send transports and get their sick and wounded men – prisoners of war – that our government offered them at any time they would send transports. It further can be said, without fear of contradiction, that, at the time this petition for retaliation was before the United States Senate, President Lincoln and all his officials had full knowledge that the Confederate government was feeding to its prisoners of war the same rations the Confederate soldier received in the field. What more could our government do? What more could be demanded of them?

The late Senator Sumner offered a substitute for the Lane resolution of retaliation, which can be found in the United States Senate Reports, 1864-65. It reads:

"Be it resolved, That the treatment of our officers and soldiers in Rebel prisons is cruel, savage, and heartrending beyond all precedent; that it is shocking to morals; that it is an offence against human nature itself; that it adds new guilt to the great crime of rebellion, and constitutes an example from which history will turn with sorrow and disgust.

"Resolved, That any attempted imitation of Rebel barbarism in the treatment of prisoners of war would be plainly impracticable on account of its inconsistency with the prevailing sentiment of humanity amongst us; that it would be injurious at home, for it would barbarize the whole community; that it would be utterly useless, for it would not affect the cruel authors of the revolting conduct which we are asked to overcome; that it would be immoral, because it would proceed from vengeance alone; that it could have no other result than to degrade the national character and the national name, and to bring down upon our country the reprobation of history. And being thus impracticable, useless,

immoral, and degrading, it must be rejected as a measure of retaliation, precisely as the barbarism of roasting and eating prisoners of war is always objected to by civilized powers.

"*Resolved*, That the United States, filled with deepest grief and sorrow for her cherished citizens who, as officers and soldiers, have become the victims of heaven defying outragers, hereby declare their solemn determination to put an end to rebellion, of which it is natural fruit; that to secure this end they pledge anew the best energies and all the resources of the whole people, and they call upon all to bear witness that they renounce all vengeance and every evil example, and plant themselves on the sacred landmarks of Christian civilization under that God who is ever present with every prisoner, and enables heroic souls to suffer for their country."

Of all the hypocritical utterances, this is the worst. Certainly Mr. Senator Sumner knew that at the very moment he was denouncing retaliation against the Confederate government, his own government was torturing, by starvation and wanton cruelty, at Hilton Head, S.C, and at Fort Pulaski, Ga., six hundred Confederate officers, prisoners of war.

The laws of all nations say that prisoners of war shall, and must, be treated fairly and humanely, and with strict justice. No earthly power can change this. It is the law of God, and the human power that violates this law is guilty of murder.

No excuse can be given by the apologists for Mr. Stanton, who ordered the inhuman treatment inflicted upon the Immortal Six Hundred Confederate prisoners of war on Morris Island, at Fort Pulaski, and Hilton Head. The law of God was defied; the law of nations violated. History will judge the officials guilty of the crime, and the Confederate prisoners of war, murdered by the cruelty of Stanton and Foster, will be the witnesses before the bar of God to condemn them. From the verdict of heaven there can be no appeal.

The following order was posted in our prison:

Provost-Marshal's Office,
Hilton Head, S.C., February 7, 1865.

General: – The major-general commanding the Department of the South directs me to inform you that the rations of the prisoners of war held in your department for retaliation (here was interlined some hieroglyphics) have been increased by four ounces of meat per diem and the addition of four ounces of potatoes. You will please give the necessary instruction to the officer in charge of the Rebel prisoners here, and in custody at Fort Pulaski, Ga.

I am very respectfully your obedient servant,

Wm. Gurney, Provost-Marshal-General,
Lieut.-Col. 127th N.Y. Vols.

This order brought joy to our hearts. We were starving. Four ounces of meat and four ounces of potatoes to be added to our corn meal diet! It would save us from death. We had been reduced by the corn meal until a majority of our number had a very slim hold on life. It gave us all new hope, in fact, a new lease on life. During all our bad treatment I never heard one of the six hundred who remained true to the end utter one complaint against the Richmond government. We all knew it was doing its best to make the Yankees treat us fairly and humanely.

After our arrival at Hilton Head, as I stated before, our camp was near that of the 144th New York Volunteers (our guard). We were hardly located before Captains Tom Perkins and Campbell, with Colonel Folk, of North Carolina, and Lieutenants Killmartin, Brinkly, and John Casson organized a party and began digging a tunnel in their tent to enable them to get outside of the guard line and escape. They worked day and night on the tunnel, and in two days they would have completed it; but the camp was moved into the barracks at Hilton Head, and their efforts came to naught.

Capt. Tom Perkins was one of the most daring brave men I ever knew. He would take the most desperate chance to get away of any man in the prison. He was the most determined of men, yet to his comrades he was as gentle as a woman. He was a man positively without fear, and the men associated with him in his plans to escape were just as brave as himself. After a few days in the log barracks, Perkins and a party set about planning to escape. With nothing but pen knives for tools these men succeeded in cutting through two of the thick logs that formed the floor of their cell. They finished their work, but concluded not to leave the prison until about the middle of November. On the night of November 20th, just after the clock at the provost-marshal's office struck ten, Colonel Folk, of North Carolina; Capt. Tom Perkins, and Lieutenant Killmartin left their cell and safely passed the guard line of the prison. At midnight Captain Campbell, Lieutenant Casson, and Lieutenant Brinkly followed. After passing the guard line in safety, they came to the high fence surrounding the prison barracks, and all passed over the fence safely and began to flatter themselves they had now reached safety, ending all trouble. But they soon found their trouble had just begun. Right in the rear of our prison was a large workshop in which convict prisoners of the United States Army were made to work. Our men went into this shop and out the back door, when they found themselves confronted with a second high board fence, and upon this fence was a parapet on which the sentinels on guard over the prison workshop walked. They eluded the guards, and had gotten safely over this fence and found themselves in a large field, when, to their surprise and consternation, they discovered they had taken the wrong direction, and, before they were aware of it, they stumbled upon a sentinel. This compelled them to make a hasty retreat, which threw them further out of their course, and they landed in a large swamp, waist deep, in which they floundered some time before they found solid ground, and this they did by crawling on their hands and knees. They finally found themselves near Mitchellville, a negro settlement, a growth of the Yankees harboring runaway negroes. Covered as they were with mud, they passed boldly through this village, the negroes not being able to tell if our men wore the blue or gray. They made no stop in the village. Passing through the village safely, they turned, as they thought, towards the south. Daylight now began to approach and they looked about for a hiding place. They found one in a clump of large bushes about one mile from the negro settlement. In this clump of bushes they remained all day without food or water, compelled to lie close to the ground to keep themselves from being seen by the soldiers and negroes constantly passing on the road which was within fifty feet of their hiding place. Had the negroes discovered them, not one man would have been left alive, so bitter was the hatred of the runaway negroes for the "Rebs." After the painful hours of the day had passed into night with her black robe thrown over the world, they started out in the dark to hunt the right road south. They had gone from their hiding place but a mile or two when they came onto a negro cabin. Being almost famished for water, they concluded to stop and ask for water. One of the party started for the cabin, but before he reached the door a negro woman came out with a bucket in her hand, leaving the door open behind her. In the light they saw a negro cavalry sergeant in the room. They at once retreated back into the road. They had not gone a mile from this cabin when they found they were on the outskirts of a village, which proved to be Mitchellville. Again they retreated a mile or so back. Now hunger and thirst began to tell upon them, and they were compelled to stop for rest. They were completely broken down. They hid in some bushes and all fell asleep from exhaustion. When they awoke they were chilled, numbed, and in great pain, which made it difficult for them to walk. They, however, again took up the line of march, as they thought, to the south. They staggered on for some time, when they came in sight of a large building, which they concluded would afford them shelter, but, hearing the sentinel on picket calling "halt," they retreated back into the road, and laid down for a moment or two. Daylight was breaking, and they must again seek shelter. They saw in the distance a small clump of trees, and they made for it. From this shelter they could see soldiers and negroes passing up and down the road. Now a new trouble presented itself to them. Their wet clothing became heavy and uncomfortable. Hunger and thirst was wearing them out, and they dare not go out from their hiding, in daylight, to seek food. In looking into the haversack they found about a spoonful of wet corn meal for each man, and this was divided amongst them.

When night came the boys again began their march. Captain Campbell, who was a scout of note, took up a position on the road, that he might ascertain by the travel in which direction the town lay. They had all gotten together and were about to start, when two cavalrymen galloped into sight. They laid down in the ditch alongside of the road. After these horsemen passed the boys fell in behind them, trusting to fate to discover to them the outer picket post towards Charleston. After a long tramp they discovered they were going in the wrong direction, and were compelled to seek shelter in a swamp to keep from being picked up by a company of infantry coming towards them. After consultation in the swamp it was concluded best to await the coming of some lone person on the road, and go boldly out to him and ask for information. Again the morning light was coming, and they must seek shelter. They were too weak to walk far, so they just laid down in the swamp grass and soon fell asleep, and did not awake until late next day, when they found their limbs so swollen and numb they could hardly walk, and then only with great pain. Yet they had no idea of going back to prison. From their place of hiding in the swamp they saw a clump of timber. This they safely reached and in its shelter remained the day and night. Next morning, after they had reached the timber, Lieut. Hugh Brinkly was discovered by some negro wood choppers, who informed the white soldiers of the presence of a white man in the woods, dodging about amongst the trees. A large body of troops was thrown around the timber, from which escape was impossible, and our boys, broken down, weak, hungry, and thirsty, were recaptured and brought back to prison – the human torture house. While our boys were in custody of the 144th New York Volunteers, who had captured them and treated them kindly, a Confederate deserter came up to ask about the capture. He was dressed in citizens' clothes. After looking at our boys for some moments this scoundrel pulled a pistol out of his belt and, pointing it at Captain

Captain Leon Jestremeska
10th Louisiana

Campbell's head, deliberately pulled the trigger, and would have killed Campbell but for the timely aid of one of the 144th New York, who knocked the pistol out of the fellow's hand. This fellow was acting as spy for the Western Yankee army, and had recognized Captain Campbell as one of the Wheeler scouts.

After a march of a few miles our men were turned over to the provost-marshal and put back into close confinement in the barracks for a few days, when they were again released to the general prison.

After a few days of rest the same party, with the addition of Captains Kitchen, of North Carolina, Dupriest, Lieutenants Akers, Oliver, and Sergeant Denham began another plan of escape. After the organization had been arranged, as a matter of prudence they concluded to start out a scout, let him get proper locations, and then return to the prison to report. Then the whole party should leave. This being arranged, one evening just after the five o'clock roll call of the prison was made, Captain Campbell, arrayed in the uniform of a Yankee lieutenant, with Captain Perkins and Sergeant Denham in the uniform of privates (how they procured them no one has ever known), walked boldly out of the prison, passed the sentinel, and reached the outer guard about the prison before being halted. When the sentinel at the outer gate halted them Captain Campbell said, "I am Lieutenant Thomas, 22d New York Volunteers. My men and myself got inside of your post line looking for the well." The guard saluted Campbell and they passed out the gate. While getting the proper direction our boys stumbled on some Yankee soldiers cooking supper. Captain Campbell saluted them, asked several questions, said good night, and started with his two comrades down the road. Now that this danger was past another problem presented itself: how to pass the provost-marshal's office guard, and officers that would most likely be sitting on the porch at the office. The boys put on a bold front, walked slowly down the road past the office, saluted the guard and a group of officers sitting on the porch, they thinking Campbell was what his uniform made him look – a Yankee officer of the newly arrived troops from the East.

The boys went into the town of Hilton Head, mixed with the troops, talked with the officers, learning all they could that would help them on their final trip. In the distance our men saw some old breastworks and told the officer who had pointed them out that they would run over and take a look at them. Saying good evening, they started for the breastworks; but before reaching them darkness overtook them, and before they knew it they walked into a lake of water. In their struggle to reach the shore they attracted the attention of the sentinel on duty, who challenged them and demanded one should advance and give the countersign or he would shoot. Captain Campbell told the sentinel to call the sergeant of the guard. The sentinel obeyed, and in a few moments the sergeant came up with a lantern. Seeing Captain Campbell in the uniform of a Yankee lieutenant, he saluted him and asked what was the matter. Campbell told the sergeant a story about his men wanting to look over the old breastworks and he gratified them by coming with them; but in the darkness they lost their way and walked into the lake. The sergeant listened attentively to Campbell's story, was convinced he was all right, piloted Campbell and his companions over the lake shore without going past the reserve guard. Before leaving prison Campbell had prepared himself and comrades a pass. This he showed the sergeant, who grew very polite and insisted in putting the boys on the right road to camp. After the sergeant left our boys they pushed up the road and soon found themselves in Seabrook; and all this due to the polite sergeant, who never suspected he was aiding Rebel prisoners of war to escape.

While on their way to Seabrook they heard before them the gallop of horses, and hardly had time to conceal themselves before two cavalrymen dashed past, evidently couriers from Seabrook. After a consultation by our boys as to the next move to make, they concluded to try and capture some old darky to guide them into and about Seabrook, so they could locate the boats and sentinel over them. They had not gone down the road very far when it seemed like Providence sent them the very man they were looking for in the person of a very gullible old darkey, credulous, like all his race. Campbell stopped him and introduced himself as Lieutenant Thomas, 22d New York Volunteers, the newly arrived regiment from the East. He then told the old darkey that if he could get them a good boat or show him (the Lieutenant) where a boat could be obtained in Seabrook, they would take him to Pinkney Island, where they had buried a lot of fine whisky, part of which the darkey was to have for his trouble in getting the boat and helping to get the whisky over to the mainland. They told the old negro he could sell his share of the whisky to the soldiers for five dollars per bottle. They impressed the old negro with the necessity of silence, as the whisky had been smuggled from New York, and if the matter got to the ears of the General, they would all be shot and the negro with them. He took in the story, and swore to be silent and true, get the boat and pilot the Lieutenant and his men over to the island and never say "nuffin to nobody, and git the boat hisself without any white man knowing 'bout it."

Capt. Tom Perkins went into Seabrook with the old darkey, who showed him the wharf where the boats were moored, and pointed out the sentinel over them. He also showed Perkins how he (the darkey) could slip under the bridge without the sentinel seeing him. After Perkins had gotten all the information he wanted out of the old negro they returned to the point where they had left the lieutenant and man. Here our boys parted from their guide, with a solemn promise to meet them the next night at midnight at a point near Seabrook and then go for the whisky. The old negro put them on the road to Hilton Head and went to his home in Seabrook to dream of the good whisky he was to get and sell the "Lincum sogers."

On the way down the road Capt. Tom Perkins collapsed. The corn meal and pickle diet had broken him up. From the time the boys left prison they had walked over twenty miles. After a rest of an hour or so Perkins revived, and our fellows started back to prison to communicate the information gained to their comrades. They got as near the prison as they could before daylight without discovery. They then hid until good daylight, then walked boldly into the Yankee guards' barracks, next to our prison, and from there passed over into the prison without being discovered. They had wonderful stories to tell us on their return to prison. They had been out of the barracks for over thirteen hours – never missed even by the sergeant who called the prison roll. But later in the day some spy in the prison communicated the story of the boys to the provost-marshal. He was dumbfounded as to how our boys got hold of the uniforms; it was real funny to see the agitation of the provost-marshal-general when he found he had been outwitted by the cunning of the "Reb."

On January 20, 1865, Col. Van Manning received positive information from one of the guards that Lieut. J. W. Davis, 20th Va. Cav., was going to take the oath of allegiance and had made application to take it and be released. A meeting of prisoners was called to meet in Capt. Tom Perkins's cell, and a committee appointed to wait on Lieutenant Davis and invite him to come before the prisoners and refute, if he could, the charge Colonel Manning had made. Davis promptly accepted the committee's invitation, came before the prisoners, and solemnly declared on honor that he had made no application to take the oath, and had never had such idea. When Colonel Manning read a copy of the application to him he broke down, admitted the truth, and became very defiant. Colonel Manning suggested to the meeting that, as Lieutenant Davis had premeditatedly intended to dishonor his uniform of the Confederate States Army and insult by such act his brother officers, prisoners of war, that the bars and buttons be cut from his coat, and his coat turned inside out, and that he be ostracized by his fellow prisoners. This suggestion was quickly carried out by Tom Perkins and Pete Akers. Colonel Manning suggested to Davis that he get the provost-marshal to remove him from the prison at once, as the prisoners were not in good temper to tolerate or overlook his insult to them by taking the oath. Like a whipped cur Davis ran and put himself under care of the guard, who soon had the fellow out of our prison.

The following day, after Davis had been removed from the prison, Colonel Manning, Capt. Tom Perkins, Captain Kitchen, of North Carolina, Captain Campbell, Lieutenants P. B.

Akers and John Casson, the committee that called the meeting and disgraced Davis, were taken from our barracks and locked up in a cell in the Yankee convict prison, where criminals of all sorts were confined – men who had broken the laws of God and man. These refined gentlemen, Confederate officers, prisoners of war, were locked up with criminals without the least investigation, by the provost marshal, of the charges Davis made against them. These gentlemen were all put in one cell, not over three feet wide and six feet long, and there they were kept, in this cramped condition, for seven days and nights. From five o'clock in the afternoon until ten o'clock in the morning their cell door was closed and not allowed to be opened except by order of the provost-marshal. In this cell all the men could not lay down at once, comfortably, but by tight squeezing they could lay spoon fashion. In this cell was put each night a foul smelling tub for sink purposes, and there it remained from five o'clock each evening until ten o'clock next morning before it was taken out. The cell floor was made of heavy pine logs, smoothed with the axe, from which the rough knots were not cut very close. They had no blankets, and the hard logs was not a downy bed. This cell had been occupied by some convict negros, and was swarming with vermin, which accentuated discomfort and misery. Yet we hear much said about the tortures of Andersonville, by the Northern people. No such treatment was ever inflicted upon Union prisoners of war *in any Confederate prison of the South*. Just above the cell in which our comrades were confined was a room in which white and negro convicts were confined. Daily they polluted the ears of our comrades with the vilest epithets such scoundrels could utter about our Southern women. They even cut a hole through the floor and spit upon our men, and when the prison authorities were complained to about this indignity they simply smiled and made no effort to stop it; they even rather encouraged these vile scoundrels in their meanness and insults to our helpless men. Davis, the deserter, one day did worse than spit upon our men in the cell. Our men protested to the sergeant who had charge of the convict room, but he would take no notice of the protest. Finally the conduct of the convicts towards our men became so unbearable that Colonel Manning got the sergeant to ask Lieutenant Thompson, U.S.A., assistant provost-marshal, to come and see him, which he did. Our men protested against such insults as the convicts perpetrated upon them, but Thompson simply ordered the cell door closed, and paid no further attention to the protest, and this devilish torture went on. Finally the provost-marshal-general made a general inspection of the convict prison, with his assistant, Thompson. When the door of the cell in which our men were confined was opened, Colonel Gurney asked Thompson why those Confederate prisoners of war were confined in convict cells. Thompson hesitated for a moment before he replied, and then lied by saying the men had formed a conspiracy to escape and murder the guard. Colonel Manning at once denounced Lieutenant Thompson as a liar, and his story as a mean, cowardly lie. When Colonel Gurney heard Colonel Manning's story, he ordered Thompson to instantly remove the prisoners from the filthy cells to a room on the floor above, where they were confined seventeen days, surrounded by the galvanized scoundrels – deserters who had taken the oath of allegiance. This fellow, Thompson, inflicted upon Colonel Manning all the little mean indignities he dared without Colonel Gurney finding him out; and all this for the sole reason that Manning had proved and denounced Thompson a liar and coward.

These brave men never allowed this fellow to see how much he really made them suffer. They were that class of men referred to by Judah P. Benjamin who, when he left the United States Senate, said to the people of the North: "You may, with your immense armies, invade the South; sack our cities, towns, and villages; render homeless our wives and children; you may drive the black car of war throughout our land; but the subjugation of our people is impossible."

The most fearful test a man can be put to is that of starvation. The corn-meal-pickle ration was this test; it was the trying ordeal of the manhood of those six hundred Confederate mortals. They stood the test. The seventeen who took the oath were the dross of the gold; they must wear their badge of dishonor; they can not rid themselves of it, they can not hide it. In the world's history these fellows will be classed as cowards; in the glorious history of the Confederacy they will be written down as deserters – none can defend them. Dear old Murray, let's say together, "God bless those of the six hundred who remained true unto the end." Their story will be written on the scroll of fame; it will go down through all time. Generations will sing their praise and crown them martyrs to principle for their devotion and fidelity in those days of torture.

P.B.A.

Escape From the Federals

I was Captain of Company H, 10th Louisiana Regiment, Infantry, Stafford's Brigade, Edward Johnston's Division, Jackson's (afterwards Ewell's) Corps, of the Army of Northern Virginia. With three-fourths of the regiment, I was taken prisoner at the Bloody Angle, at the battle of Spottsylvania, May 12, 1864. I was taken to Fort Delaware and was one of the six hundred Confederate officers picked out to be placed under the fire of the Confederate batteries on Morris Island, for alleged retaliation.

These officers were embarked in August on the small transport *Crescent*, where four men were allowed a space of four by six feet to lie in. We had been some nineteen days on this floating purgatory when we were landed on Morris Island, and marched ankle deep in sand for six miles to our place of confinement, a stockade that had been erected between the Union batteries Gregg and Wagner, where we remained for some six weeks, under the occasional fire of mortar batteries in Charleston and the premature explosions of shells fired from battery Wagner. As a refinement of cruelty, we were guarded by the 54th Massachusetts (negro) Regiment. Later, a part of the prisoners were sent to Port Royal for wintering and the rest to the damp casemates of Fort Pulaski. I was with the latter.

Early in March, 1865, it was reported that the six hundred were to be exchanged at a point on the James River, and they were reunited and embarked on the big transport *Illinois*, which was already crowded with prisoners taken by Sherman at Savannah, some of whom were sick and wounded. In due time the vessel reached Norfolk, where orders were received to return the prisoners to Fort Delaware. This was sad news indeed to the six hundred, who hoped to be back in Dixie soon.

The vessel put to sea and after dark I went on the upper deck for fresh air. I was soon approached by an Irishman, who was of the crew and was a Southern sympathizer. He said to me: "They're treating you like dogs. I'd get away if I were you."

I replied to him that I would do so if he could show me how, and that I had already made four fruitless attempts. He then told me that in the forward part of the deck, where I was quartered, I would find a hatch through which I could descend to the forepart of the hold, where the anchor chains and sail duck, ropes, etc., were stored. That if I concluded to make the attempt and would let him know, after a while – after the prisoners would be landed at Fort Delaware, the day following – he would bring me food for the trip to New York, where the transport was to go to take on supplies. That before reaching New York he would come down to supply me with clothes and to give me a few dollars. "Then," he concluded, "if you're smart, you'll be able to get back South." I thanked him and told him that I would let him know as he suggested. Thereupon, I went down for a consultation with some friends. Three of them agreed to make the attempt with me. They were: Capt. Thomas F. Perkins, 11th Tenn. Cav., Capt. Emmett E. DePriest, 23d Va. Inf., and Lieut. Cicero M. Allen (a Louisianian), 2d Ark. Cav. We decided not to inform my Irish friend, for fear that by some indiscretion he might have our attempt revealed. We swapped clothes with other friends, gathered some crackers and canteens of water, some matches and candles, and arranged with some of the Georgians to personify us at roll calls, and, after bidding our friends good-bye and receiving their warm wishes for our success, we went down to the designated place of concealment. We fixed places to lie in with the aid of candle light, but soon afterwards Captain Perkins, who had been suffering with flux, was violently seized with pains in the bowels and his ailment grew more pronounced, to an extent that caused us to insist upon his return to the deck above us and seek the assistance of the surgeon. The gallant fellow urged his right to risk his life in the endeavor, and that the responsibility rested wholly upon himself. We finally resolved to inform him that we could not agree to his view and that we had rather abandon the attempt than witness his increasing sufferings and danger, and that we would proceed to do so. He then consented to be assisted up the hatch. We then fell into a sleep from which we awoke by the cessation of the vessel's rolling and pitching, and the rumblings above indicating that we were at Fort Delaware and that the prisoners were being landed. For several hours we lay upon the anxious bench, but when the vessel began to move once more we felt that our absence had not been observed and that we had only to fear a telegram to search the vessel on her arrival at New York. At times during the rest of the voyage we would light the candle for an instant, eat some crackers and go back to sleep. Finally we were awakened by the firing of a cannon and soon after the ship's motion told us that we were in New York harbor. We could hear the whistles of passing crafts, and when we felt it to be afternoon, we ascended to the deck above and sought refuge there in a dark corner. After dusk one of the trio made a reconnaissance to the upper deck and reported the vessel to be fast to the pier with her stern swinging a few feet outward. We had been in the hold for more than three days and nights, and it was with joyful feelings that we emerged upon the upper deck and in turn jumped to the wharf and walked rapidly into the city. We soon crossed Broadway and hastened to go down into a cellar saloon and eating place. We called for cocktails and had a substantial meal. We were in rags and looked like tramps. Fourteen dollars in greenbacks was our aggregate wealth. We went to a cheap lodging house and got a room under assumed names. There we gazed at each other and rejoiced at being free men again. Allen had been a prisoner for fifteen months and DePriest and I ten months. It was then Sunday, March 13, 1865.

The next day we found friends who gave us clothes and money. DePriest left us to go to Baltimore, where he expected to meet friends, and Allen and myself concluded to stay a few days longer to recuperate.

At the end of the time we had set, we proceeded to Baltimore, thence to a place near Point of Rocks, on the Potomac, where we thought of entering Virginia and rejoining the Confederate forces. There news came that Richmond was about to be evacuated, and we felt that we would soon have Grant's army to elude to get to our friends. We decided to return to Baltimore. There our friends supplied us with funds and railroad tickets and we went on through to Louisville. Thence we took a steamer for Cairo. At Evansville cannons were being fired, as we landed, announcing the surrender at Appomattox. A Union officer was addressing a large crowd that was rejoicing over what we regarded as dreadful news. At Cairo we got aboard another boat and went down to Memphis. Finding it difficult to get out of the lines there we went back aboard, and on her trip up we were landed at Randolph, in West Tennessee, in the middle of the night. Thence we made our way safely to Meridian, Mississippi, and reported to Gen. Richard Taylor, whose army had retired to that place after the evacuation of Mobile. The General gave us thirty days' furlough almost on the eve of the surrender of his forces.

Then we crossed the Mississippi with the intention of joining Kirby Smith's army in the rumored continuance of the war in the Trans-Mississippi country. But before the expiration of our furloughs that officer also surrendered. The war was over.

Allen died at Lake Providence, La., not long after the war. Perkins, who became prominent in politics in Tennessee, died in the nineties. DePriest also died in the nineties, at Richmond.

I had the good fortune of meeting Allen and Perkins at times after the war, but never had the satisfaction of meeting De-

Priest, from whom, however, I received several messages.

Leon Jestremeska.
Baton Rouge, La., December 26, 1904.

Fernandina, Fla., January 18, 1905.

Maj. J. Ogden Murray,
    Winchester, Va.

My Dear Comrade and Friend:

When I go back to those days of the ordeal of starvation of the Six Hundred Immortals, and think of the ordeal we went through on Morris Island, Hilton Head, S. C, and Fort Pulaski, Ga., by order of Secretary Stanton, my heart grows bitter.

I can never forget November 20, 1864, when two hundred and twenty of us were taken from the prison of Fort Pulaski and sent to Hilton Head. When we reached Hilton Head we were unloaded upon the wharf, then under guard marched through the town, and placed in a camp one mile in the rear of the village. Our shelter was the same old A-tents we had on Morris Island; we were surrounded by the same old 54th negro troops; our ration two ounces of fat meat with a small quantity of hominy grits, most vilely cooked, and some beans. A few frying pans were given us, but were not sufficient for the camp use, so we had to let each mess have its turn with the frying pans. Our camp was located in a very exposed place. On the evening of November 29th we were moved from this bleak camp into barracks, built in the yard of the provost-marshal's office. The building was a large log structure of two stories, with hospital in the second story. The lower floor was built in cells, six by eight feet. A long pine board table was run down the room before our cells. This was our dining room, or mess hall. Between the table and our cells there was a space of two or three feet, and up and down, night and day, a sentinel with loaded gun paced. They would not allow us to close the cell doors; we had no blankets, the weather was cold, and there was no stove allowed in our quarters. On December 4th about forty or more of our party – the sick and wounded – were sent to Hilton Head, and exchanged. Time hung heavy on our hands at that place. We were allowed no exercise outside of our cells, and no incident that I can now recall occurred to break the monotony of the prison until December, when we were put on the rotten corn meal and pickle ration; ten ounces of rotten corn meal, one-half pint onion pickle – no grease, no salt, no meat of any kind. There were plenty of imprecations heaped upon the heads of those who ordered us such a ration, but there was no sign of a break in our ranks.

A party composed of Captains Perkins, Jestremeska, and Casson and some others, cut a plank out of their cell floor and would have made their escape from the prison but for a Lieut. J.W. Davis, who betrayed them. This fellow took the oath of allegiance. Some of our party did get out of the prison, but were recaptured, brought back, and the whole lot crowded into a small cell, four by eight, which had been used to confine some negro convicts. When it was discovered that this fellow – Davis – had betrayed the boys, Col. Van Manning and Lieut. Pete Akers cut the stripes from his collar and buttons from his coat, and literally kicked him out of prison before the guard could interfere to save him. This action on the part of our men got them into a cell in close confinement for many days. The corn meal diet was rough on our fellows, and scurvy got hold of us badly. One day I saw one of our men sitting very quietly in one corner of the room. Thinking he was sick, I went over to speak to him and do whatever I could for his comfort. I found he had a long string in his hand, on which he had a fishhook baited with a grain of corn. This he dropped through a chink in the floor. He was simply catching rats. For a while I thought the poor fellow was crazy, but when he yanked in a rat the problem of why he was quiet was solved. He caught rats and ate them to keep from starving.

There was a fine large cat, that belonged to the provost-marshal's office, that often came into our prison. One day this cat very mysteriously disappeared; next day my mess had meat for

Captain J. W. Mathews
25th Virginia

dinner, and we invited some other fellows to dine with us. In February, 1865, our ration was increased by two ounces of meat and two ounces of potatoes; but it came too late to drive away scurvy. About this time Colonel Manning, Pete Akers, Tom Perkins, and the others were released from their close confinement. March 4, 1865, we were loaded on board of the steamer *Ashland*, taken to Hilton Head Harbor, and transferred to the steamship *Illinois*, and sent back to Fort Delaware prison. On comparing numbers – leaving out those exchanged and those who deserted – we found that twenty-five percent. of our number had died from the brutal treatment. The *Illinois* was a troop ship, dirty, but not one hundredth part as filthy and dirty as was the steamer *Crescent City*, that brought us from Fort Delaware to Morris Island, in August, 1864.

You can tell the story of the trip better than I can. You had a diary. Tell it, dear old comrade. The world must know how brutal we were treated; and do not forget, you must put in big type the seventeen deserters who took the oath.

Sincerely your comrade and friend,

W. D. Ballantine.

CHAPTER FIVE

Account of Escape From Fort Pulaski,
by W. E. Stewart of Easton, Maryland

Easton, Maryland
July 13th, 1897

J. Ogden Murray, Esq.,
      My dear Comrade:

I certainly was delighted to hear from you, and to know that you intended to write a book about our treatment from the time we left Fort Delaware until the end of imprisonment.

I knew Col. Fulkerson, was in the same mess with Col. Manning, Fellows was on Gen'l Beall's staff who was our Brigadier General at Port Hudson. But I do not think that Fellows was with us at Morris Island, or at Fort Pulaski. The other gentlemen whom you mentioned I have forgotten. I was Major of the 15th (Port Hudson) Arkansas Regiment. There were three 15th Arkansas Regiments, numbered from the different calls for troops. When I escaped from the so-called hospital, Lieut. Wm. H. Hatcher also escaped with me. Hatcher was from Virginia, a place called Thaxton or Thaxton Switch, not far from Lynchburg. He belonged to a Virginia Regiment. I do not know whether he is still alive. I saw him in Baltimore some twelve or fifteen years ago, but he did not then look very strong, and I have not since heard from him.

I was captured at Port Hudson and sent to Johnsons Island, and sent from Johnsons Island with the sick and wounded to be exchanged at Point Lookout. Two boat loads were exchanged, then exchange was stopped, and quite a number of the prisoners were sent to Fort Delaware. Most of us were put in the pen, but I was placed in the fort; Col. Fulkerson was in the fort. I have forgotten the date when we left Fort Delaware, and in fact do not recollect any of the dates from the time we left, so you will have to supply them, and I want to get your book when published. But many circumstances I shall never forget. I recollect when we were marched aboard of the iron steamer – I think her name was the *Crescent*. It was a hot day, we were kept in her hold, Col. Woolfolk was in the bunk with me; I do not know what became of him, he was from Paducah, Ky. I think he made some arrangement with the crew by which he was smuggled back with the steamer – he never landed at Morris Island. I think we were on the boat eighteen days; on the route, you will remember, the steamer got aground, and when we found it out, it was agreed that Col. Manning, Col. DeGurney, and I think, yourself, should demand that the steamer should be surrendered to us. Our escort was a man-of-war called, I think, the *Dictator*. She lost us and about the time we expected to get our liberty she hove in sight and our plans were frustrated. Of course, you remember the little A-tents without flys on Morris Island; I heard that fourteen cart loads of pieces of shell were hauled off the ground where we were penned when the place was cleaned, for our accommodation. I can almost hear ourselves now counting off, and marching to get the hardtacks and the little pieces of meat, and the soup, one-half pint, for dinner. I think it took fourteen hardtacks to weigh a pound, and it was Col. Hallowell, I believe (a white-eyed villain from Boston, I think), who remarked that we got our fresh meat from the worms in the soup.

Then our removal to Fort Pulaski, the twenty-one casemates, I think, from which the cannons had been removed – the four cook stoves, the two ounces of flour bread, and ten ounces of corn meal, and the pickles – no meat, grease or vegetables –

our sickness in the damp fort, a reservoir in one of the casements – the doctors coming in one day with pills, another with powders, and stating that medicine was no use, that we were starving. I believe if Foster had not been removed, and Gilmore put in his place that all the prisoners would have been starved to death. I have heard that Gilmore's surgeons reported that the prisoners were starving and that desiccated vegetables were ordered. I know that the scurvy broke out and many were sorely afflicted. I had a touch of it and my gums have never been all right since.

I was taken very sick, and one day I was removed, wrapped in a blanket – I could hardly see, taste, or smell – carried in a horse cart from the fort to what was intended for a hospital. It was a small house, I suppose, a quarter of a mile from the fort. I found about eight or ten sick prisoners. We had beds and a fire – the same rations, only the bread was in loaves, and the corn meal was baked in large cakes. After awhile I began to improve and could walk about. I made gutta percha jewelry (I was considered a tip-top hand at it) and gave some to Col. Carmichael, I think, and possibly some to Col. Brown, but I know I made some for the Doctor. I have forgotten the number of the Regiment, but Col. Brown and Lieut. Col. Carmichael, and the Doctor, were kind-hearted men, but had to do as they were ordered. After Brown's Regiment was removed another Regiment took its place. I do not know the number or the names of the officers. Col. Brown's doctor told me he would see the new doctor, and tell him about me. I had made so much jewelry for the officers and men that I had some influence and I think I got several sick removed from the fort to the house.

The night I escaped from the Island, a salute in honor of the fall of Charleston was fired – I have forgotten the month and day; we had to get away in short order; it was, I think, the same day that the new regiment arrived to guard us. I think it is called ten miles from the Island to the South Carolina shore – that is the route we took.

Hatcher and myself roomed together; the new doctor came to the hospital where we were; he looked at and examined the prisoners, and he told Hatcher and myself that we were well enough to go back to the fort, and that he would send us back. Neither one of us was well and we were very weak. I told Hatcher that if in our condition we went back to the damp fort, we would surely die – that we must get away that night or get killed in attempting it. He agreed with me. There were sentinels, then a boat guard and a gunboat not far from the island. We gathered up a haversack full of scraps of bread, and had a canteen full of water and were preparing for our trip. About the time we were ready to leave the doctor came in on us. I pretended that the things were in such a condition, because I was hunting for a letter. The doctor did not suspicion us and in a short time left, so now we were ready. I shall never forget a poor fellow named Davis from Florida. I gave him my uniform suit; he was very ill and could not walk. He asked us to take him along, but, of course, he could not go and we left the house. It was, I reckon, 8:30 or 9 o'clock at night. We crawled out of the house and through the grass until we got to the shore. We had to go past guards and we could hear the sentries on the boat wharf. We went up the shore, towards the fort hunting for a boat; finally we found one on the shore. It was a large boat and as Hatcher and myself were so weak we could not launch her, we had to leave her. We prowled around and in a little while found a small canoe, about large enough for one man – a very light and frail affair. I hardly think the boat was ten feet long and she was very narrow. I told Hatcher to untie the boat; he crawled in the grass to the bow of the boat, and then crawled back to me and said the boat was chained and locked. I asked him if he had any keys; he said he left his keys at the hospital. I told him to crawl back and get them and I would wait in the grass for him, so he went back to the hospital and brought his keys, but none of them would fit the lock, so I told him to stay in the grass and I would go back to the hospital and get a file and cold chisel. I went back and brought them. We filed away and it seemed to us that you could hear the noise one hundred yards; finally we filed through the link; then we got two stones and put a hat over the chisel and drove the chisel into the link until it was opened wide enough to let the chain be parted. The little canoe was chained to a large ship's row boat which was a wreck, and high up on the marsh. We soon launched the little craft and Hatcher got in the middle and I took a seat in the stern. Now as we were lower, we could see the sentinels on the wharf and the gunboat, but they could not see us so well. We concluded that if we could pass the boat guard, and not be discovered by the gunboat, we would escape. We paddled lightly, were not seen, and then we went at it with all our might. I think the current runs about eight miles an hour in the Savannah River; we had fair tide and wind and we fairly flew. After awhile we got out of sight of everything, and then we concluded that we were going out to sea, and that we would be swamped and drowned, but we kept on and finally came to land on our right. Hatcher said it was an island. I thought it was the South Carolina side of the river. We kept the land to our right, and finally came to a very suspicious place – it looked like a tower – and when we neared it we heard a noise just like men cocking their muskets. I told Hatcher to get down in the boat and I put the oar under my arm, and every moment expected to receive a volley, but we concluded that it must have been some animal walking over the dry canes. After a while we saw a gunboat in the river; we went by it and heard the sentry cry out "half past eleven and all is well." I think we kept on but the tide changed and we could hardly make any progress, so we concluded to land. We pulled the boat ashore, and cut down the tall grass and covered the boat with it. I asked Hatcher if he could keep a course. He said he had traveled over the mountains in Virginia and never got lost, so I took the canteen and oar and Hatcher took the haversack and off we started. We ran all night and it seemed to us that we must have jumped over or into a hundred ditches. When day broke we discovered that we had been traveling over an immense marsh which had been burnt off, and we were at the edge of where the grass was as high as our heads. We learned after we got out of it that we had been in an immense rice plantation full of ditches. Before starting through the high grass or, as it seemed, an ocean of

marsh, Hatcher and myself held a council of war. We were sure
that we could not be captured or found in that marsh, but the
question was, could we ever get out of it? Hatcher thought we
were on an island, I thought it was a part of the South Carolina
main land, so the first thing we did was to divide our rations into
six parts, for we thought it would take us at least three days to
get around it, if it were an island, and if it were part of the main
land it would take us the same length of time to get through the
marsh and reach dry land; so, as before stated, we divided our
rations into six parts and agreed not to eat but one ration a day,
so we started. I think it was Sunday night we got away, but am
not sure; if it were not Sunday night, then we started through that
wilderness of marsh and grass, Monday morning. We walked all
day and were very thirsty, for it seems that the ocean and river
water mingled and tasted salty; after drinking nearly a canteen
full, in ten minutes, you felt as if you were famishing and had
never taken a drink of water. After walking all day – sometimes
the water being over our shoes, then again very deep, night found
us in the water and marsh. We cut down grass and piled it up
until it was above the water, then got on top of it and went to
sleep. I guess we slept nearly a couple of hours and awoke nearly
chilled to death. We could not keep our teeth from chattering.
When daylight came we were hungry and thirsty; we ate our ration and started again through the tall grass, above our heads;
Hatcher got a briar in his eye and we thought his eye was out, but
he did not go blind at the time we thought he would. The grass
constantly getting between our legs and striking us all the time
came to feel as if we had been struck by sticks. My legs gave out
and I had to lift them up with my hands to avoid the grass. If we
came across a muskrat track we would follow it as far as we
could; when darkness came we were still in that marsh, so we had
to sleep as we did the night before. At daybreak we again ate a
ration; we were very hungry and thirsty and started through the
marsh; about 9 or 10 o'clock the marsh got firmer, and but little
water on it, and in a little while we reached a forest high and dry.
We took off our clothes and wrung out the water, then started

Major W.E. Stewart
15th Arkansas

through the woods. We now knew that we were on the South Carolina side of the Savannah River, and we knew that we were in the Federal lines, because, as I said when we left, the troops at the fort were firing a salute in honor of the fall of Charleston. Sherman had gone from Savannah to Charleston. I forgot to say that we were dressed in Yankee clothes – we were constantly afraid we would run into the Yankee army. We never saw but one squad during the day; we saw where Sherman's army had camped and we saw the chimney of many houses that had been burned, everything seemed to have been destroyed. At about sundown, we came to where two roads crossed and we were afraid to venture down a road until dark, so we hid in the woods, and we were then so hungry that we agreed that if we could to get a full meal the Yankees might capture or kill us, and we determined to go to the first place that we saw a light.

When night came we started down a road; we had not gone very far before we heard a dog barking. We started for the sound and in a little while we saw a light and it was in a house occupied by a colored man. We inquired where we were; he asked us which way we came in, we told him, and he said that was the road taken by Sherman's army. He said we were about eight miles from Savannah. We pretended that we were Federal soldiers from Savannah out on a foraging trip, that we lost our way, and would have to be at camp at roll-call in the morning or we would be put in guard house. Incidentally we told him we had come out without any money and that we were very hungry. I had a new penknife in my pocket and said that I would give it to him for our supper. He looked at the knife and said he would do so. His wife and himself went out of the room and in a little while she brought in a great dish full of rice and a good quantity of fresh pork. We soon ate every bit of it. Hatcher had the toothache, but he said he would not allow that to keep him from eating, so he kept at it until we had eaten all, and then the woman went out and brought in as much more, and we ate nearly all of that. The old man and his wife seemed astonished at our appetites. We put what was left in our haversack, bade the old man and his wife good night and started off. It was the first information we had about "where we were." We traveled all night and next morning went to sleep in some pine leaves in the woods not far from the road. We saw quite a number of refugees, negroes, and some soldiers passing on the road. I reckon it was about 3 or 4 o'clock when we awoke; we remained in our hiding place until dark, when we resumed our journey. We had traveled until after midnight when we came to a house which was occupied by a colored man. I gave him some thread and needles in exchange for supper. I asked him if some white people did not live in the neighborhood. He said that just up the road an old white lady and her daughter were living – that the daughter's husband was a Captain in the Rebel army. He said that your folks (he thought we were Yankee soldiers) had burnt down the "big" house and that old Mrs. Zant (I think that was the name, but am not sure) and her daughter were living in a small house on the roadside. We left and after awhile came up to the house. It was very dark and raining hard – it rained nearly every night we were out; we rapped at the door and after awhile we heard some one say from the inside of the house, "I am an old woman sixty-five years of age." She seemed to be scared; she doubtless thought we were Yankees and were going to burn down that house, as her "big house" had been burned. She never opened the door, but I believe we half-way convinced her that we were escaped Confederate prisoners; for she said to us, "Why don't you go across the river, for you will starve on this side?" We asked her if we could get across the river, and she said, "You go right out to the gate and turn to your left, and the first house you come to is where my old colored man lives, and he will put you across the river, and if you cannot get across come to my house in the morning and I will give you your breakfast." We did as directed, found the old colored man, and asked him to put us across the river. He told us that some one had taken his boat, but if we went up the road about four miles, Mr. Yomans (I think that was the name) had a boat and would put us over the river. So off we started for Mr. Yomans'; we were very tired and our feet were sore, we trudged along the mud-

dy road in the rain until daybreak, but didn't see Mr. Yomans'
house. We then came to the conclusion that we passed it in the
darkness, so we concluded to turn back; after walking back some
long distance, we thought possibly we had not come to Mr.
Yomans' place and turned back again. After walking a little way
we saw some people coming and we hid in the woods until they
came up. There were an old man and his wife, a pretty girl about
fourteen, without shoes, and a boy some twelve years old, and a
good sized dog in the company. When they came up we went out
of the woods and met them. We said we were looking for Mr.
Yomans. He said he was the man, and he said we had passed his
house about two miles back. We told him we were escaped prisoners from Fort Pulaski and wanted to get across the river. Just
as soon as we told him we were escaped prisoners, the old lady
spoke up and said to her husband, "John, you put these men
across the river," and said to us, "I have a son a prisoner at Fort
Delaware, and maybe some one will help him." The old man said,
"I will put you across the river if I get hung for it." He told us
that he was out trying to catch a hog. We asked him if we could
not assist him; he said his wife and the children could catch the
hog with the dog, so we started back to reach Mr. Yomans' boat;
the boat was in a bayou and we had to go a long distance to reach
it; the river was overflowed, and it was a tough job to get to the
boat. It was a small affair – a little larger than the boat we took
at the fort. Hatcher got in the bow of the boat, I sat in the middle,
and Mr. Yomans in the stern. It seemed the canoe would upset all
the time on account of the heavy load as the boat was only intended for one man. As we went down the bayou, I looked and
saw something on top of a cypress tree which had been cut off,
and thought it was some sort of an (animal;) I called Mr.
Yomans' attention to it and he said it was his molasses jug – that
he had to keep everything hidden away as his house was constantly plundered.

    We went down the bayou until we came to the Savannah
River; it was rushing down, carrying long and large trees; there
was an overflow and it looked dangerous to cross in our little

boat, and just as we were about to enter the river – and it all happened in less time than it takes me to write it – the boat ran on a cypress knee, and there she was fixed – on a pivot. Mr. Yomans said, "Gentlemen, keep quiet." I asked Mr. Yomans how far we were from dry land and I think he said about twelve miles. I told him I would keep quiet – that a cannon ball could not budge us. He attempted to back the boat off the cypress knee – off she came, and down she went, and Mr. Yomans caught a cypress knee and cried to us to look out for the boat which had sunk out of sight. Hatcher had also found a cypress knee and I got hold of a small tree. We formed a sort of triangle, I do not know how deep the water was – all of a sudden, the boat popped up by Mr. Yomans; he spied it and shoved one end of it over to me, and said that we would work the boat backward and forward, and thus get some of the water out of it, but after getting a little water out of the boat Mr. Yomans would slip off his perch, and she would fill again; so we had to bail the boat with our hands – the water was cold and it took us a good while to do it, then Mr. Yomans told me to bear down on my end of the boat, we were up to our neck in water, and he would try to balance himself on the cypress knee and get into the boat; he was successful in this, and after the water had run off his clothes he bailed the boat out and told us to get in. I told Hatcher that I was stronger than he – that he had better swim over to where I was and get in, because I thought that I could stand the water longer; I was almost frozen and exhausted. So Hatcher swam to where I was, I wrapped the chain of the boat around the little tree, hugged the chain and tree, and told Hatcher to get on my shoulder and then in the boat. I told him if he felt the chain going down to get off. Hatcher made several attempts but failed – he was very weak. Finally he told us that we would have to leave him, but after awhile he succeeded in getting into the boat; then I climbed up the tree and got in. We then started across and safely landed at a place or landing called "Red Bank." I gave Mr. Yomans my gloves, a handkerchief, the file and cold chisel, and told him I wished I could give him more. He said he did not charge us a cent – that he was glad to help us.

We bade him good-bye, he went back home and I have never seen or heard of him since.

We stopped at places in Georgia and got food, and whilst walking up the Georgia Central Railroad, we saw a Confederate Lieutenant whom I knew in prison, whose name was Branch; we remained all night with him, and after a few more days of travel we reached Waynesboro; there we saw Rebel soldiers with guns. We were taken to Augusta and carried before General Fry; he had been a prisoner and I knew him. We were ragged and muddy, clothes all torn and generally played out. Hatcher and myself stayed in Augusta for a week. Finally, one day I went down town and on my return was told by the landlady that Hatcher had been ordered to go to Richmond, and he told her to say good-bye to me, and that was the last I saw of him until I met him in Baltimore, as before stated. I remained in Augusta for several more days, and was ordered to go to the Trans-Mississippi Dept.

After many hardships I finally reached Marshall, Texas, was assigned to a regiment there and surrendered.

Thus, my dear brother, you have an account of our escape from Fort Pulaski; it may interest you, I have written hastily, and if you desire to use any of it, just put it in shipshape form.

I wish you well and hope soon to have the pleasure of reading your work. I am, comrade,

Truly yours,
(Signed) W. E. Stewart,
Easton Maryland.

CHAPTER SIX

Diary kept by Capt. A. M. Bedford, Third Missouri Cavalry,
While on Morris Island, S.C., at Hilton Head and Fort Pulaski.

Beginning the 20th of August, 1864, six hundred officers,
selected out of thirteen hundred, confined at Fort Delaware, are
taken out of prison and placed on board the steamer *Crescent*,
bound for Hilton Head, S.C. Left the wharf at 3 p.m. All of said
officers, except sick and wounded, are placed in the hull of ship
nearly without air, and many in the dark, having a sickly and
deadly smell. Ran until 7 p.m. Anchored in Delaware Bay. Lay at
anchor all night.

August 21st. – Weighed anchor 3 a.m. Ran to the mouth
of Bay, arrived there at 8 a.m. Anchored waiting Convoy. Admiral Convoy arrived at 6 p.m., weighed anchor; ran all night.

August 22d. – Continued on our journey.

August 23d. – Continued on our journey. Very warm and
sultry in our position. Men fainting occasionally.

August 24th. – Ran on sand bar 3 a.m., off Cape Romain,
S.C. Got off sand bar 8 a.m., after heaving overboard several
tons of coal. Ran in sight of Charleston 4 p.m. Could see the
Yankee fleet lying inside the bar; could see very distinctly the
flash of the guns. We continued to run until 9 p.m. Anchored off
the harbor of Port Royal, S.C.

August 25th. – Took on a harbor pilot. Ran into the harbor, anchored off Hilton Head, 8 a.m. Lay at anchor the balance
of the day. A beautiful day. Pleasant on upper deck, warm below.

August 26th. – Still at anchor, a great deal of grape about exchange. Captain and pilot of ship arrested for running on sand bar. Another steamer came along-side. Had a court-martial to try said captain and pilot, don't know the result of their labors. The nights of the 25th and 26th, were the hottest nights we ever experienced, had to fan all night, and our shirts were wet with perspiration. Several men fainting, Capt. Henry Allen, Lieut. David Bronaugh, and Lieut. Carter (a young preacher). I should have mentioned the escape of Col. Woolfork, while on the bar on the morning of the 24th; also that we are guarded by 157th Ohio Militia, and a company of deserters, commanded by one Capt. Prentiss, an overbearing tyrannical rascal, who let his men pillage our baggage, rob men of all their clothes, and in one instance one of our men caught a Yankee stealing his hat. He was pointed out to this scoundrel, but he refused to make him give it up. He talked to men as though they were dogs. We would insist on going on deck for a little fresh air, but were denied the privilege. Sometimes we would be allowed to go up twenty-five at a time. That did not more than answer for the calls of nature, as we had to go above for such business. We are subject to all insults that a lot of degraded men calling themselves soldiers could offer and protected by the beast of a Captain commanding them.

August 27th. – Capt. Prentiss, with militia and deserters relieved to-day by Capt. McWilliams, with a detachment of 157 New York, which was quite a relief to us. But not so to the old cook, who had been selling us hot water from 25 to 50 cents per coffee pot full, we would have ground coffee in them and it would have made weak coffee. As soon as our new Commander found it out he put a stop to it, and had water heated for us without price. Our new guard is as kind to us as men could be. They would do anything in their power to make us comfortable. They had their orders from General Foster, and could not do much in that way. They always spoke respectfully to us, and no insults were offered from any of them. They told us they had smelt our powder, and some of them had tried Libby Prison, and they knew how to treat a prisoner.

August 28th. – Still at anchor. More grape about exchange, and going back to Fort Delaware, and many other reports. Weather clear and warm. Sergeant Smith goes ashore to buy something to eat, sugar, tea, coffee, tobacco, cigars, shirts, etc.

August 29th. – No change, except being ordered on deck once a day to clean out the ship and receive rations which consisted of a few hardtack, a very small piece of bacon or beef, not sufficient for one meal, but had to do us twenty-four hours.

August 30th. – No change, except the sick and wounded (about forty), are sent ashore to Buford Hospital.

August 31st. – No change, except Capt. commanding received orders to have on full head of steam to be ready to start next morning by daylight.

September 1st. – Steam up, all ready to move. The Captain refuses to start until he has read written orders, which was done about 10 a.m. Weighed anchor and left, we did not know where, but about sunset we crossed the bar off Charleston, ran in among the Yankee fleet and anchored.

September 2d. – Still at anchor, all on tiptoe expecting to go right through to Dixie. Bought a gum cloth for $5.00, from J.E. Underhill, Company B., 157 New York.

September 3d. – No change, but not in Dixie yet. The flag of truce went in this morning in full view of us, came out and went to sea, and then we all felt very flat.

September 4th. – Still at anchor and Mr. Grape is very busy, but I will not give any of his dispatches. Bought a canteen for 60 cents and a ring.

September 5th. – No change. Hot water to drink as usual.

September 6th. – No change, except water a little hotter. Hot enough to make tea or burn our flesh when we spilt it on ourselves. We poured it from one cup to another to cool it, and make it wet a little. Some put it in the sea in a canteen, well stopped and it would soon be fit to drink.

September 7th. – Rained last night. No water, except what each man could catch in his oilcloth during the rain last night up to twelve o'clock, at which time we were landed on Morris Island, and were received by the 54th Mass. Regt. (negro). We marched two and one-half miles along the eastern shore of the Island and many of our officers gave out owing to their confinement on the boat and want of rations. We passed in front of Fort Wagner, being then in between it and Fort Sumter, we continued in same direction, but a few hundred yards when we were run into a pen made of pine poles planted in the ground, about twelve feet in length, making a substantial picket fence with a parapet on it, and mounted thereon was a line of negro sentries, and on the ground another line of like sentries. Inside of said pen is a grass rope, about twenty feet from the fence, between this rope and fence we were told by the Colonel of said regiment was certain death to any of us, except we were escorted by a Yankee officer. Inside of said rope are 160 A-tents. In these we are put, four to the tent. The Yankees fired more than usual since we have been in hearing of this place, we suppose trying to draw fire from our batteries, but got no answer as yet. Weather clear and nice. I am in good health, but growing weak from shortness of rations.

September 8th. – Was aroused this morning at daylight by the Colonel whipping one of his black Yankee soldiers for being asleep on the fence. The darky said he was not asleep, but just studying. At a little after sunrise in came the negro drummers and gave us a rousing reveille and then followed by a colored Sergeant, got us out in line, orders to left dress front, count us. Presently along came the Captain, a white man. The Sergeant saluted him, made his report. The Captain returned the salute, took down the report. The Sergeant orders to break ranks, march. This is gone through three times a day.

September 9th. – No change in rations. Three roll calls or counts. Sutler came in, sold some ginger cakes, tobacco, and stationery, at an enormous price. Some of the Yankee officers told us they had official news that Atlanta was occupied by the 20th Army Corps and Generals Hardee and Finigin killed, and in the evening commenced firing solid shot. They said they were firing salutes, but after awhile we could see shells coming over us

Lieutenant W.H. Chew
Georgia

from Moultrie and other batteries, and we had quite a lively time all night. Shells passing each way over us. Two shells from Moultrie exploded over us, the pieces falling in among us, but no one was hurt. Two shells from Wagner exploded in the mouth of gun and the pieces whistled over us, but no one was hurt among us. Weather pleasant and dry. I am well and growing weak.

September 10th. – As the Yankees are continually boasting about how well they feed us, I will attempt to give a correct account of each meal. Roll call one and one-half hours by sun for breakfast, three crackers issued, one tablespoonful of rice. Twelve o'clock roll call. Rations for dinner, one-half pint bean soup, two crackers, wormy and full of bugs. Five o'clock roll call. Rations for supper, two ounces of bacon, two crackers, wormy as usual. Shelling from our mortars all last night bursting about the right place to do execution. Don't know what amount of damage done. Heard of one Yankee losing his leg, a horse shot under him during the day. All quiet with our batteries, but not so with Yankees. They commenced to shell early in the direction of Fort Sumter and Charleston. Weather clear and pleasant. I am well, but getting weak.

September 11th. – Shelling from our mortars last night directed at Wagner. One piece of shell striking the fence around us. Six thirty a.m., roll call. Rations for breakfast, two crackers, very wormy and two ounces of very old salt beef (stinking). Twelve o'clock roll call. Rations for dinner, one-half pint of bean soup, two crackers (full of worms and bugs). A.J. Armstrong and myself had to pick out the worms before eating. An occasional shot has been fired at Charleston from Battery Gregg, up to noon to-day. Water full of wiggle-tails to-day. Five p.m., roll call. Rations old salt beef, two ounces, one cracker, wormy as usual. Some little firing last night from the Yankee batteries, but don't think they got any reply from ours. One gun kept up firing into Charleston at intervals of half an hour all night.

September 12th. – Six thirty a.m., roll call. Rations for breakfast two ounces old salt beef, so badly spoiled that we could not eat half of it. Three crackers, musty and full of worms – not fit for hogs. One of our officers showed his rations of crackers to the Colonel in charge of us (Col. Hallowell, 54th Mass.). His reply was, "Do you know that fifty of our officers are now in Charleston, in cells fed on bread and water?" The prisoners wished to know the reason. His reply was, "Because they are Yankees." Weather warm and clear. I am well, but feel weak and hungry, falling off very fast. Can't buy what we want, it is forbidden. Twelve o'clock roll call. Rations for dinner, one and one-half pints of soup for four men (bean soup, very good). Two crackers as usual, very full of worms. Very little cannonading going on to-day. Distant artillery firing going on west of us. We are not permitted to buy anything from the South, except tobacco and stationery, except on an order from Surgeon. Can get a little tea, imitation of coffee and sugar at 50 cents per pound; black tea at 75 cents per one-quarter of pound. Half past six roll call. Rations, 2 ounces pickled pork (half done), two crackers, very wormy as usual. Weather clear and pleasant. I am well and think I can stand it.

September 13th. – Some firing last night. Very windy, but clear and cool and a beautiful morning. Roll call. Rations two ounces of fat pickled pork, two crackers, musty and wormy. Twelve o'clock. Some distant firing in the west this morning. Roll call. Rations, two crackers, some better than usual, over one gill of soup, and two ounces of pickled pork. Half after six roll call. Rations, two crackers, two ounces of pickled pork each, good. Bought one-half gallon of syrup for two ($2.00) dollars, very good. I feel a great deal better. Beautiful evening, all quiet. Washday to-day.

September 14th. – Some firing last night by the Yankees. Half after six roll call. Rations, two crackers, good, two ounces pickled pork, good, but a fat negro put it on our plates with his hands. Twelve o'clock, two crackers, one-half pint of thin soup. Six o'clock roll call. Rations two crackers, two ounces pickled pork (fat), and a little vinegar. We bought some tea and had some to-night. I feel first-rate, most well. Very beautiful day. All sorts of grape, which is not good for us.

September 15th. – Occasional shot last night. Some distant firing this morning. All well. Roll call, half after six. Rations, one cracker, two ounces of pickled pork, good and very fat. Beautiful morning. Distant firing. Twelve o'clock roll call. Rations, two crackers, tolerable good, one-third of a pint of soup, very good. Firing occasionally by the Yankees. Been very warm and cloudy, with a sprinkle of rain. Six o'clock roll call. Rations, one cracker, hardly two ounces of meat, good. Wrote to my wife, very hungry, never any other way. Negro issues out the medicine, gives us our orders and we obey. Considerable firing, don't know whether our batteries replied or not.

September 16th. – Half after six roll call. Rations, two crackers, one and one-half ounces pickled pork, both good. Am very hungry, every time I sleep I dream of something good to eat. Our men at Sumter, sharpshooting the Yankees at Gregg. All well. Negro put meat on our plates with his hands. Twelve o'clock roll call. Rations, a little over a gill of cooked rice, one ounce meat. Starvation staring us in the face. Very weak. Rebels shelling battery Gregg. Sharpshooting Yankees. Six o'clock. Evening rations, two crackers, two ounces pickled pork, good. Beautiful day, all well. Good grape, we will exchange shortly. Some little firing last night by the Yankees.

September 17th. – Beautiful morning. All well. Six o'clock roll call. Rations, one ounce pickled pork, good, two crackers, a little wormy. Negro handles the meat with his hands. Twelve o'clock roll call. Rations, one-half pint bean soup, two crackers, a little wormy. Soup good. A fire in the direction of Charleston this evening, I suppose it is a house burning. Six o'clock rations, one gill of rice, two ounces of meat, good, two crackers, best meal we have had for a month, as we bought a little syrup at the rate of $4.00 per gallon, we also had a little black tea, paid 75 cents per one-quarter of pound. Some firing last night by the Yankees.

September 18th. – Roll call. Rations one ounce of meat (or two mouthfuls), two crackers, wormy. All well, but we are weak from our treatment. Hope it will not last long. Twelve o'clock roll call. Rations, one-half pint of soup, two crackers, bugs and a few worms in them. This is the Sabbath. Very heavy rain. Read thirteen chapters in the Bible. Yankees fire occasionally at Charleston. Five o'clock rations, two ounces meat, one-half pint of rice and one cracker, very wormy. All well. A shot occasionally at Charleston last night, also this morning.

September 19th. – All well. Pleasant morning. Roll call. Rations, two crackers, two ounces meat, good. Some distant firing in the southwest. Twelve o'clock roll call. Rations, one cracker, one-half pint of soup, good, crackers wormy. Sometimes a shot from one gun to Charleston. Weather very warm and cloudy, and occasional sprinkle of rain. Six o'clock roll call. Rations, one-half pint scorched mush, two ounces pork, good. Hard living, hard treatment for a prisoner of war, taken in a civilized warfare, but by the help of God, we can stand it. All quiet last night.

September 20th. – Warm and a little cloudy. All well. Six o'clock roll call. Rations, one cracker, the wormiest of them all, full of webs and bugs (not fit for hogs to eat), one ounce meat, good, but so little it will hardly sustain life. Who could have the heart to starve a man, but a Yankee. Very warm, cloudy, has the appearance of rain. Twelve o'clock roll call. Rations, one-half pint soup, good, two crackers, some wormy. Five o'clock roll call. Rations, two ounces pork, very fat, but good, one cracker, tolerably good. If they don't improve I don't think men can stand it. Rations too short. Yankee Colonel in to see us this evening, told us what he got in prison, said it was very rough. He was exchanged five or six weeks ago. The crackers we get will not make more than two good mouthfuls, they are so small and thin.

September 21st. – A good and gentle rain fell last night. Warm and cloudy this morning. All well. Half after six roll call. Rations, two ounces of meat, two crackers, both good. Benson made the negro Sergeant mad and he said, "By Jesus Christ, I will satisfy this tent for once," so he gave us a double handful, at least two crackers apiece. That satisfied us and we wish he would get mad again. They handle the meat in their hands and the grease runs between their fingers, and makes a dirty sight for men to eat. Twelve o'clock roll call, one cracker full of worms and bugs (look like they were made ten years ago, not fit to eat by any one), one-half pint soup, good. Bought a pocket handkerchief for $3.00. A monitor has been firing on our batteries this evening, but no reply from the batteries. Very warm to-day. Five o'clock roll call. Rations, two ounces pork, good, one and one-half pint of soup for four men (soup and meat, a fine supper).

September 22d. – Some firing last night by the Yankees. A nice shower of rain just before day. All well. Warm and cloudy. Half after six roll call. Rations two crackers, and two ounces of pork, both good. Excitement about leaving at half after ten. Orders to pack up. At eleven orders to start. We marched back the way we came. It appeared to be the longest two miles I ever traveled as I was so weak. We were placed on board the steamer *General Hooker* and from there to a schooner nearby. Half of the crowd on one and half on the other. We were told we could stay up on top until night, then we had to go in the hull. At three o'clock we got one cracker and nearly one-half pint of soup, both good, but it takes three times as much to satisfy our hunger. We got no supper. There were a few wormy crackers given out to some, but did not go half-way around. I did not get any. At night we were crowded into the hull, where we nearly smothered, could not sleep, and in the night here came a negro through both hatches and falling on two of our men, crippling one tolerably bad. Every once and awhile some one would holler out as a big rat ran over them. Heard negroes quarrel.

September 23d. – They soon issued one cracker, and one ounce of meat and in one hour we got two ounces of salt beef, and one cracker, said it was double rations, as we did not get supper. All well and a very warm day. Very anxious to know the result of the flag of truce. The boats in sight. Twelve o'clock and we were soon landed, many sad hearts. We waited an hour or two, then came rations, one-half pint of soup and one cracker, both good, but too small to fill up a man. About four o'clock we commenced our march back to our old stockade and about sunset we arrived, each man knowing his quarters. Soon we had roll call and finding six men missing created some confusion in camp, but the Yankees soon telegraphed back to the boat and found them before dark. Rations, one cracker, one-half pint rice, two ounces pork, good. Last night we rested fine, being tired and sleepy. One gun kept up firing on Charleston all night and an occasional shot this morning.

September 24th. – All well, except Armstrong had a spell of colic last evening and is not quite over it. Roll call. Rations, two ounces salt beef and one cracker, tolerable good. A nice day. Twelve o'clock roll call. Rations, one cracker, one-half pint of soup, good, cracker, very wormy. Five o'clock, three-quarters pint rice, two ounces pork, both good. Cloudy and a few drops of rain. Yankee Colonel in command, said this evening "throw all bones and worms out of your crackers into the sink barrel." It is a curious way to make sport over a starving people.

September 25th. – Some firing last night by the Yankees. A beautiful morning, clear and cool. Half after six roll call. Rations, one cracker, wormy, two ounces pork, good, a light breakfast, it makes me ask the question, "Who will have these sins to answer for?" All well. This is the Sabbath. I have read thirty chapters in the Bible since last Sabbath. Twelve o'clock roll call. Rations, one-half pint of soup, not good, beans raw, two crackers, wormy. Some firing to-day, no respect for the Lord's day. Five o'clock roll call. Rations, one-half pint of rice, two ounces pork, good, rice without grease or sweetening. A beautiful and pleasant day.

September 26th. – All well. A beautiful morning, clear and pleasant. Some firing all night. They seem to be mounting more guns. I could hear them working nearly all night. Heard some small arms early this morning, think it was the Rebels sharpshooting the Yankees. Half after six roll call. Rations, one cracker, two ounces pork, both good. Twelve o'clock roll call. Rations, one-half pint of soup, three and one-half crackers for dinner and supper. Some firing to-day at the city. A nice day. New hopes of exchange. Five o'clock roll call. Rations one-half

Colonel Abe Fulkerson
Tennessee

pint rice, half done, two ounces of pork, good.

September 27th. – All well. A beautiful morning. Some firing last night at the city. Half after six roll call. Rations, two ounces pork with the promise of crackers at noon. Orders were issued yesterday for us to have four and one-half crackers per day giving them in the morning, so we see the order violated in the beginning. Crackers come five to the man, wormy. Twelve o'clock roll call. Rations, one-half pint soup. Five o'clock roll call. Rations, two ounces pork, good, one-half pint rice. Lieut. W. P. Callahan of the 15th Tenn. died last night. The first death out of the six hundred. Bought three loaves of bread for three rings and feel like I have about enough to eat for some time. Capt. Buce went on special exchange to-day.

September 28th. – All well. A beautiful morning. Half after six roll call. Rations, one and one-half ounces pickled beef. A dry breakfast to one that is used to better. We made a little coffee and had a loaf of bread and did very well. We have to be shifty. Twelve o'clock roll call. Rations, one-half pint soup. Beans not done, five crackers, tolerable good. These crackers are for the day. Five o'clock roll call. Rations, two ounces pork, good and fat, one-half pint rice. A beautiful day. Firing is still kept up at the city from the Yankee guns. I will give the names of our officers at the hospital to-day. Lieut. Hunter, Capt. Logan of Kentucky, O. H. P. Calwell of Arkansas, Capt. Baker of Mississippi, A. Q. M., Lieut. Newton of Kentucky, Lieut F. P. Peake, of Kentucky.

September 29th. – All well. A beautiful morning, warm and pleasant. Firing kept up all night at the city, firing every ten or fifteen minutes. Half after six roll call. Rations, two ounces pork, very fat, some got salt beef. I feel like I had taken a light breakfast, but had a little imitation of coffee that I brought from sutler. We have to manage every way to sustain life. We had a nice shower of rain last night. Twelve o'clock roll call. Rations, five crackers for the day, some worms, one-half pint soup. Lieut. Newton returned from the hospital to-day. Shelling the city has nearly ceased for the day, resting after shelling all night. Four o'clock all called up to see if they had our names right. Five o'clock roll call. Rations, one-half pint rice, very thin and poor.

September 30th. – All well. Pleasant morning and cloudy, had a light sprinkle of rain last night. I forgot to say we got two ounces pickled beef last night. Firing kept up all night. Capt. Mason sent off on special exchange last evening. Nothing given us for breakfast. Nice shower of rain. Twelve o'clock roll call. Rations, two ounces pickled beef, one-half pint bean soup, five crackers for the day. Four o'clock. Rations, one-half pint rice soup, one ounce pickled beef or two mouthfuls.

October 1st. – All well, warm and pleasant. Had a nice shower last night. Understood two Yankees were killed the other day by a premature shell. Half after six roll call. Rations, two ounces beef. Lieut. Cargil went to the hospital last evening. Twelve o'clock roll call. Rations, five crackers for the day, good. One half pint bean soup if the beans had been done. Lieut. Peake died in post hospital this morning. Shelling as usual to-day. Five o'clock roll call. Rations, one-half pint rice soup, three ounces bacon for night and morning.

October 2d. – Nice morning, very warm. Rebels shelled Gregg last night and did it in order, shells falling in the right place to do execution. Half after six roll call. Our rations have been received and very short. My appetite is never satisfied, always hungry. Can't sleep without dreaming of something to eat. Twelve o'clock roll call. Rations, five crackers for the day, good, one-half pint bean soup, good. Five o'clock roll call. Rations, four ounces pork for night and morning. One-half pint rice barely enough to keep soul and body together. This is the Sabbath. Read thirty-eight chapters in Ezekiel. This week has been exceedingly warm. Another flag of truce meets to-morrow in our behalf.

October 3d. – All well. Quite warm. A small sprinkle last night and a good shower to-day. Half after six roll call. No rations as we had received them. Flag of truce meet and are together yet. Twelve o'clock roll call. Rations, one-half pint soup, five crackers. No firing to-day or last night. All quiet. Rations, one-half pint of rice, three ounces beef for supper and breakfast.

October 4th. – All well. Half after six roll call. No rations as they have been issued. Cloudy with a few drops of rain. Very warm, can sleep without cover. Twelve o'clock roll call. Rations, one-half pint soup, one cracker in place of five, both good. Five o'clock roll call. Rations, four ounces pork, good, one-half pint rice.

October 5th. – All well. Very warm. Got our crackers which were four by hard coaxing. Half after six roll call. No rations, only the four crackers I spoke of, they were due the day before. Twelve o'clock roll call. Rations, one-half pint soup, four crackers, good, fell short one cracker, don't know why, unless they thought we had a plenty as we have just received three large wagon loads consisting of bread, smoking and chewing tobacco, sweet potatoes and some sweet cakes which were all very good, but the cooked potatoes had spoiled. We felt under many obligations to our South Carolina friends and glad to see the fair ladies and kind gentlemen of that State so patriotic. We received eleven hundred pounds of smoking tobacco and the same of chewing. Thirty sacks of bread and one thousand pipes and stems. Five o'clock roll call. Rations, none as yet, if it comes I will note it.

October 6th. – All well. Our rations never came. We are cut short by receiving some provisions from Charleston. Half after six roll call. Rations, two ounces pork. Twelve o'clock, roll call. Rations, one-half pint soup, four and one-half crackers, both good. Sometimes a little vinegar, a little salt and soap occasionally. A blockade runner reported sunk on the bar last night. Five o'clock roll call. Rations, one-half pint rice, two ounces pork. A very warm day. Four and one-half crackers are for the day. I subscribed fifty dollars to the benevolent institution in Charleston to-day.

October 7th. – All well. A very heavy rain fell last night. Quite warm. Half after six roll call. Rations, four ounces pork, nothing else. Twelve o'clock roll call. Rations, one-half pint soup, four and one-half crackers, for the day and a piece of soap, four men. Some firing at the city to-day. Every fifteen minutes a gun starts her deadly missile. Sutler in to-day. Had some molasses.

Stationery men acted very greedy and unmanly. Five o'clock roll call. Rations, one-half pint rice. Washday to-day. The Rebels shelled the Yankees last night a great many bursting in the right place but after a while they began to burst too close to us. One shell bursted over us, part of the shell on one side and part on the other.

October 8th. – All well. Half after six roll call. Rations, four ounces pork. Yankees shelled all last night throwing balls into the city every fifteen minutes. Very cool to-day. Twelve o'clock roll call. Rations, one-half pint soup, four and one-half crackers, both good. Five o'clock roll call. Rations, one-half pint rice. Very cool this evening. Shelling the city is carried on day and night with some new and heavy guns.

October 9th. – Sabbath morning, very cool. Slept cold last night. All well. Half after six roll call. Rations, four ounces pork for the day, also four and one-half crackers, both good. Twelve o'clock roll call. Rations, hardly a half pint of burnt soup. We have to be shifty to sustain life, but think we can make it. Five o'clock. Rations, one-half pint rice. I have read sixty-one chapters in the Bible this week. Has been very cool all day.

October 10th. – All well. Very cold last night. Got quite pleasant to-day. Half after six roll call. Rations, four ounces pork for the day. Twelve o'clock. Rations, one-half pint soup. About three crackers apiece to-day, short rations. Five o'clock. Rations, one-half pint rice. Getting cool to-night. Some firing kept up all day at the city. No reply from our batteries.

October 11th. – All well. We were awakened to-day by our batteries firing on a Yankee Monitor. It appears the Monitor was sent out to stand picket, it got aground and by day break our men discovered it and opened fire on her for one-half hour when the Monitor got off by the help of high tide which was fortunate for her. They kept up fire on the city day and night. We see this evening quite a smoke in the city, must be a house burning. Rations this morning, four ounces pork for the day. Twelve o'clock. Rations, one-half pint soup, four and one-half crackers, both good. Five o'clock. One-half pint rice. A beautiful day. Warm and pleasant.

October 12th. – All well. Beautiful morning. We asked Sergt. (negro) for salt. He said we could not get it as they were retaliating on us as their prisoners could not get salt. Night before last the city was illuminated for what purpose I know not. Half after six. Rations, scant, four ounces pork for the day and instead of our crackers we got nearly one-half pint mush for the day. I understand some of our officers petitioned for it. I hope he will soon get his fill on the mush question. Twelve o'clock. Rations, one-half pint soup. Five o'clock. One-half pint rice. It has been a beautiful warm day. Firing has ceased to-day to some extent on the city. Old Capt. Boyd went out last evening, for what purpose I know not. Capt. Maston went out to-night but soon came in again.

October 13th. – All well. A nice and pleasant morning. Firing kept up all night. Half after six, four ounces pickled beef for the day, one-half pint mush made out of musty meal and so full of bugs and worms it would not pay to pick them out, so I shut my eyes, swallowed all and wished for more, but would desire better quality (this is for the day). To-day one Yankee was carried by, wounded at Gregg by our sharpshooters. At Sumter men swapping crackers for mush, two rations of mush is equivalent to one cracker. I think we have eaten a boat of condemned rations since we have been here and still they come. Will we ever find the end of them. Twelve o'clock, one-half pint soup, good. Five o'clock, one-half pint rice. Firing continuous to-day in the city.

October 14th. – All well. Washday. Beautiful morning. Half after six our rations change back to four crackers per day. No meat. Twelve o'clock one-half pint soup after dinner, meat four ounces pork. Five o'clock. Rations, one-half pint mush instead of rice. Wrote to wife yesterday. Cloudy this evening, looks like rain. And plenty of grape about exchange.

October 15th. – All well. A fine warm morning. Rations for the morning, four ounces pork. Twelve o'clock, mush again, one-half pint for the day in place of bread. Some men counted

Captain Louis Harman
12th Virginia Cavalry

one hundred and forty worms to the rations, others fifty. I never counted them, would not pay to take them out. I know there were plenty of them. Some men traded their rations of mush for a cracker, others gave it for a half cracker, some few threw it away. I and many others ate it and wished for more. Five o'clock. Rations, one-half pint rice. Firing continues day and night in the city.

October 16th. – All well. Nice Morning. Sabbath day. Firing continues. Half after six. Rations, two ounces pork and beef, one and one-half crackers. Glad to know the mush failed as it was poor stuff with worms and without salt. Twelve o'clock. One-half pint soup, five crackers. What has taken place I know not. We have received six and one-half crackers in place of one-half pint of wormy mush. A small quantity of salt was issued to-day. It was beginning to bear a good price as much as one dollar and half per pint. Officers came in to-day and we were called up in line to issue rations. These officers superintended the affair and said salt was issued every day and it was the fault of our wardens that we didn't get it. I believe my part of it. We had some vinegar and some soap issued to-day. Five o'clock. One-half pint rice very wormy, crackers and meat, good. Rations of meat, very small. One ration was about two good mouthfuls. This has been a day long to be remembered. Starvation has looked us fairly in the face. I have laid down at night and thought what will I come to. Shall I starve here? I have hoped and prayed for better days. I have prayed for my enemies that their hearts might be softened. I believe my prayers have been heard and answered. I am encouraged still to trust in God and all will be well. I have finished reading the Bible through twice since a prisoner. Have read thirty-three chapters this week.

October 17th. – All well. Heavy shelling last night. The Yankees shelling Sumter, Sullivan Island and the city. The Island batteries replied vigorously throwing the shells very accurate for a while, but soon lost range and began to throw them too close to be healthy. Some shells bursting over us and the pieces falling all around us and we fearful to move as the sentinels would fire on us if we came out, so we had to stand it. It is an awful situation to be in. I have been under fire many a time, but never before on quarter rations and double fire. My trust is in God. If I die I die in the Lord. If I am killed the Lord shortens my days of trouble, although I enjoy life as well as any one and will keep my lamp trimmed and burning and wait on the Lord. Half after six. Rations, four ounces beef and five crackers, both good. Twelve o'clock. One-half pint soup. Five o'clock. One-half pint rice. Weather cloudy and cool. Firing continues this evening. Some fighting with small arms last night. Sutler came in to-day. Orders were given to fall into ranks. One man did not obey soon enough. When the officer told the sentinel to fire at him, which he did but missed him. The ball passing and into the ground near a tent.

October 18th. – All quiet last night, something uncommon, and very little firing to-day. Half after six. Rations, four ounces salt beef, five crackers, both good. I said beef was good, but it was spoiled. Twelve o'clock. One-half pint soup, very good. Five o'clock. One-half pint rice. A cloudy, damp day, raining a little. We saved our rice for dinner next day, one piece of fat meat and we have a tin bucket that holds five pints we boil them in it and make a soup. With what we draw makes a tolerable meal with one cracker, then we have two for supper and two for breakfast. We make a little tea for supper and have coffee for breakfast, or imitation, and our meat and make out very well. We have to pay very high prices for everything we buy and hard to get at that.

October 19th. – All well. Some little firing last night by the Yankees. No reply from our batteries. A beautiful day. Plenty of good news. To-day's papers say Gen. Price is at Boonville, Missouri, and his cavalry north of the river. Federals concentrating at Macon City. I finished a long letter to Mrs. Bedford to-day, six pages interlined. No rations until twelve o'clock, then five crackers and three ounces of pork, both good. Five o'clock. Mush, one-half pint and full of worms as usual. We have three roll calls daily. I will leave off morning, then if any change takes place will name it. It is generally believed Sherman will have to fall back from Atlanta as our cavalry is playing havoc with the railroad in his rear.

October 20th. – All well. Some shelling last night. Yankees commenced about dusk shelling our batteries. Ours soon replied, throwing shells about the right place. About nine o'clock all was quiet and remained so up to this evening. No rations at half after six. At twelve, four ounces pork, five crackers, very good, one-half pint soup, good. Five o'clock, three days rations issued. We are going to leave to-morrow, so they say. I hope so. Rations, fifteen crackers and a pound of pork for three days.

October 21st. – All well. Beautiful morning. Yankees shelled heavy last night, trying to draw a fire from our batteries on us. Rebels too smart. We got orders the other night to fall in at roll call with our baggage. We asked permission to start fire by daylight which was granted by the Col. (order came through the Sergt.). At light one man went to the barrel to get water and was going to have his coffee in time, but a negro says, "Halt, go back" and at the same time, bang went his gun, missing the one aimed at and hitting two others, one on the knee, the other on the shoulder, but no one seriously injured. A narrow escape, only one tent between the wounded men and ours. One of the wounded was asleep. We left at six o'clock walked to the lower part of the island and were placed on board two schooners in the hull, two hundred and seventy men to the schooner. The sick and wounded went on steamer that had us in tow. These schooners had very comfortable bunks, but dark. We did very well as we were guarded by the 157th New York and could buy hardtack a little from the boat crew. It was nearly night before we got under headway. They said they were waiting for the tide to come in so they could get over the bar. Ran very slow all night and morning.

October 22d. – A nice morning, quite cool. Eight o'clock arrived at our destination, Fort Pulaski, Georgia off Savannah. Anchored out from the wharf, lay there nearly all day when the other schooner was landed and prisoners went ashore. Our schooner remained all day and all the next night. Very impatient.

October 23d. – This is a mistake. The first schooner was

unloaded on this evening 23d, ours 24th at about two o'clock, many of us on board the vessel three days and nights. Had fine, cool, dry weather. I did not think to name the wounded men. Capt. Harris and Capt. Blair are their names. I received two letters to-day, one from Clasby and one from my wife. Oldest daughter sick. Got two crackers last night and nearly a pint of rice soup. Was told these crackers were for night and morning. We being very hungry ate all.

October 25th. – Rations, two ounces meat. Three of our mess have very bad colds. A beautiful morning. I forgot to name three of our men tried to make their escape while on the boat the night before landing by sawing through the hull of the boat in three feet of the water, one got out but was about to drown when he cried out for help. Only one was overboard besides the drowning man. He had to go to his help and no more tried it as the alarm was given. Our meat we ate without anything else. At dinner we got two-thirds of pint of rice soup, eight crackers. A probability of living better. We have great room for improvement. I am very hungry and weak with headache, feel half sick. A great deal grape rumored about exchange. Nothing given for supper.

October 26th. – Slept well last night, feel much better this morning. Roll call three times a day. Half after six. Rations, two ounces pork. Twelve o'clock. Two-thirds of a pint slop called soup and six crackers, not good. They promise us ten ounces pork and soft bread every other day. The pork every day and bread every other. Fourteen ounces and twelve ounces hardtack every other day. We get nothing for supper. We nearly starve.

October 27th. – A nice morning. Very many have bad colds. I feel very weak, but hearing good news from Missouri I can stand a great deal more. Roll call three times a day. Rations for breakfast, two ounces pork. Twelve o'clock. Two-thirds of pint of soup, but did not go around. I did not get any so I live on crackers, but the Lord will provide. We got nine hardtacks. We get no supper to-night. Quite cloudy, I think it will rain.

October 28th. – All well. Nearly clear. Rained a little shower last night. Received a letter from home. All well. Half after six. Rations, four ounces bacon. Twelve o'clock. Twelve crackers and nearly a pint of rice soup. Our rations greatly improved. We made a little coffee and did admirably. No rations for supper.

October 29th. – All well. I mean my mess of four men. Nice day. Rations, meat five ounces, good, twelve crackers, a little wormy. Twelve o'clock. Two-thirds of pint thin bean soup. Very indifferent. Washday. Some of our officers went out to the sutler's store this evening with the guard. The sutler began to ask too much for his goods. When a tin cup was priced at twenty cents the guard told him fifteen cents was the price. Sutler said he had the right to ask what he pleased for his goods. The guard told him he had been a prisoner and knew how to treat gentlemen. One word brought on another and soon a fight ensued whereupon the guard gave him a complete thrashing.

October 30th. – All well. A nice morning. Quite cool. This is the Sabbath day. Half after six. Pork, three ounces. Twelve o'clock. One pint rice and nine crackers. Nothing for supper. A nice, warm evening. The Yankees had preaching in sight this evening. Wrote two letters to-day, one to Cousin Zerelda Howard and one to Bohart.

October 31st. – All well. Washday. Wrote two letters, one to Lieut. S.R. Selecman and one to Cousin Lizzie Russell. Seven o'clock. Three ounces fresh beef. Twelve o'clock. One pint bean soup, good, ten crackers with some worms. Had a fight to-day between Capt. Logan and Hammack. No one hurt serious.

November 1st. – Cloudy, damp day. Seven o'clock. Rations, three ounces beef and pork. Twelve o'clock. A loaf of soft bread. The first we have had for a long time. Weighed three eighths of pound, could eat it all as it was very good. Our rations of soup was short to-day from some unknown cause. Got about one-half pint, others got one pint good soup. Nothing for supper. Quite cool this evening.

November 2d. – All well. Cloudy, damp day. Rations, at eight o'clock, six ounces bacon, good. Two o'clock, one loaf bread, nearly a pint of soup, both very good. I could eat twice as much as I got. Hope the day will come when I can eat my fill, then I will not be studying about eating all the time.

November 3d. – All well and raining. Quite cool. Eight o'clock. Six ounces bacon, good. Twelve o'clock. One pint rice, one loaf bread, both good. A great many boxes received this evening by flag of truce for the prisoners, will be distributed to-morrow. It has been a very disagreeable day.

November 4th. – All well. Cloudy and cool. Eight o'clock. Short rations, four ounces bacon. Good news from Hood's army. All excited this morning. Also good from Gen. Lee. Two o'clock. One pint vegetable soup, one loaf bread.

November 5th. – All well. Lieut David Bronaugh came into the mess. Coulter withdrew. Weather clear and cold. Eight o'clock. Fresh beef, four ounces. Two o'clock. One loaf of bread, one pint rice, musty, bread, good. Clear and pleasant this evening.

November 6th. – The Sabbath. All well. A nice day. Plenty of grape about exchange. Wrote to my wife to-day and to Cousin Zerelda Howard. Eight o'clock. Rations, four ounces bacon. Two o'clock. One pint pea soup, one loaf of bread.

November 7th. – All well. Nice washday. Eight o'clock, six ounces fresh beef. Two o'clock. One pint rice, one loaf of bread.

November 8th – All well. The day for the election. Abe will be elected, I think. Eight o'clock. Six ounces beef and bacon. Cloudy and warm, with a little rain. Two o'clock. One pint grits or hominy, half done, one loaf bread, good, too small though for a ration.

November 9th. – All well. A nice day. We scoured up the casemate to-day. Eight o'clock. Four ounces bacon. Two o'clock. One pint pea soup, ten crackers, wormy, soup very thin, but tastes well.

November 10th. – All well. Warm and pleasant. Cloudy and looks like rain. Eight o'clock. Rations, fresh beef, six ounces. Heavy guns have been fired to-day. Suppose it is at Savannah. Two o'clock. One loaf of bread, nearly a pint of rice. We have four roll calls per day. Late in the evening. Some firing yet.

November 11th. – Very cold and cloudy this morning. All well. Eight o'clock. Rations, six ounces of good bacon. I wrote to my wife after my box to-day, also wrote to Miss Anna Thompson. Two o'clock. Ten crackers and nearly a pint of meal brand soup.

November 12th. – All well. Clear and cold. Eight o'clock. Eight ounces pork, best meat ration we have received for a long time. Two o'clock. One loaf bread, good, nearly a pint rice soup. It has moderated and a beautiful day. Lieut. Burney died this morning; disease, Chronic Diarrhœa. He is a Georgian. Lieut. Couper of the 33d North Carolina, died at Morris Island.

November 13th. – All well. Clear and very cool. Lieut. Fitzgerald, Va. (crazy), died this morning from being exposed, having no blankets and taking no care of himself. Eight o'clock. Eight ounces bacon, good. Only three roll calls per day now. Done away with one. Two o'clock. Ten crackers, good, nearly a pint of rice soup. We get all the soap we want, but our facilities for washing are bad having no way to heat water. Have to wash in cold water and dry the best we can.

November 14th. – All well. Clear and cold. Washday to-day. Eight o'clock. Six ounces fresh beef. Two o'clock. One loaf bread, nearly a pint of corn brand soup. Scorched our bread. Does for two small meals or one large one.

November 15th. – All well. Cloudy. Eight o'clock. Six ounces pork, very fat and good. Two o'clock. One pint rice, one loaf bread, not well done, but very good. A nice evening.

November 16th. – All well. Clear and beautiful day. Eight o'clock. Seven ounces bacon, good. Two o'clock. Nearly a pint pea soup and onc loaf bread. Good iron doors arrived to fence us off from the Yankees. Lieut. Bryan died at Buford Hospital, Hilton Head, S.C. several weeks ago, have just learned the fact. Six out of our number that left Fort Delaware have gone the way of all the earth.

November 17th. – All well. A nice day. Eight o'clock. Fresh beef, six ounces. Two o'clock. One loaf bread, one pint rice. This day eighteen months ago I was taken prisoner.

November 18th. – All well. A nice day. Eight o'clock. Six ounces pork, very fat and good. Two o'clock. One loaf of bread, good, one pint slop called soup, made of corn brand. Iron gate taken down to-day that was put up between us. The gates that were put up between us and the Yankees yet stand.

November 19th. – All well. Rained last night. Foggy this morning with a little rain. Eight o'clock. Seven ounces pork, fat and good. Two o'clock. All excitement about leaving roll call. About one hundred and fifty called out to leave. Many conjectures about where we were going. In about an hour fifty more were called, I being among the last fifty. Rations, one loaf bread, two-thirds of pint of mush or grits, not good, only for the hogs. About four we were called out to leave for our new home, knowing not where it would be, but soon ascertained we would go to Hilton Head. About four o'clock we left the wharf, at about seven anchored off Hilton Head.

November 20th. – All well. Left two of our mess behind. Rained last night. I slept fine, was not crowded. It is a cloudy, disagreeable day. We were guarded by 144th New York Volunteers, treated very well only got no rations on the boat at three p.m. We went ashore, marched one-half mile to our old Morris Island tents, three men to the tents. About dark the sound of coffee was given. We got over a pint of good coffee, a pint of sugar to three men and made out very well. Wanted meat and other things. Eight o'clock p.m. Roll call and then for bed. We made our bed down on the wet ground, having oilcloth to go under us and rested well.

November 21st. – All well. Still rainy and foggy. Roll call at seven. At eight, coffee again. I should have said we got twelve crackers to the man last night. Our mess is P.H. Benson, Wm. H. Allen and myself (A.M. Bedford). Wrote a letter home to-day.

November 22d. – All well. Clear and very cold. Slept cold last night. Many of our officers nearly froze as they had no blankets. I loaned one of mine to Capt. Hodges of Virginia. We have four roll calls per day. Eight o'clock roll call. Rations, one pint of good coffee, nine crackers. Two o'clock. Over a pint of good bean soup, about one and one-half ounces pickled pork. Last night we got a pint coffee. One ounce pickled beef, one pint coffee to-night, and twelve crackers issued for the coming day.

November 23d. – All well. Clear and very cool. Slept with my blankets on last night and like to froze. Rations very short here. Ice one-half inch thick this morning. Twelve o'clock. Soup made of grits or fine hominy and crackers. One-half ounce pickled pork, very fat. We got a pint of coffee this morning, the best we will have issued to us. We will have to buy all we get. I understand we will not be allowed to receive any box or money coming from our friends now. Had coffee of our own make to-night.

November 24th. – All well. Clear and cold. Slept with clothing on last night and got very cold. Had some coffee of our own. Ice three-fourths inch thick. A beautiful day. Inspection to-day. No one came to inspect us. Washday with me. Two o'clock. One pint of good bean soup, but very thin, two ounces pork, fat and good. They say they give us one-fourth pound before cooked. Five o'clock. Fifteen crackers for two days.

November 25th. – All well. Another beautiful morning. Very cold last night. I slept with my clothing on and nearly froze. Yankees will not give us blankets nor allow us to receive money to buy them, no boxes allowed. We had a little coffee and molasses of our own and a few crackers left, which made our breakfast. Had considerable frost last night. Two o'clock. One pint soup, two ounces pork.

November 26th. – A nice morning. Excitement about moving into quarters in town. About eleven, we moved down, halted inside of barracks. Roll call and kept us there until half after four p. m., then put in quarters, room like staterooms on a steamboat six, and one-half by six and two bunks, four men in a room. No rations to-day. Always save a day's rations by moving us. Our building is two stories high. The hospital is above us. Our door is made of thick slats about two inches apart with a padlock hanging to it. I don't think the key was turned on us.

November 27th. – All well. After a long time roll call and our rations, ninety-seven loaves to one hundred and nine men, one pint coffee nothing else. I want meat. Allen and I bought us a pair of blankets on the 25th, gave twelve dollars for them. A beautiful Sabbath day. We were kept from going out until eight o'clock, one at time. Two o'clock. One pint soup, very thin. Two roll calls per day.

November 28th. – All well. Nice day. Twelve crackers issued, four ounces pickled beef. Two o'clock. Over a pint of thin pea soup. Received a letter from my wife and one from Joe Bennett. Wrote home to my wife.

November 29th. – All well. A beautiful day. Five men missing at roll call this morning. I will give their names to-morrow. Rations, two ounces pickled beef. Eight crackers. Yankees excited about the men being missing. One o'clock. One pint bean soup, very thin. Roll call four times to-day. Yet we find six men missing.

November 30th. – All well. A lovely day, clear and warm. Grape about going back in tents this morning. Names of men missing, Col. Folk, Capts. Campbell and Perkins, Lieuts. Martin, Casson and Brinkley. I hope they are in Dixie and freed from Yankee tyranny. Rations, three ounces pickled pork and bacon, ten crackers. One o'clock. Three ounces bacon, in place of soup. Col. Folk and Capt. Perkins recaptured. We are guarded very close, sentinels walking in our house day and night.

December 1st. – All well. A beautiful day. Yankees had a fight yesterday with the Rebels at the Long Bridge, ten miles from Savannah. I think they got a good grubbing. We hear all sorts of news. Eight o'clock. Rations, three ounces meat, ten crackers. I hear they have all the men but one that tried to make their escape.

December 2d. – All well. Nice weather. They have recaptured all the men now. Yankees did get a whipping. Rations, three and two-third loaves of bread to four men. One pint rice and three ounces meat for the day.

December 3d. – All well. Same amount of bread, soup and meat for the day.

December 4th. – All well, except colds. Three of us have

a dry, hacking cough. Cloudy and warm, I think it will rain. Rations, loaf of bread the same as usual. Had some important business on hands but did not attend to it.

December 5th. – All well. Clear and pleasant. Been quite dry for two weeks. They continue to fight in the direction of Savannah. We can hear the artillery every day. Our rations are the same daily.

December 6th. – All well. Received a letter from Cousin Z. Howard. I answered it. Still hear firing in the same direction. Rations the same. Meat rations, less two ounces per day, after cooked is a big estimate. Delightful weather.

December 7th. – All well, except colds. Benson complaining of one of his ears. Fighting continues in the direction of Savannah. Rations, the same salt beef, hardly fit for dogs to eat. Seven wounded men and three well men brought in here to-day, say they have a tolerable hot fight, that is, one of the three men captured. Nice weather. I wrote home to my wife to-day.

December 8th. – All well. Benson complaining of his ear, nearly all have bad colds. A delightful day. Meal issued to-day in place of bread. About one and one-half pints to the man. Meal not good, wormy.

December 9th. – All well. Quite a sudden change, very cool. Loaf bread and meat as usual. Very windy. A few Rebel prisoners brought in this evening. They say Sherman is getting close to Savannah, Ga. I think he will have a rough time before he gets there. One of the wounded men brought in died last night, one of them is blind, being shot through both eyes.

December. 10th. – All well. Very cold this morning. How do men do without blankets? I nearly froze with two over me and one under and a gum cloth. We have no fire, only a little in the yard for cooking purposes. Only twenty allowed out at the time from each division one hundred each, that is the fiftieth man. They give us no blankets nor fire. Our prison is getting worse. Received a letter from Bohart to-day; he is one of my best friends. Rations as usual. Answered Bohart's letter. Our meat rations are very slim, hardly two ounces after cooked. Very cold for this climate.

December 11th. – All well. Rained all last night. No meat to-day. Soup at twelve, one pint, very poor. We do our own cooking, but have nothing to cook to make a good meal. This is the Sabbath and as we have no fires the house is so cold we can't read. Our house is a mere shell and so damp. Every one has colds. Wrote to Sister Lucy in California.

December 12th. – All well. Very cold weather. We suffered severe to-day. All slept cold. Col. Manning talked to the provost-marshal about our treatment but did not affect anything. Hardly any meat issued to us. We shivered all day, could not exercise as we were under a hospital with our sick and wounded and can't go out doors only twenty at a time and have to do our cooking out there. I can't do the subject justice.

December 13th. – Benson not very well to-day, has a very bad cold. Clear and cold. Slept some warmer last night. Prepared for it. Rations, about as usual. A loaf of bread and some crackers. Some heavy firing in the direction of Savannah.

December 14th. – All well. Pleasant weather. All excited about leaving for exchange. The sick and wounded, about forty out of two hundred, were taken. Continual firing to-day. Wash-day. Rations as usual.

December 15th. – All well, except colds and a continual coughing, tickling in the throat. Some firing this morning. Clear and pleasant. No sutler has been allowed to come around and sell us anything for several days. Another screw loose somewhere. Our rations very short and not allowed to buy anything.

December 16th. – All well, but continue to cough. Just got over a coughing spell. Some firing this morning in same direction. Weather warm and beautiful. No meat issued to-day. Yankees learning us to do without eating. Some Yankee officers made their escape from Columbia, S.C, and came in a few days ago, give as bad account as possible, but can't come up to ours. We learn Hood is besieging Nashville, Tenn.

December 17th. – All well. Weather beautiful. No meat to-day. We had a little grits for dinner, very nice, boiled without meat. Three and one-half loaves of bread to four men. This is our day's ration. Who can love a Yankee, after such treatment? All quiet to-day in direction of former disturbances. We got one-tenth pint grit, that is a a pint to ten men. Who can live on that?

December 18th. – All well. Weather beautiful. This is the Sabbath. Some firing. No news. That is generally the way when there is nothing good for the Yankees. No meat to-day. Bread as usual. Nothing else yet. I wrote to my wife. Received a letter from her also. Wrote one to California. L.M. Lewis at Richmond, Va.

December 19th. – All well. Beautiful weather. No meat yet, some grits. Hear we will be reduced to bread and water, nearly at that now. Washday. No firing to-day.

December 20th. – All well. Beautiful morn. Thirteen guns fired in honor of Gen. Sherman and staff and Admiral Dalgren and staff, both of these notable characters are here so the Yankees say. Nothing but bread to-day. Three and one-half loaves to four men. More Yankee officers coming in to-day having made their escape from prison, Columbia, S.C. Cloudy this evening and turning cold fast.

December 21st. – All well. Wind got to the south and moderated. Bread and water are our rations now. We had corn meal issued to-day. They say we will get ten ounces corn meal and four ounces bread per day and some pickle in the place of meat or molasses. Can man live on corn meal and pickle? No way to bake it, nothing to cook in, and no wood to burn. We are without fire in an open barn of a house eighty feet long and twenty-five feet wide for one hundred and eight men. Seventeen of these have been sent South and ten out of the other building making twenty-seven, not as many as I first supposed. Wind in the north getting very cold.

December 22d. – All well. Like to froze last night. It is giving us all very bad colds. I think it the coldest night we have had. We have a frying pan. Made up our meal after sifting out the wevil and when the bread was done it was crumbed up like it was for chickens. It would not turn. We had some coffee without sugar. Our bread and a few pickles constituted our breakfast. It ate very good to us. The sutler is in this morning. The first time for two weeks or ten days. Some of Sherman's men arrived here last night, discharged and going home. They say Savannah is closely invested by Sherman's men and will soon fall, as they have Fort McCallister and have opened communication with the sea.

December 23d. – All have very bad colds. Had to get up four times last night with cramp in my legs, it nearly killed me. I have enough cold to kill common men, men of delicate constitution. Savannah has been evacuated by our troops.

December 24th. – All complaining and coughing. I feel like having a spell of sickness. Bread and water continues to be our rations with a few pickles. We eat twice a day. We have nothing to cook in, but a frying pan. Sometimes we get a little green wood and make a little coffee, which without sugar, makes our meal. They don't allow us to receive anything from our friends, money, clothing, eatables, blankets, nor anything that adds to our comfort. We are for retaliation and they are using us. Fifty of our officers and 600 privates came in to-day, captured near Savannah. It has moderated considerable. I go to bed to-night feeling very bad.

December 25th. – Christmas morning and the Sabbath. All feel better of their colds. A dreary Christmas for us. Our breakfast was coffee, without sugar, and corn bread without grease, baked in our frying pan. Coffee cost us 70 cents. We had some pickle. Some ate while others refused. We have slept with our clothes on for three or four nights. Wrote home to my wife.

December 26th. – Our colds not so well, more tight. We have taken more cold since we have been here than we ever did before in the length of time. Had a nice rain last night, and the appearance of more to-day. We washed on the strength of some grape of leaving in a day or two for another prison. Rations continue the same – bread and water. Our Provost-Marshal gone to the field (Joseph T. Pratt). Our present one Maj. Thompson.

December 27th. – We continue to bark. Cold very tight. I never slept any last night until four this morning, thinking of our condition and things generally. It has cleared off and moderated and we have a beautiful day. Some grape about exchange. We still have three roll calls per day. Our division has 111 men in it. House 80 feet long, 24 feet wide, doors closed from one-half hour by sun, till sun up in morning. We are in close confinement. Twenty allowed out at a time to cook. A great rush of a morning. Hard-hearted wretches.

December 28th. – Lieut. Eakin sick. Weather warm and raining. Had a hard time to get our breakfast this morning, such as it was. Our rations continue bread and water. Sherman's men threw their meat to our boys, after they were stopped handing it over. We kept hearing bad news from Hood's army, enemy captured 17,000 prisoners, 21 General Officers and 51 pieces of artillery.

December 29th. – Clear and beautiful, but very cold, nearly as cold as a few days ago. Our breakfast consisted of corn bread, without salt or grease, baked in a frying pan, coffee, without sugar, and pickle. That any one knows is fine living. All better this morning.

December 30th. – All getting better of their colds. Clear and moderated, a beautiful evening.

December 31th. – All still cough. Turning very cold. Weather clear. We have the privilege of all being out during the day, which is a great privilege, more than we have had for sometime. We are closed up half hour by sun, and opened about the same time next morning. Our officers were talking the other night, when the negro guard ordered them to hush them damned lies or he would do some shooting. They spoke a few words like they did not hear. He brought down his gun and told them to dry-up, which they did.

January 1st, 1865. – A very cold morning, but clear. Our rations issued to-day for five days, corn-meal and pickles, is all we get, only the four ounces of bread and one ounce of salt. This is the Sabbath, wrote home to-day.

January 2d. – Very cold, but calm and clear. I have a very bad cough and have had the blues about it, fearful of consumption.

January 3d. – All getting better of colds. Weather moderated, cleared off. Our rations continue the same, ten ounces of meal, four ounces of bread, and a few pickles. Hard living.

January 4th. – A beautiful morning. It clouded up and rained last night, but clear this morning. This is my second son's birthday. Our officer's have eaten five or six cats in the last few days. Say they are good as rabbit.

January 5th. – Benson complaining of pain in side. Eakins still on sick list. Nigs on guard and very saucy, need killing. We have to give the road to them, they threaten to bayonet us. They promenade the room all night. We don't crowd them, but would kill the saucy ones, if we had a half chance. Some I pity, as they are so dissipated. One told us that Sherman's army ran him down and shot at him, and forced him into service. They said that Wheeler's cavalry was killing all that returned, or he would have gone home. He wished he was at home then.

January 6th. – Benson and Eakins still complaining. Cloudy and raining a little. We have shavings to sleep on now, and I am as proud of them as I used to be of a feather bed. I never rested better than I did last night. Have just finished my pillow slip by sewing my shirt-tails together and filled it with shavings for a pillow.

January 7th. – Eakins very poorly. Clear and cold. My eyes very weak, can scarcely see after night. A great many of the privates, some 48, took the oath yesterday.

January 8th. – Eakins a little better. Quite cold this morning. This is the Sabbath and some 75 privates took the oath. I wrote home to my wife and cousin Lizzie Russell to-day.

January 9th. – Our colds not much better. My eyesight failing fast, can hardly see after night. Fifteen guns fired in honor of Secretary Stanton, this evening.

January 10th. – Rained all last night, cloudy this morning. Ten days more to be fed on meal. What will become of me the Lord knows.

January 11th. – Quite a change in the weather, getting

cool, wind blowing, quite disagreeable. Sun shone for a few hours to-day. Three roll calls, as usual.

January 12th. – A little warmer. Wash day. Wrote to Mrs. Egerton at Baltimore. More news about exchange.

January 13th. – Still a little warmer. All getting better of their colds. Had some fine soup yesterday and to-day, but to-morrow we starve as the vegetables have given out. Potatoes are worth $7.00, per barrel. I used to give them away. They weren't worth anything.

January 14th. – Cool weather. Three years ago I was sworn into the Confederate service. We still live on corn meal and pickles. The Provost-Marshal says, he would reduce us to less, if he thought we could live. The object is to just spare life. I think sometimes it is better to starve men to death, than treat them this way.

January 15th. – Another Sabbath. Beautiful day, getting some warmer. My eyes no better, can hardly see after night, very weak in daytime.

January 16th. – Eyes same. Wrote to Baltimore to-day. Our rations the same.

January 17th. – Twenty months a prisoner. Bought a stove to-day, first time I have been thawed out this winter. Thirty-seven guns fired to-night, about nine o'clock. They say they have news of the fall of some Fort near Wilmington, N.C. We are allowed to receive boxes and money now. Wrote to my wife to-day.

January 18th. – Tolerably pleasant to-day. No snow has fallen this winter. Wrote to W. P. Howard at St. Louis, and Col. Wolford, making inquiry about a box and a keg of syrup, sent by my uncle in Florida, to me.

January 19th. – All getting better of colds. Raining this morning, not very cold.

January 20th. – Still cloudy and raining occasionally. Our officers hearing of Lieut. Davis applying for the oath, five of them, Captains Campbell, Perkins, Kitchen, Lieutenants Akers, and Casson, called him into a cell and cut the buttons off of his coat, took off his bars, and turned his coat wrong side out. He (Davis) reported them. They soon arrested the above named, with Col. Manning. I don't think the Colonel had anything to do with it. These gentlemen were soon locked up in cells without trial to sleep on pine poles. My eyes are some better. Head swims a great deal. I stagger as I walk and almost fall down. Weakness is the cause and the cause of weakness is shortness of rations. Ten ounces of meal and four ounces of flour per day to the man, for eleven days, and that is all of January, with a few poisonous pickles. This will make one and one-half months that we have been kept on such rations. I think it will wind us up by spring. Received two letters from wife, one notifying me of a $50.00 check being sent (it is not to be found); also $1.00 worth of stamps.

January 21st. – Cloudy and still raining. I feel very unwell, spinning in my head, sore throat, and weakness. Wrote home to my wife about check and telling her to send my box.

January 22d. – Still cloudy and raining. I received two letters from home, one only twelve days out. They are generally out a month.

January 23d. – Cloudy, rained all last night, and raining occasionally. Took a dose of medicine to-day, feel like I was going to be sick. Am very weak, can hardly walk.

January 24th. – It is clear and cold this morning. On Sunday the 5th of this month, Captains G.R. Campbell and T.F. Perkins, and a private, Deniem, procured Federal uniforms and passed out about dark. One of these Captains had an officer's uniform. These three gentlemen, passed down to Seabrook, eight miles distant, meeting with a negro and telling what the arrangements were, which was to get a boat across the river and proceed toward Savannah, where they had a large box of fine liquor, in bottles, of which they promised the negro one, and $10.00 to find the boat and pilot them. All the time abusing the Rebels and saying he never expected to take one of them, and they joining in with him. They came across the Negro Recruiting Officer and he encouraged them never to take a Rebel. They did not succeed in getting a boat, then it was what to do. They concluded to return, which they did and made it successfully. Capt. Perkins fainting on the road. Had a hard time to get him back. They traveled about twenty miles that night, which was a big tramp for men that had been fed on pickles and corn meal.

January 25th. – Clear and cold. I feel very bad to-day. We still hear grape about the late prisoners going North.

January 26th. – Clear and very cold. I feel some better to-day. I wrote to my wife and to S. R. Selecman at Johnson's Island. Our rations continue the same, ten ounces of mean, spoiled meal, four ounces of good flour, and a few pickles, this is per day; two ounces of salt for ten days. Have not had soup since the 15th of December. Meat and nearly everything else were played out then.

January 27th. – Clear and very cold. I have been quite sick, but feel much better. Had my washing done for the first time in twelve months. We drew four ounces of pickled beef and four ounces of Irish potatoes this evening, the first we have had since the 14th of December; making forty-four days living on ten ounces of corn meal, spoiled at that, four ounces of bread or flour, and a few pickles; two ounces of salt for ten days. Hard living, nearly half the men sick and would have died had it not been for the Yankee surgeon informing Gen. Foster, if he did not increase the rations, it was no use to give medicine, as they all would die. The order soon came for us to receive the above rations.

January 28th. – Clear and very cool. I think I am improving slowly. All the rest keeping up. To-day all of Sherman's capture sent North, the unlucky boys remain on hand. Lieut. Campbell is very sick and they say will die.

January 29th. – This is the Sabbath. Clear and cold. I am not much better. Got some cough drops to-day that helped me very much.

January 30th. – Clear and beautiful. Moderated very much. Took three doses of quinine. Rations very short to-day. We have a little soup without bread.

January 31th. – Clear and beautiful, not very cold. I keep

Lieutenant Geo. F. Keiser
5th Virginia

about the same. Better of a morning and worse of evenings. I make a drunken man complete, head swims and I am so weak I stagger when I walk. Rations issued to us for ten days; one-quarter pound of pickled pork, one-quarter pound of potatoes, ten ounces of damaged meal, four ounces of good flour, a few pickles, and half as much salt as we use. No soap has been issued for us since the 14th of December.

February 1st. – Clear beautiful morning. Heavy frost last night. I feel some better this morning.

February 2d. – Cloudy or rather foggy, not very cold. Allen sick. I am not much better, am weak. I think I have scurvy, it is quite common among us.

February 3d. – Cloudy and raining, not very cold. Allen no better. I keep the same. Wrote home to my wife.

February 4th. – A little foggy, warm and pleasant. I am not very well to-day, eyes very bad, especially at night. Allen on the mend. Music in town to-night. The brass band playing most beautifully. A beautiful night up to twelve o'clock, then it commenced raining. I coughed nearly all night.

February 5th. – This is the Sabbath. Feel much better this morning. A nice pleasant day, all getting along tolerably well, considering.

February 6th. – Cloudy. All keep up, but very weak. Little cool.

February 7th. – Rained all last night, very cool and cloudy. Rations very short. We nearly starve for something to eat. What will we do if it gets no better?

February 8th. – Clear and cool this morn. We had a little corn bread for breakfast, and borrowed a little grease skimmed off the fat, and made gravy, which constituted our breakfast.

February 9th. – All moving along about the same. Great deal of grape about exchange and peace, Lincoln meeting our peace Commissioners at Fort Monroe. A great deal of speculation, fearful it is all talk.

February 10th. – This is the day for drawing rations. We draw, ten ounces of meal, four ounces of flour, four ounces of potatoes, four ounces of pork, making twenty-two ounces of provisions per day, per man. We get two tablespoons of salt for ten days, we make it do now. We have commenced drawing meat, we get no soap. Weather clear and very cold.

February 11th. – Clear and more pleasant, nice day. Lieut. Campbell still lives, but very low. Thirteen guns fired. Received a letter from big Jack to-day.

February 12th. – Clear and cool. I am still on the sick list.

February 13th. – Clear and cool for this climate. Flour is worth fifteen cents per pound, Irish potatoes, $3.00 per bushel, or $8.33 per barrel (three bushel in one barrel), beans ten cents per pound, they are cheapest for us to buy. Money gone and can't buy anything. Received letter from my wife. All well.

February 14th. – This is Valentine Day and it is raining. I feel quite poorly, have a distressing cough.

February 15th. – Rained all last night hard. I feel a little worse, hope it will not last long. Cloudy and warm this morn. Cleared off and a fine day. Great exchange news. We will soon be free once more, I think. Wrote home to my wife to-day.

February 16th. – A lovely day, clear and pleasant. News is we get full prison rations, until we leave. Not come yet, rations short.

February 17th. – Clear and pleasant in the morning, wind raised and blustery. I have been a prisoner twenty-one months.

February 18th. – Clear and beautiful. I feel better than I have for ten days.

February 19th. – Clear. Lieut. W. C. Campbell, died last night at ten o'clock with diarrhœa. Feel worse, caught cold last night and nearly wore myself out coughing. We learn of the fall of Charleston and to-day about one hundred guns were fired. We are still expecting to start on exchange shortly.

February 20th. – Full prison rations were given to us to-day, making size last six months. We have seen the elephant in all his forms. I feel much better. Eyes no better. Weather clear and cool. We get for rations per day, one-half pound of meal, one-half pound of flour, ten ounces of pork and bacon, one-half pint of beans or peas, for eight days; also half bar of soap for four men.

February 21st. – Received a letter from Capt. Furnish and one from J. L. Bennett, and answered them both. Cloudy and cool. I feel better to-day.

February 22d. – Washington's Birthday. Many salutes fired. Cloudy and pleasant. Great many washing, preparing for exchange.

February 23d. – Cloudy and raining a little. Lieut. John Long of the 10th Regiment died of inflammation of the bowels, death quite sudden.

February 24th. – Cloudy and raining a little, pleasant. I feel much better, almost like a new man. Received my check for $50.00; one from Brother Joe Bennett, and one from my wife yesterday.

February 25th. – Cloudy this morning and a little cool. I think it will clear off soon. Wrote to my wife to-day.

February 26th. – Cloudy and raining, quite pleasant. I am improving, but yet not much better.

February 27th. – Very foggy and warm this morning. No grape about leaving, on the mend slowly.

February 28th. – Cloudy and dark with some rain. All called out to give our names, rank, regiment, and whether we wanted to go to Fortress Monroe for exchange or to take the oath and go to New York. Not many went to the latter place. All keen for exchange. I went out to the sutler's store to-day. Cashed my check (or duplicate); found goods very high; shoes, $7.00 per pair, coarse gingham shirts $2.40. Everything in proportion. Our ten days rations the same as the last, we get plenty of soap now and salt, our meat rations are very good at present, beans, musty, but too few to make a noise about.

March 1st. – It rained all last night. Capt. Baly is very sick. Cloudy this morning. Washday. The first time I washed for sometime. I feel much better to-day.

March 2d. – Cloudy and a little rain, warm and pleasant. All anxious to start to Dixie. All that receive money can get a chance to spend it before we leave.

March 3d. – Clear and beautiful. I had the privilege of going to the sutlers store, bought pants, haversack, and other articles, soon spent $50.00. We are expecting to be called out to start to Fortress Monroe, every minute.

March 4th. – Little cloudy, wind feels like rain. While I was out yesterday I found at the express office, two boxes; one for Capt. Low and one for Lieut. Pens of Pulaski. I notified the Provost-Marshall of the fact. Called out about four o'clock to leave, marched to the wharf, and soon put aboard of a steamer, but finding it too small to accommodate us we were put aboard of the large steamer *Illinois* about seven p.m. Lay all night up to twelve o'clock the next day.

March 5th. – Cloudy and pleasant. A great many are sea-sick. I am in fine health. This is the Sabbath.

March 6th. – Ran all last night, but met a strong breeze this morning, our speed is not so great. Cloudy this morning. I keep well so far.

March 7th. – A beautiful day. Awfully crowded and a bad smell, many sick aboard. Arrived at Fortress Monroe at midnight, anchored in Hampton Roads.

March 8th. – Cloudy and raining, pleasant weather. Waiting for orders, no orders come yet. We move a little before dark for the mouth of the James River, anchored all night.

March 9th. – Cloudy and pleasant. About eight o'clock weighed anchor and started for Norfolk. Arrived about nine o'clock, anchored off the city. Awaiting orders and they say they are wanting coal. Horrible smell on board this morning.

March 10th. – I slept on upper deck, it rained nearly all night on us. Still cloudy with a little rain; also grape afloat. Sunset clear. Loading coal last night and to-day. Many of our officers go ashore to see their friends, and some of their friends come aboard to see them.

March 11th. – Clear and beautiful. Very cool last night. About eight o'clock, weighed anchor. Bound for some new prison, can't tell yet. Soon found we were on the road for Fort Delaware. Men dying to-day. Lieut. Edwards was soon thrown overboard, but they did not let the Commander know the other man was dead until the next morning.

March 12th. – Clear and beautiful. Nobody allowed on deck, only as they pass to and from the privy. Arrived at the Fort at ten o'clock. One private died on board to-day. It took until night to unload and examine us.

March. 13th. – Wrote to Selecman, wife and to Howard of St. Louis. A beautiful day. I am improving fast. Ate a good supper with friend Wm. Casey. Last day no roll call. Our rations very short here (about half enough).

March 14th. – Clear and very beautiful. Wrote to Brother Thomas to-day. All well.

March 15th. – Cloudy and a little rain, warm and pleasant. All of our sick and wounded pardoned to go in exchange. Rations quite short, but very good.

March 16th. – Very cloudy and damp. Warm and pleasant, it is now clearing off. Wrote to Cousin Lizzie Russell and J. M. Bohart.

March. 17th. – All well. Clear and quite cold. I slept cold last night, don't feel so well by it. Twenty-two months ago I was made a prisoner. Eight of our number have died since we arrived here and more will soon. The seed of death was sown in the department of the South or near Charleston.

March, 18th. – All well. Clear and cool. Mouse got in my hat last night, and cut his way out, spoiling a new hat. Rations very short, about four or five ounces of meat and ten ounces of bread is all we get. All that have money can live well, as we have a sutler that keeps nearly everything, but prices are enormous. Coffee, $1.20 per pound, sugar, sixty cents, cheese, fifty cents, butter, ninety, lard, thirty-five, bacon, thirty-five cents per pound. Shoes from $7.00 to $15.00 per pair. Paper $1.00 per quire, envelopes fifty cents per bunch, they have fallen some in price in the last few days, on their goods. Wrote to Sister Lucy.

March 19th. – A beautiful, pleasant Sabbath day. Heard Lieut. Thomas preach to-day.

March 20th. – Clear and very warm. A beautiful day. All

well.

March 21th. – All well. Another beautiful day, warm and pleasant. The sick and wounded leave to-day and some few other officers, together with 600 privates. Wrote home to-day.

March 22d – Clear and cold. All well. At night the officers had a concert for the benefit and use of the Hilton Head sick and destitute. Raised about $100.00 and one hundred pounds of tobacco, which was distributed among them.

March 23d. – All well. Quite cold and windy. Disagreeable. Our rations yesterday shorter than common, two mouthfuls of meat and six crackers, per day. Wind blew the fence down between us and privates yesterday. Raining a little.

March. 24th. – All well. Cold and windy. Exchange played out. Heard of Sherman's defeat.

March 25th. – Clear and a little warmer, cloudy during the day.

March 26th. – Sabbath day. Quite cool and clear. All well. Wrote to Brother Thomas for money.

March 27th. – All well. Washday. All called and a thorough search. Two men found over in the privates' pen. Quite ragged. All our old clothes taken from us. All of the parade officers called out to be ready to start to Dixie in a few moments warning. Wrote to Capt. Burnes at Johnson's Island this lovely day.

March 28th. – All well and improving in flesh. It has the appearance of raining. Officers called out, not gone yet.

March 29th. – Officers still here. All well. Still looks like rain, but none yet.

March. 30th. – This is quite a rainy day, warm, growing weather. Parole officers not left yet. Wrote to my wife.

March 31st. – Still raining and warm. All well.

April 1st. – Cloudy and cool. Roll call, one a day. Paroled prisoners still here.

April 2d. – Clear and cool. A beautiful Sabbath morning.

April 3d. – A beautiful day. All well. Hear bad news. They say Richmond's fallen. I don't believe it, yet the Lord knows. Received a letter from J. L. Bennett.

April 4th. – Another nice day. We will have to move out directly to white-wash. We have good order in our division now. No one is allowed to spit on the floor, or spill water, under penalty of damage of five cents, this to be paid in money, or extra duty performed. Wrote to J. L. Bennett, to-day.

April 5th. – All well. Pleasant weather. Richmond has fallen and the Yankees think the rebellion crushed. They will find more have to die before that is done. No meat for dinner, a half-pint of bean soup and a small piece of bread makes our dinner.

April 6th. – Warm and raining. All well. Concert tonight, proceeds for the use and benefit of the sick and destitute. This makes three times they have performed, making $100.00 and a hundred plugs of tobacco. Scurvy rages very bad among the Hilton Head prisoners.

April 7th. – Warm and cloudy. All well. No news this morning. Raining.

April 8th. – A beautiful day. All well. News here yesterday that Lee and all his army were captured. Received letter from home and answered it.

April 9th. – Cloudy, with a little rain, very cool. No news of importance. All well.

April 10th. – Still cloudy with a little rain. Eight officers called out this morning that were Captains in Arkansas, for exchange, together with eighty privates. All well. To-day we were notified we could send for boxes of all kinds of provisions and clothes. Wrote a letter to my wife, one to Howard, at St. Louis, and one to Clasby.

April 11th. – All well. Cloudy and looks like rain. Oh, we hear such bad news. Gen. R. E. Lee, has surrendered his army to U. S. Grant. What will become of us nobody knows. Many conjectures about our punishment. It is enough to know our army has gone and our cause hopeless. Are we wrong? I think not, but we are overpowered. I cannot see the error of our way yet. God help us is my prayer, and submit to our fate.

April 12th. – All well. Cloudy yet, weather unsettled. Very

muddy. All news bad yet. None good for us.

April 13th. – All well. Clearing off, quite cool. News is the field and staff officers to be put in another prison for retaliation.

April 14th. – Clear and cool. Some frost last night. Wrote to Howard at St. Louis and to J.L. Bennett.

April 15th. – All well. Cloudy and raining. All astonished at seeing the flag at half mast this morning. News soon came of the death of President Abraham Lincoln. No one believed it at first, but soon found out it was a stern reality and all seemed to regret it, as they thought it worse for us. Secretary Seward was stabbed at the same time in his bed, he being thrown from his carriage a few days previous and badly hurt. His son was killed. A barbarous deed.

April 16th. – All well. Clear this morning, but soon clouded and raining. They are firing a gun every half hour in remembrance of the President, commencing at sun rise. Wrote to my wife.

April 17th. – Clear and beautiful. No news of importance. All well. That is our mess. Wind cool.

April 18th. – Clear and beautiful, rather cold. They stopped us getting coal, can't make coffee now. They are moving out the fence and moving the sutler's store. We hear Mobile has surrendered with 6,000 prisoners; also Mosby's command and hear Joseph E. Johnston has to, but doubt if soon.

April 19th. – Clear and beautiful. All well. Warm and pleasant. Extra rations have been cut off from those that have been buying them on account of the President being assassinated. That is their version of the story.

April 20th. – Cloudy and quite cool and rainy. Took out the stoves this morning.

April 21th. – Cloudy and quite cool. All well. Made application for the oath this morning. The most solemn act of my life.

April 22d. – All well. Cloudy. No news.

April 23d. – Sabbath. Heard Capt. Harris preach. Wrote to my wife.

April 24th. – All well. Clear and moderate. Roll call once a day and hardtack all the time. Only six a day, being one-half pound of bread with four ounces of meat and a pint of thin soup, is our rations per day.

April 25th. – All well. A lovely day, warm and pleasant. All anxious to know our fate. News reached us yesterday of the surrender of J.E. Johnston to Sherman, but was not accepted by the Federal Government. Grant was immediately sent to take command. Received and wrote to cousin Mary A. Taggart, Ky., and to J.L. Bennett, in Mo.

April 26th. – A beautiful day. All well. Get hardtack nearly all the time.

April 27th. – All well. Nice washday. Called out to give us the advantage of oath. Got down to the letter "G," half had taken it. Wrote to my wife.

April 28th. – All well. Beautiful weather. No news.

April 29th. – All well. Cloudy and rained very hard in evening. We hear Johnson has surrendered. Wrote to J. L. Bennett.

April 30th. – All well. Clear, clouded up before night.

May 1st. – Cloudy and raining, very disagreeable. My time for making coffee. Had a hard time of it.

May 2d. – Clear. All well. Offering the oath again, all took it, but 115 out of 1,900.

May 3d. – All well. A nice morning. All expect to start home soon.

May 4th. – All well. Nice weather, warm and pleasant. The galvanized Rebels are leaving here every day.

May 5th. – All well. Nice weather. W.H. Allen left our mess yesterday. By our concert we learn of the surrender of Gen. Jeff. Thompson, to-day. Wrote to my wife.

May 6th. – All well. Nice weather. No news.

May 7th. – All well. Clear and beautiful. Heard of the surrender of Gen. Kirby Smith to the United States forces. All of the Confederate army is gone and we must have peace now. Had grape to-day of the Hilton Head prisoners. Had to be sent to Richmond for retaliation. I hardly think it so as we have suffered death twice already.

May 8th. – All well. Cloudy and rained a little. No improvement.

May 9th. – All well. Cloudy and raining. A disagreeable day.

May 10th. – All well. Cloudy, weather unsettled. Heard to-day of the surrender of Dick Taylor Commanding. Wrote to my wife. About twenty-seven officers were released to-day. All those that applied before the fall of Richmond.

May 11th. – Cloudy and in the evening it rained.

May 12th. – All well. Rained all night last night, clearing off beautiful this morning. Some more of the galvanized left this morning for home.

May 13th. – Clear, nice beautiful day. All well. Wrote to Gen. Hitchcock to-day at Washington.

May 14th. – All well. A lovely morning. Wrote to Gen. Craig at St. Joseph. No news of importance.

May 15th. – All well. A beautiful day. Wrote to John Taggart to have released, and wrote to my wife.

May 16th. – All well. Nice weather. We learn they have Jefferson Davis in prison.

May 18th. – All well. A nice morning, turned cold this evening and looks like rain. Capt. Carson died this morning.

May 19th. – All well. Cloudy and cool, mist of rain falling. No change in rations or roll call.

May 20th. – Cloudy and heavy rain. Wrote to my wife.

May 21st. – All well. Cloudy and raining. Some few leave here every day on special release. This is the Sabbath.

May 22d. – Cloudy. No news.

May 23d. – All well. Clear and beautiful, nice day.

May 24th. – Clear and beautiful. Quite cool last night. Benson and I wrote to Pennybaker at Washington.

May 25th – All well. Clear. Cloudy this morning, looks like rain. We have hardtack often these days. My mouth is very sore, have scurvy in it. Wrote to Gen. Craig and my wife.

May 26th. – All well. Cloudy and raining a little. Received two letters from home to-day. Heard of the death of my dear sister. She died on the 26th of March, with consumption.

May 27th. – Cloudy and raining and very cold for this time of the year. One of the sentinel's gun fired accidentally and killed one and wounded another. They are too careless with their guns. One man taken out day before yesterday, hand-cuffed and tied him up by the thumbs for writing a contraband, I understand it is very abuse.

May 28th. – All well. Clearing off. Some meals we get no meat for dinner, we get a little thin soup and bread. Wrote to my wife for money. Sabbath day. Heard two sermons to-day.

May 29th. – All well. Clear and beautiful morning, a pleasant day. Wrote to J. H. Selecman, for money to-day. Just learned of the surrender of Gen. Kirby Smith. All that are released have to furnish their own transportation.

May 30th. – All well. A beautiful day. My release came to-day, a welcome visitor. I start for home in the morning.

May 31st. – A beautiful day. All well. I started for Philadelphia at eight o'clock in the morning, arrived at eleven o'clock. Took the cars at half after three for St. Louis, via Chicago.

June 1st. – Quite cool this morning at sunrise. Clear and a beautiful day.

June 2d. – Clear and nice. Arrived in Dunkirk at eight a.m., left half after six p.m.

June 3d. – A nice day, clear and warm. Arrived in Cleveland at five a.m., departed at nine a.m.

June 4th. – Arrived at Chicago at six a.m. Departed at seven fifteen p.m. Clear and beautiful. Arrived at St. Louis at nine a.m.

June 5th. – Departed on steamer *Jennie Dine* for Hannibal.

A. M. Bedford.

Capt. D.C. Grayson's 10th Va. Regt., Diary corroborates this Diary in all things we had to eat at Fort Pulaski. The rations at Hilton Head, were little better than we received.

APPENDIX

List of the Immortals

The six hundred Confederate officers who were placed upon Morris Island, South Carolina, under the fire of their own guns shelling that point, and subsequently starved upon 10 ounces of rotten corn meal and pickle at Hilton Head and Fort Pulaski, Georgia, by order of the United States authorities, 1864-65.

Maryland Confederate Troops

Name	Rank	Regiment	Captured – Date	Residence
W.W. Goldsboro	Major	1st Md.	Gettysburg, Pa., Jul. 4, 1863	Baltimore
Geo. Howard*	Capt.	1st Md. Cav.	Hawes Shp, Va., May 27, '63	Baltimore
W.H. Griffin	Capt.	B.B.	Yellow Tavern, May 27, '64	Baltimore
Eugene Diggs	Capt.	2d Md. Cav.	Martinsburg, W.V. Oct. '63	Prt Tobacco
E.J. Duly	Lieut.	1st Md. Cav	Hanover Jct., Va., May, '64	——
J.E.V. Pue	Lieut.	1st Md. Cav.	Gettysburg, July, 1863	Ellicott Mlls

Virginia Confederate Troops

Name	Rank	Regiment	Captured – Date	Residence
C.B. Christain	Lt Co	49th Va. Inf.	Cold Hbr, Va., May 30, '64	Amhurst Co.
J. Calvin Council	Lt Co	26th Va. Inf.	Petersburg, Va., Jun. 15, '64	St. Stephens
Rich. Woodman	Major	26th Va. Inf.	Cold Harbor, May 30, 1864	Monroe Co.
Peter V. Batte	Major	44th Va. Inf	Petersburg, Jun. 15, 1864	Petersburg
W.H. Hood °	Major	Militia	Petersburg, May 15, 1864	Petersburg
D.A. Jones	Major	Staff	Spotts. C.H., May 10, '64	Petersburg

* Took oath of allegiance.   ° Exchanged at Hilton Head, Dec. 14, 1864

Virginia *continued*

Name	Rank	Regiment	Captured – Date	Residence
Thom. P. Branch	Lt Co.	Staff	Drury's Bluff, May 16, '64	Petersburg
McD. Carrington	Lt Co.	C. Battery	Spotts. C.H., May 12, 1864	Charlottesvl
E.E. DePrest [1]	Major	23rd Va.	Spotts. C.H., May 12, 1864	Richmond
W.E. Carter	Major	Pg Battery	Spotts. C.H., May 12, 1864	Clarke Co.
Geo. W. Mercer	Major	29th Inf.	Cold Harbor, June 6, 1864	Rural Retrt
J.H. Johnson	Major	25th Inf.	Spotts. C.H., May 12, 1864	Pendt. Co.
J.J. Dunkle	Major	25th Inf.	Spotts. C.H., May 12, 1864	Pendt. Co.
H.E. Dickenson	Major	2nd Cav.	Chickahominy, May 12, '64	Liberty
J.H. Matthews	Major	25th Inf.	Wilderness, Va., May 5, '64	Beverly
H.A. Allen	Major	9th Inf.	Gettysburg, July 3, 1863	Portsmouth
R.E. Frayser °	Major	Sgnl Corps	Spotts. C.H., May 20, 1864	New Kent
J.R. Christain	Major	3rd Cav.	Spotts. C.H., May 8, 1864	New Kent
Lewis Harman	Major	12th Cav.	Violersville, May 5, 1864	Staunton
A. Doybins	Capt.	42d Inf.	Spotts. C.H., May 12, 1864	Jacksonville
J.W. Helm	Capt.	42d Inf.	Spotts. C.H., May 12, 1864	Jacksonville
A.K. Humes	Capt.	21st Cav.	Leetown, W.V., July 3, 1864	Abingdon
W.P. Duff	Capt.	50th Inf.	Spotts. C.H., May 12, 1864	Jonesville
D.C. Grayson	Capt.	10th Inf.	Spotts. C.H., May 12, 1864	Luray
H.N. Finks	Capt.	10th Inf.	Spotts. C.H., May 12, 1864	Madison CH
F.W. Kelley	Capt.	50th Inf.	Spotts. C.H., May 12, 1864	Tazewell Co
T.M. Gobble	Capt.	48th Inf.	Spotts. C.H., May 12, 1864	Abingdon
W.S. McConnell	Capt.	48th Inf.	Spotts. C.H., May 12, 1864	Estellville
W.S. Guthrie	Capt.	23d Inf.	Spotts. C.H., May 12, 1864	Prnc Edwrd
James Dunlap	Capt.	26th Inf.	Cold Harbor, June 3, 1864	Union, W.V.
A.K. Edgar	Capt.	27th Inf.	Spotts. C.H., May 12, 1864	Lsbg, W.V.
J.A. Lipps	Capt.	50th Inf.	Spotts. C.H., May 12, 1864	Wise C.H.
J.O.B. Crocker	Capt.	9th Inf.	Gettysburg, July 3, 1863	Norfolk
T.B. Horton	Capt.	11th Inf.	Milford Station, May 21, '64	Cmpbell Co.
R.C. Gillespie *	Pvt.	45th Inf.	S.W. Va., October 25, 1863	Ft. Wrth, Tx
R.H. Miller	Capt.	44th Inf.	Spotts. C.H., May 12, 1864	Bcknhm CH
J.M. Hillman	Capt.	44th Inf.	Spotts. C.H., May 12, 1864	Amelia
T.H. Board	Capt.	58th Inf.	Spotts. C.H., May 12, 1864	Bedford
J.M. Hughes	Capt.	44th Inf.	Spotts. C.H., May 12, 1864	Bedford
Isc. Kuyendall °	Capt.	7th Cav.	Wire Bridge, Feb. 18, '64	Rmney, WV
J.M. Lovett	Capt.	22d Inf.	Capon Bridge, June 31, '64	Hmpshr Co.
W.T. Mitchell	Capt.	6th Inf.	Yellow Tavern, May 11, '64	Pttslvnia Co.
T.A. Moon	Capt.	6th Inf.	Yellow Tavern, May 11, '64	Halifax Co.
A.M. King	Capt.	50th Inf.	Spotts. C.H., May 12, 1864	Halifax Co.
B.G. Brown	Capt.	7th Inf.	Gettysburg, July 3, 1863	Albrmrl Co.
C.D. McCoy	Capt.	25th Inf.	Spotts. C.H., May 12, 1864	Chrlttsville
W.C. Nunn °	Capt.	5th Cav.	Trevillian Sta., June, 1863	Litt. Plymth
Perylon Alfriend	Capt.	39th Militia	Petersburg, June 9, 1864	Petersburg
Bruce Gibson	Capt.	6th Cav.	Yellow Tavern, May 11, '64	Upperville
Geo. W. Nelson	Capt.	Staff	Gettysburg, July 5, 1863	Hanovr C.H.
C.J. Lewis	Capt.	8th Cav.	Shepherdstown, July 3, '63	Charleston
Thom. D. Moss	Lieut.	23d Inf.	Spotts. C.H., May 12, 1864	Louisa C.H.
Henry Fry	Lieut.	37th Inf.	Spotts. C.H., May 12, 1864	Whlng W.V.
W.E. Hart	Lieut.	Pg Battery	Spotts. C.H., May 12, 1864	KngWm CH
B.C. Maxwell	Lieut.	Cutshaw Bt	Spotts. C.H., May 12, 1864	Westmorlnd

[1] Escaped.   ° Exchanged at Hilton Head, Dec. 14, 1864.   * Took oath of allegiance

Virginia *continued*

Name	Rank	Regiment	Captured – Date	Residence
J. Ogden Murray	Capt.	7th Cav Stf	Valley Pike Va., Nov. 1863	Richmond
W. Ashburn	Lieut.	16th Inf.	Wayne Co., Va., Feb. 15, '64	Tzewell Co.
B.D. Merchant	Lieut.	4th Inf.	Antioch, Dec. 29, 1864	Man. Jnctn.
James H. Childs [2]	Lieut.	4th Cav.	Markham Sta., Jan. 6, 1864	Warrenton
S.F. Carson	Lieut.	5th Inf.	Morton's Ford, Feb. 6, 1864	Steel's Tvrn
Jesse Childs	Lieut.	4th Inf.	Spotts. C.H., May 12, 1864	Richmond
Geo. H. Killian	Lieut.	5th Inf.	Spotts. C.H., May 12, 1864	Waynesboro
J.W. Gilkerson	Lieut.	25th Inf.	Spotts. C.H., May 12, 1864	Mint Sprint
D.M. Layon, Adj.	Lieut.	25th Inf.	Spotts. C.H., May 12, 1864	Mt Meridian
R.B. Howlett	Lieut.	5th Cav.	Yellow Tavern, May 11, '64	Cobb's Crk
O.H.P. Lewis	Lieut.	31st Inf.	Highland Co., Nov. 10, 1863	Beverly
M.W. Boggs	Lieut.	20th Cav.	Loudoun Co., July 16, 1864	Wheeling
J. Annington	Lieut.	42d Inf.	Gettysburg, July 3, 1863	Cmpbl C.H.
D.W. Garrett	Lieut.	42d Inf.	Gettysburg, July 3, 1863	Mrgntn, WV
H.T. Coulter °	Lieut.	53d Inf.	Gettysburg, July 3, 1863	Kng Wm CH
M.E. Bowers	Lieut.	25 th Inf.	Wilderness, May 5, 1864	Franklin
W.L. Hunter	Lieut.	43d Cav.	Aldie, Va., Apr. 23, 1864	Waynesboro
W.L. Bernard	Lieut.	37th Cav.	Leesburg, Va., July 16, '64	Rocky Mt.
T.S. Mitchell	Lieut.	42d Inf.	Spotts. C.H., May 12, 1864	Marksville
P.M. Dalton	Lieut.	42d Inf.	Spotts. C.H., May 12, 1864	Patrick Co.
H.L. Hoover	Lieut.	25th Inf.	Spotts. C.H., May 12, 1864	Staunton
T.J. Kirk	Lieut.	25th Inf.	Spotts. C.H., May 12, 1864	Bowlng Grn
T.C. Chandler	Lieut.	47th Inf.	Spotts. C.H., May 12, 1864	Bowlng Grn
A.A. Angle	Lieut.	42d Inf.	Spotts. C.H., May 12, 1864	Rocky Mt.
G.W. Finly	Lieut.	50th Inf.	Gettysburg, July 3, 183	Clarksville
W. McGauley	Lieut.	9th Cav.	Ashland, Va., 1864	Warsaw
J.C. Allen	Lieut.	7th Cav.	Near Romney, Feb. 2, 1864	Edenburg
L.B. Doyle *	Lieut.	5th Inf.	Spotts. C.H., May 12, 1864	Lexington
C.B. Eastham	Lieut.	10th Inf.	Spotts. C.H., May 12, 1864	Harrisonbrg
J.H. Hawkins	Lieut.	10th Inf.	Spotts. C.H., May 12, 1864	McGeahysvl
T.S. Doyle	Lieut.	33d Inf.	Spotts. C.H., May 12, 1864	Staunton
J.W.A. Ford	Lieut.	20th Cav.	Near Wash., D.C., July 1864	Lewisburg
A.W. Edwards	Lieut.	15th Cav.	Near Richmnd, May 11, '64	Princess Ann
W.H. Morgan	Lieut.	11th Cav.	Milford Station, May 21, '64	Cmpbell Co.
J.D. Grever	Lieut.	50th Inf.	Spotts. C.H., May 12, 1864	Tazewell Co
C.P. Harper	Lieut.	21st Inf.	Spotts. C.H., May 12, 1864	Mcklnbr Co
Isaac Coles	Lieut.	6th Inf.	Brandy Station, June 9, 1863	Pittsylv. Co.
S.M. Dent	Lieut.	5th Cav.	Yellow Tavern, May 11, '64	Alexandria
C.D. Hall	Lieut.	48th Inf.	Spotts. C.H., May 12, 1864	Lee County
Edward Bell	Lieut.	10th Inf.	Spotts. C.H., May 12, 1864	Petersburg
H.C. Howlett	Lieut.	5th Cav.	Chesterfield, Va., 1864	Petersburg
E.C. Andrews	Lieut.	4th Inf.	Morton's Ford, Feb. 6, 1864	Elk Creek
J.W.O. Funk [3]	Lieut.	5th Inf.	Spotts. C.H., May 12, 1864	Winchester
J.F. Lytton	Lieut.	5th Inf.	Spotts. C.H., May 12, 1864	Long Glade
J.W. Gillock	Lieut.	27th Inf.	Gettysburg, July 3, 1863	Lexington
J.W. McDowell	Lieut.	26th Inf.	Cold Harbor, June, 1864	Grn. Br. Co.
A.G. Hudgins °°	Lieut.	C.S.N.	Albermarle Sound, May, '64	Richmond
Drury Lacy	Lieut.	23d Inf.	Spotts. C.H., May 12, 1864	Prc. Ed. C.H.

[2] Went blind from bad treatment.   [3] Died from bad treatment.
° Exchanged Fort Pulaski, Dec. '64. °° Exchanged Morris Island. * Took oath of allegiance

Virginia *continued*

Name	Rank	Regiment	Captured – Date	Residence
S.J. Hutton	Lieut.	37th Inf.	Spotts. C.H., May 12, 1864	Gld Spgs Dp
M.H. Duff	Lieut.	37th Inf.	Spotts. C.H., May 12, 1864	Wshngtn Co.
E.A. Rosenblam	Lieut.	37th Inf.	Spotts. C.H., May 12, 1864	Wshngtn Co.
S.A. Johnson	Lieut.	23d Inf.	Spotts. C.H., May 12, 1864	Louisa Co.
J.W. Groome	Lieut.	23d Inf.	Spotts. C.H., May 12, 1864	Louisa Co.
A.B. Cooke	Lieut.	23d Inf.	Spotts. C.H., May 12, 1864	Louisa Co.
R.C. Bryan	Lieut.	48th Inf.	Spotts. C.H., May 12, 1864	Abingdon
J.T. Fulcher	Lieut.	37th Inf.	Spotts. C.H., May 12, 1864	Abingdon
J.S. King	Lieut.	37th Inf.	Spotts. C.H., May 12, 1864	Abingdon
S.H. Hawes	Lieut.	Pgs Battery	Spotts. C.H., May 12, 1864	Richmond
F. King	Lieut.	Fry's Bttry	Spotts. C.H., May 12, 1864	KngWm Co.
R. Massey	Lieut.	Fry's Bttry	Spotts. C.H., May 12, 1864	Coovesville
Geo. F. Keiser	Lieut.	Ctshw's Bt	Spotts. C.H., May 12, 1864	Greenville
J.F. Ganneway	Lieut.	5th Va. Inf.	Spotts. C.H., May 12, 1864	Chathm Hill
R.W. Legg	Lieut.	50th Inf.	Spotts. C.H., May 12, 1864	Turkey Cve
R.S. Bowie	Lieut.	37th Inf.	Spotts. C.H., May 12, 1864	Abingdon
F. Fansa	Lieut.	37th Inf.	Spotts. C.H., May 12, 1864	Weston
W.L. Enos	Lieut.	26th Inf.	Petersburg, June 15, 1864	Gloucstr Co
A.B. Cantham	Lieut.	26th Inf.	Petersburg, June 15 1864	Kg & Qn CH
Jno. M. Lambert	Lieut.	52d Inf.	Cold Harbor, May 30, 1864	Greenville
W.P.R. Leigh	Lieut.	5th Cav.	Kng & Queen C.H., Jun. 7 '64	Gloucstr Co.
W.N. Hendricks	Lieut.	25th Inf.	Wilderness, May 5, 1864	Fair Mount
J.G. Brown	Lieut.	49th Inf.	Mechanicsville, May 30, '64	Front Royal
W.H. Hatcher	Lieut.	42d Inf.	Spotts. C.H., May 12, 1864	Liberty
W.B. Carder	Lieut.	4th Inf.	Gettsyburg, July 3, 1863	Marion
F.J. King	Lieut.	42d Cav.	Charles City, Dec. 10, 1863	Martinsville
T.M. Gravely	Lieut.	42d Inf.	Spotts. C.H., May 12, 1864	Henry Co.
J.P. Kelly	Lieut.	4th Inf.	Spotts. C.H., May 12, 1864	Newberne
Pat Hogan	Lieut.	4th Inf.	Spotts. C.H., May 12, 1864	Lexington
J.W. Mauck	Lieut.	10th Inf.	Spotts. C.H., May 12, 1864	Harrisonbrg
J.W. Kratzer	Lieut.	12th Cav.	Spotts. C.H., May 12, 1864	Harrisonbrg
S.D. Bland	Lieut.	18th Cav.	Pendleton Co. WV, Jan., '63	Franklin
C. Fraetas	Lieut.	3d Inf.	Howlett's Farm, June, 1864	Petersburg
S.W. Gary	Lieut.	3d Inf.	Gettysburg, July 3, 1863	Norfolk
F.C. Burnes	Lieut.	56th Inf.	Gettysburg, July 3, 1863	Charlotte Co
J.H. Allen	Lieut.	45th Inf.	Logan, Va., Dec., 1863	Ballardsville
H.G. Brinkly	Lieut.	41st Inf.	Nansemond, Va., Sept., '63	Norfolk
C.F. Crisp [4]	Lieut.	10th Inf.	Spotts. C.H., May 12, 1864	Luray
S.F. Finks	Lieut.	10th Inf.	Spotts. C.H., May 12, 1864	Madison CH
Jno. Long	Lieut.	10th inf.	Spotts. C.H., May 12, 1864	Bridgewater
J.J. Henritey	Lieut.	37th Inf.	Spotts. C.H., May 12, 1864	Lebanon
J.A. Burnett	Lieut.	50th Inf.	Spotts. C.H., May 12, 1864	Bluntsville
W.S. Gilmer	Lieut.	37th Inf.	Spotts. C.H., May 12, 1864	Lebanon
W.W. George	Lieut.	26th Inf.	Cold Harbor, June 3, 1864	Princeton
W.G. Herrington	Lieut.	25th Inf.	Cox's Farm, July 12, 1864	Shelby
R.C. Campbell	Lieut.	53d Inf.	Gettysburg, July 3, 1863	Kng Wm Co
J.W. Frazier	Lieut.	Capt.	Rapidan, Oct. 11, 1863	Loudoun Co
C.P. Johnson	Lieut.	1st Cav.	Burlington, Dec. 3, '63	Hmpshre Co
P.B. Akers	Lieut.	11th Inf.	Milford Station, May 21, '64	Lynchburg

[4]After the war was Speaker of the United States House of Representatives.

Virginia *continued*

Name	Rank	Regiment	Captured – Date	Residence
L. Green	Lieut.	5th Cav.	Near Richmond, May 12, '64	Petersburg
H.C. Jones	Lieut.	50th Inf.	Spotts. C.H., May 12, 1864	Gladesville
J.W. Harris	Lieut.	58th Inf.	Spotts. C.H., May 12, 1864	Bedford CH
J.S. Hix	Lieut.	44th Inf.	Spotts. C.H., May 12, 1864	Goochland
T.A. Applebery °	Lieut.	44th Inf.	Spotts. C.H., May 12, 1864	Fluvanna Co
J.W. Hughes	Lieut.	44th Inf.	Spotts. C.H., May 12, 1864	Cobham Dp
W.A. Dawson	Lieut.	27th Inf.	Spotts. C.H., May 12, 1864	Callards
D.B. Conway	Lieut.	4th Inf.	Spotts. C.H., May 12, 1864	Elk Creek
Jno. A. Donaghe	Lieut.	10th Inf.	Spotts. C.H., May 12, 1864	Purnassus
J.L. Hempstead	Capt.	25th Inf.	Wilderness, May 5, 1864	Dubuque, Ia.
W.B. Dobson	Lieut.	5th Cav.	Yellow Tavern, May 11, '64	Danville
R.B. Hart	Lieut.	5th Cav.	Yellow Tavern, May 11, '64	Stevenville
J.W. Davis *	Lieut.	20th Cav.	Frd'k City, Md., July 10, '63	Clarksburg
Hopkins Harding	Lieut.	19th Inf.	Gettysburg, July 3, 1863	Scottsville
F.R. Haynes	Lieut.	24th Cav.	Gloucester Co., Oct. 5, 1863	Cobb's Crk.
T.J. Bery	Lieut.	25th Inf.	Wilderness, May 5, 1864	Salt Lick
N.D. Embry	Lieut.	25th Inf.	Milford Station, May 21, '64	Pineville
A.R. Humphries	Lieut.	26th Inf.	Cold Harbor, June 3, 1864	Lewisburg
C.D. Fitzhugh 5	——	———	Antietam, Md.	Hgrstwn, Md

South Carolina

Name	Rank	Regiment	Captured – Date	Residence
M.G. Zeigler	Major	H. Legion	Stony Creek, Va., May 7, '64	Cokesburg
W.P. Emanuel	Major	4th SC Cav	Louisa C.H., June 11, 1864	Charleston
P.B. Martin	Capt.	H. Legion	Petersburg, May 7, 1864	Spartanburg
D.C. Moore	Capt.	H. Legion	Garrett's Stat., May 8, 1864	Polksburg
S.B. Mecham	Capt.	5th Inf.	Wilderness, May 6, 1864	Yorkville
W.L. Campbell	Capt.	11th Inf.	Petersburg, May 13, 1864	Waterboro
Thos. Pinckney	Capt.	4th Cav.	Hawes Shop, May 28, 1864	Charleston
J.M. Mulvaney *	Capt.	27th Inf.	Petersburg, June 24, 1864	Charleston
T.M. Easterday	Lieut.	5th Cav.	Trevillians, Va., May 12, '64	Charleston
W.H. Covington	Lieut.	23d Inf.	Petersburg, June 18, 1864	Bennetsville
H.J. Clifton	Lieut.	21st Inf.	Petersburg, June 11, 1864	Timminsvlle
W.S. Bissell °	Lieut.	2d Inf.	Gettysburg, July 4, 1863	Charleston
S.T. Anderson	Lieut.	1st Cav.	Martinsburg, July 19, 1863	Chester Dist.
J.B. Gallman	Lieut.	5th Inf.	Wilderness, May 5, 1864	Unionville
N.B. Lusk	Lieut.	12th Inf.	Wilderness, May 5, 1864	Cherokee
J.A. Garrett	Lieut.	H. Legion	Rocky Creek Sta., May 4, '64	Spartanburg
J.G. Hallford	Lieut.	8th Inf.	Cold Harbor, May 20, 1864	Timminsvlle
W.E. Johnson	Lieut.	7th Cav.	Old Church, May 30, 1864	Kershw Dist
William Epps	Lieut.	4th Cav.	Louisa C.H., June 11, 1864	Knight Free
David Gordon	Lieut.	4th Cav.	Louisa C.H., June 11, 1864	King Distrct
M.P. Galloway	Lieut.	23d Inf.	Petersburg, June 17, 1864	Mrlboro Dist

° Exchanged Hilton Head, Dec. '64.   * Took oath of allegiance.
5 This man was captured going south; did not belong to Confederate Army.

North Carolina

Name	Rank	Regiment	Captured – Date	Residence
Jno. A. Baker *	Col.	3d Cav.	Petersburg, June 21, 1864	Wilmington
G.N. Folk °	Col.	6th Cav.	Kinston, June 22, 1864	Morganton
T.S. Hargrove	Lt Col	4th Inf.	South Bridge, June 26, '64	Oxford
J.R. McDonald	Major	51st Inf.	Gaines' Mill, Va., 1864	Fayetteville
H.D. Fowler	Capt.	1st Inf.	Spotts. C.H., May 12, 1864	Rallsville
T.L. Johnson	Capt.	1st Inf.	Spotts. C.H., May 12, 1864	Edenton
W.H. Day	Capt.	1st Inf.	Spotts. C.H., May 12, 1864	Halifax
J.L. Cantwell 6	Capt.	3d Inf.	Spotts. C.H., May 12, 1864	Wilmington
John Cowan	Capt.	3d Inf.	Spotts. C.H., May 12, 1864	Wilmington
H.W. Horne	Capt.	3d Inf.	Spotts. C.H., May 12, 1864	Fayetteville
W.G. McRae	Capt.	7th Inf.	Wilderness, May 6, 1864	Wilmington
J.G. Knox	Capt.	7th Inf.	Wilderness, May 6, 1864	Rowan
W.H. Kitchen	Capt.	12th Inf.	Spotts. C.H., May 12, 1864	Scotlnd Nck
J.W. Lane	Capt.	16th Inf.	Wilderness, May 6, 1864	Hendrsnvlle
F.C. Lewis	Capt.	18th Inf.	Spotts. C.H., May 12, 1864	Wilmington
C.B. Bromly	Capt.	20th Inf.	Gettysburg, July 3, 1863	Concord
Alec T. Cole	Capt.	23d Inf.	Spotts. C.H., May 12, 1864	Rockingham
N.G. Bradford	Capt.	26th Inf.	Gettysburg, July 3, 1863	Lenoir Co.
S.S. Bohannon	Capt.	28th Inf.	Spotts. C.H., May 12, 1864	Yadkin
W.B. Demar	Capt.	31th Inf.	Gaines' Farm, June 1, 1864	Yadkin
J.E. Hodges	Capt.	32d Int.	Spotts. C.H., May 12, 1864	Deep Creek
H.M. Dixon	Capt.	35th Inf.	Petersburg, June 17, 1864	Moore Co.
C. McN. Blue	Capt.	35th Inf.	Petersburg, June 17, 1864	Moore Co.
W.J. Alexander	Capt.	37th Inf.	Gettysburg, July 3, 1863	Wilksboro
S.H. Hines	Capt.	45th Inf.	Spotts. C.H., May 10, 1864	Milton
W.F. Murphy	Capt.	51st Inf.	Bermuda H'd, June 16, 1864	Clinton
DS Cockenham °	Capt.	54 th Inf.	Rapp'k Bridge, Nov. 7, '63	Clinton
J.K. Kyle	Capt.	52d Inf.	Spotts. C.H., May 21, 1864	Fayetteville
J.C. Blair 7	Capt.	1st Cav.	Yellow Tavern, May 21, '64	Boone C.H.
S. Hartsfield	Capt.	3d Cav.	Hanover Court House, 1864	Kinston
J.W. Moon	Capt.	3d Cav.	Greenville, S.C., Dec. 17, '63	Wilmington
W.B. Allen	Lieut.	6th Inf.	Rapp'k Bridge, Nov. 7, '63	Wake Co.
S.P. Abernathy	Lieut.	30th Inf.	Kelly's Ford, Nov. 7, 1863	Wake Co.
Robt. C. Carr	Lieut.	43d Inf.	Gettysburg, July 4, 1863	Maynolin
David A. Coon	Lieut.	11th Inf.	Gettysburg, July 4, 1863	Lincolnton
AL Leatherwood	Lieut.	29th Inf.	Clay Co., N.C., Feb., 1864	Ford Hendry
J.A. Hartsfield	Lieut.	1st Inf.	Spotts. C.H., May 12, 1864	Ballsville
J.A. Latham	Lieut.	1st Inf.	Spotts. C.H., May 12, 1864	Plymouth
J.O. Frink	Ensgn	18th Inf.	Spotts. C.H., May 12, 1864	Cerogoda
Geo. W. Corbell	Lieut.	18th Inf.	Spotts. C.H., May 12, 1864	Caintuck
N.S. Mosely	Lieut.	12th Inf.	Spotts. C.H., May 12, 1864	Warrenton
Frank McIntosh	Lieut.	18th Inf.	Spotts. C.H., May 12, 1864	Richmnd Co
Jno. M. Geyther	Lieut.	1st Inf.	Spotts. C.H., May 12, 1864	Tarboro
Jno. T. Bullock	Lieut.	23d Inf.	Spotts. C.H., May 12, 1864	Tranquility
Jno. F. Grubb	Lieut.	14th Inf.	Spotts. C.H., May 12, 1864	Shelly
J.D. Malloy	Lieut.	51st Int	Drury's Bluff, Va., 1864	Buck Horn
H. Earp	Lieut.	24th Inf.	Petersburg, June, 1864	Smithville

* Took oath of allegiance, Fort Pulaski, March, 1865. ° Exchanged Hilton Head, Dec. '64.
6 This officer did much for our sick men; made this roll. 7 Shot by sentinel on Morris Island.

North Carolina *continued*

Name	Rank	Regiment	Captured – Date	Residence
J.D. McMullin	Lieut.	1st Inf.	Spottsylvania C.H., 1864	Wilmington
C.P. Mallett	Lieut.	3d Inf.	Spottsylvania C.H., 1864	Fayetteville
J.M. Hobson	Lieut.	2d Inf.	Spottsylvania C.H., 1864	Rocksville
F.F. Patrick	Lieut.	32d Inf.	Spottsylvania C.H., 1864	Columbia
H.J. Jenkins	Lieut.	Wymn Batt	Gate City, N.C., June 9, '64	Murfreesbro
J.W. Brothers	Lieut.	67th Inf.	Kinston, N.C., 1864	Kinston
T.B. Henderson	Lieut.	4th Inf.	Washington, Dec. 16, 1863	Jacksonville
J.M. Allen	Lieut.	4th Inf.	Gettysburg, July 4, 1864	Fairfields
B.W. Burkhead	Lieut.	22d Inf.	Hanover Jct., Va., May, '64	Ashboro
R.A. Glenn *	Lieut.	22d Inf.	Spottsylvania C.H., 1864	
W.T. Anderson	Lieut.	5th Inf.	Spottsylvania C.H., 1864	Snowhill
J.H. Daiden	Lieut.	3d Inf.	Spottsylvania C.H., 1864	Fayetteville
N. McLeod	Lieut.	26th Inf.	Wilderness, May 6, 1864	Carthage
G.W. Avant	Lieut.	35th Inf.	Petersburg, Jun 17, 1864	Chatham
Alex. H. Brown	3d Lt.	2d Inf.	Kelly's Ford, Va., 1863	Lynstreth
G.N. Albright	Lieut	6th Inf.	Rapidan Station, 1863	Melville
J.M. Brugin	Lieut.	22d Inf.	Gettysburg, July 4, 1863	Marion
J.B. Coffield	Lieut.	1st Inf.	Spottsylvania C.H., 1864	Tarboro
Geo. L. Cooke	Lieut.	44th S.S.	Hanover Junction, 1864	Graham
D.T. Bullard	Lieut.	18th Inf.	Spottsylvania C.H., 1864	Owenville
J.Q. Elkins	Lieut.	18th Inf.	Spottsylvania C.H., 1864	Whitsonville
G.H. Lindsay	Lieut.	54th Inf.	Drury's Bluff, 1864	Madison
M. Ballison	Lieut.	62d Inf.	Cumberland Gap, 1863	
W.H. Ivey	Lieut.	2d Cav.	Spottsylvania C.H., 1864	Jackson
W.T. Doles	Lieut.	32d Inf.	Spottsylvania C.H., 1864	Nash Co.
N.H. Fennell	Lieut.	61st Inf.	Bermuda Hundreds, 1864	Linsville
F.F. Floyd	Lieut.	51st Inf.	Bermuda Hundreds, 1864	Wilmington
G.P. Highly	Lieut.	51st Inf.	Cold Harbor, 1864	Lumberton
J.B. Lindsay	Lieut.	31st Inf.	Cold Harbor, 1864	Wadesboro
B.A. Gowan	Lieut.	51st Inf.	Bermuda Hundreds, 1864	Whiteville
J.H. Bloodworth	Lieut.	4th Cav.	Brandy Stat., Va., Oct. '63	Wilmington
W.C. Gordon	Lieut.	6th Cav.	Jacksons Mill, W.V., 1864	Morganton
H.Y. Gash	Lieut.	6th Cav.	Jacksons Mill, 1864	Hendrsnvlle
A.J. Hanser	Lieut.	1st Inf.	Spottsylvania C.H., 1864	Lincolnton
T.P. Barrow	Lieut.	3d Inf.	Spottsylvania C.H., 1864	Washington
J.M. Hargett	Lieut.	1st Inf.	Spottsylvania C.H., 1864	Newbern
E.A. Carver	Lieut.	1st Inf.	Spottsylvania C.H., 1864	Forrestville
R.H. Lyon	Lieut.	3d Inf.	Spottsylvania C.H., 1864	Black Rock
J.F. Heath	Lieut.	67th Inf.	Swift Creek, N.C., 1864	Newbern
W.B. Chandler	Lieut.	37th Inf.	Wilderness, May 6, 1864	Yancyville
A.J. Gurganus	Lieut.	3d Inf.	Spottsylvania C.H., 1864	Onslow Co.
Geo. M. Crapon	Lieut.	3d Inf.	Spottsylvania C.H., 1864	Smithville
L.J. Henderson	Lieut.	3d Inf.	Spottsylvania C.H., 1864	Onslow Co.
Z.H. Loudermilk	Lieut.	3d Inf.	Spottsylvania C.H., 1864	Randolph
J.E. King	Lieut.	3d Inf.	Spottsylvania C.H., 1864	Onslow Co.
C.M. Busbey	Lieut.	5th Inf.	Spottsylvania C.H., 1864	Raleigh
C.C. Lane	Lieut.	3d Inf.	Spottsylvania C.H., 1864	Snow Hill
H.C. Andrews	Lieut.	28th Inf.	Spottsylvania C.H., 1864	Orange
J.A. Blair	Lieut.	16th Inf.	Falling Waters, Va., 1863	Macon Co.

* Took oath of allegiance, Morris Island.

North Carolina *continued*

Name	Rank	Regiment	Captured – Date	Residence
J.C. Haines	Lieut.	5th Cav.	Jack's Shop, Va., 1863	Clinton
J. Coggin	Lieut.	23d Inf.	Gettysburg, 1863	Montgomery
W.P. Jones	Lieut.	35th Inf.	Petersburg, 1864	Moore Co.
J.B. Davis	Lieut.	7th Cav.	Petersburg, 1864	Wilson
T.D. Crawford	Lieut.	C.S.N.	Washington, N.C., 1864	Washington
E.S. Hart	Lieut.	23d Inf.	Spottsylvania C.H., 1864	Barrck's Mll
M.P. Johnson	Prvt.	1st Cav.	Bostic Station, Nov., 1863	Charlotte

Georgia

Name	Rank	Regiment	Captured – Date	Residence
D.F. Booton	Major	3d Cav.	East Tenn., Jan., 1864	Rome
W.J. Dumus	Capt.	53d Inf.	Knoxville, Tenn., Nov., '63	Forsyth
W.C. Nutt	Capt.	53d Inf.	Knoxville, Nov., 1863	Griffin
W. Barnes	Capt.	55th Inf.	Cumberland Gap, Tenn., '63	Atlanta
J.P. Allen	Capt.	55th Inf.	Cumberland Gap, 1863	Dawson
T.N. Kent	Capt.	48th Inf.	Gettysburg, 1863	Wrightsville
J.L. Lenemood	Capt.	18th Inf.	Knoxville, 1863	Cobb Co.
J.D. Ashton °	Capt.	4th Cav.	Summerville, Ga., 1863	Burke
W.J. Gorham	ADC	Gen. Thom.	Wilderness, 1864	Hamilton
T.M. Carter	Capt.	44th Inf.	Wilderness, 1864	Jackson
J.J. Henderson	Capt.	31st Inf.	Spottsylvania C.H., 1864	Ironville
D. McDonald	Capt.	61st Inf.	Spottsylvania C.H., 1864	——————
T.W. Harris	Capt.	12th Inf.	Spottsylvania C.H., 1864	Oglethorpe
J.R. McMichael	Capt.	12th Inf.	Spottsylvania C.H., 1864	Buena Vista
Alex. Gibson	Capt.	4th Inf.	Spottsylvania C.H., 1864	La Grange
G.W. Lewis	Capt.	31st Inf.	Spottsylvania C.H., 1864	Bambridge
H.B. Dedwyler	Capt.	38th Inf.	Spottsylvania C.H., 1864	Elberton
J.H. Conneley	Capt.	44th Inf.	Spottsylvania C.H., 1864	Griffin
J. Edmonson	Capt.	44th Inf.	Spottsylvania C.H., 1864	Fayetteville
C.R. Ezell	Capt.	4th Inf.	Spottsylvania C.H., 1864	Jasper
A.J. McLeod	Capt.	57th Inf.	Gaines' Farm, 1864	Camilla
R.L. Miller	Capt.	7th Cav.	Trevillian Station, 1864	Scarboro Co.
H.K. Harrison °	Capt.	7th Cav.	Louisa C.H., Va., 1864	Chatham
T.W. Hopkins	Lieut.	7th Cav.	Louisa C.H., 1864	Chatham
W.J. Bozwell	Lieut.	55th Inf.	Cumberland Gap, 1863	Penfield
S.U. Branch	Lieut.	8th Inf.	Gettysburg, July 4, 1863	Savannah
B.L. Brown	Lieut.	59th Inf.	Gettysburg, July 5, 1863	Fort Gaines
T.J. Carr	Lieut.	43d Inf.	Champ Hill, Miss., 1863	Jefferson
J.J. Maddox	Lieut.	38th Inf.	Locust Grove, Va., 1864	Milton
Jno. G. Morgan	Lieut.	45th Inf.	Wilderness, 1864	Clinton
J.J. Bass	Lieut.	35th Inf.	Wilderness, 1864	Monroe
G.M. Roughton	Lieut.	49th Inf.	Wilderness, 1864	Sandersville
D.W. Garrett	Lieut.	11th Inf.	Wilderness, 1864	Morgan
M.D. Joy	Lieut.	12th Inf.	Spottsylvania C.H., 1864	Wiliford
C.C. Grace	Lieut.	12th Inf.	Spottsylvania C.H., 1864	Perryville
W.W. Hulbert	Lieut.	4th Inf.	Spottsylvania C.H., 1864	Augusta

° Exchanged, Fort Pulaski, 1864.

Georgia *continued*

Name	Rank	Regiment	Captured – Date	Residence
R. Childs	Lieut.	4th Inf.	Spottsylvania C.H., 1864	Clinton
N.B. Durham	Lieut.	44th Inf.	Spottsylvania C.H., 1864	Clarke
E. Jeffers	Lieut.	61st Inf.	Spottsylvania C.H., 1864	Macon
M.M. Mosely	Lieut.	3d S.S.	Spottsylvania C.H., 1864	Homer
J.D. DeLoach	Lieut.	61st Inf.	Spottsylvania C.H., 1864	Tattnall Co.
W.H. DeLoach	Lieut.	7th Cav.	Louisa C.H., 1864	Bryan Co.
P.P. Logan	Lieut.	18th Inf.	Gaines' Farm, 1864	Canton
J.W. Maxwell	Lieut.	50th Inf.	Cold Harbor, 1864	Canton
H.J. Moses	Lieut.	51st Inf.	Gaines' Farm, 1864	Blakely
W.R. Avaunt	Lieut.	61st Inf.	Gettysburg, July, 1863	Macon
J.B. Bently	Lieut.	22d Inf.	Gettysburg, July, 1863	Lincolnton
A.J. Barton	Lieut.	55th Inf.	Cumberland Gap, Sept., '63	Gainesville
J.F. Davies	Lieut.	14th Inf.	Wilderness, 1864	Amhrst, Va.
A.M. Green	Lieut.	12th Inf.	Spottsylvania C.H., 1864	Yngsbr, NC
W.C. Cherry	Lieut.	4th Inf.	Spottsylvania C.H., 1864	West Pt., Ga.
D.T. Harris	Lieut.	21st Inf.	Spottsylvania C.H., 1864	Forsyth
F.N. Graves	Lieut.	61st Inf.	Spottsylvania C.H., 1864	Lumpkin
D.W. Goodwin	Lieut.	44th Inf.	Spottsylvania C.H., 1864	Greensboro
T.J. Gurr	Lieut.	51st Inf.	Cold Harbor, 1864	Houston
W.H. Chew	Lieut.	7th Cav.	Trevillian Station, 1864	Augusta
G.H. Ford	Lieut.	7th Cav.	Trevillian Station, 1864	Wayne
R. Hervie	Lieut.	7th Cav.	Trevillian Station, 1864	Bogan

Florida

Name	Rank	Regiment	Captured – Date	Residence
W.D. Ballantine	Capt.	2d Florida	Gettysburg, July, 1863	Pensacola
William Baily	Capt.	5th Inf.	Gettysburg, July, 1863	Leon Co.
G. Finley	Capt.	1st Cav.	Mis. Rdg., Tenn., Nov., 1863	Marianna
J.G. Talbot	Capt.	5th Inf.	Wilderness, 1864	Lake City
T.S. Armstead	Lieut.	8th Inf.	Wilderness, 1864	Marianna
Saunders Myers	Lieut.	4th Inf.	Miss. Ridge, Nov., 1863	Bnbrdg, Ga.
S.M. Davis	Lieut.	4th Inf.	Miss. Ridge, Nov., 1863	Quincy
R.A. Hall	Lieut.	4th Inf.	Miss. Ridge, Nov., 1863	Applchicola
A.S. Bull	Lieut.	5th Inf.	Wilderness, 1864	Tallahassee

Missouri

Name	Rank	Regiment	Captured – Date	Residence
Peter Ake	Capt.	3d Mo.Cav.	Arkansas, Nov., 1863	Ironton
M.J. Bradford	Capt.	10th Inf.	Arkansas, Nov., 1863	Raleigh
J.G. Kelly *	Capt.	Staff	Smithville, N.C., 1864	St. Louis
S. Lowe	Capt.	3d Battery	Rodney, Miss., 1864	Independnce
A.M. Bedford	Lieut.	3d Cav.	Big Black, Miss., 1863	Savannah
Peter G. Benton	Lieut.	8th Inf.	Helena, Ark., July, 1864	Cassville
W. Halliburton *	Lieut.	Frin's Btry.	Arkansas, 1863	Dent C.H.
Geo. C. Brand	Lieut.	2d Cav.	Holly Springs, Miss., 1863	Boonville

* Took oath of allegiance, Fort Pulaski, Ga.

Alabama

Name	Rank	Regiment	Captured – Date	Residence
R.T. Campbell	Capt.	49th Inf.	Port Hudson, La., July, 1863	Village Spgs.
J.N. Chisholm	Capt.	9th Inf.	Gettysburg, July, 1863	Florence
J.W. Burton °	Capt.	6th Inf.	Gettysburg, July, 1863	Montgomery
C. Ed. Chambers	Capt.	13th Inf.	Gettysburg, July, 1863	Tuskegee
L.S. Chetwood	Capt.	5th Inf.	Spottsylanvia C.H., 1864	Clayton
J.W. Fannin	Capt.	61st Inf.	Spottsylanvia C.H., 1864	Tuskegee
A.J. Armstrong	Lieut.	46th Inf.	Champ Hill, Miss., 1863	Columbia
W.T. Bishop °	Lieut.	16th Inf.	Bexar, Ala., 1864	———
H.A. Chadburn	Lieut.	10th Inf.	Mt. Pleasant, Tenn., 1863	Faundsdale
Jn. P. Breedslove	Lieut.	4th Inf.	Gettysburg, July, 1863	Tuskegee
J.J. Andrews	Lieut.	Staff	Florence, Ala., 1863	Florence
A.J. Kirkman	Lieut.	4th Cav.	Missionary Ridge, 1863	Florence
Paul H. Earle	Lieut.	28th Inf.	Missionary Ridge, 1863	Huntsville
E.J. Mastin	Lieut.	Staff	Charleston, 1863	Huntsville
D.E. Bates	Lieut.	J. Darthy	Spottsylanvia C.H., 1864	Selma
J.L. Haynes	Lieut.	14th Inf.	Petersburg, 1864	Talledega
J.D. Bond	Lieut.	57th Inf.	Petersburg, 1864	Haynesville
W.H. Allen	Lieut.	49th Inf.	Port Hudson, 1864	Guntersville
A.C. Foster °	Lieut.	2d Cav.	Lauderdale, Ala., 1863	Florence
J.L. Leonard °	Lieut.	7th Cav.	Swanborn, N.C., 1864	Tuskegee
W.B. Bass	Lieut.	15th Inf.	Wilderness, 1864	Tuskegee
R.H. Adams, Jr.	Lieut.	Engineers	Mt. Pleasant, 1863	Farmsdale

Mississippi

Name	Rank	Regiment	Captured – Date	Residence
T.H. Johnson *	Major	1st Inf.	Port Hudson, July, 1863	Fernand
Thos. Boyd	Capt.	1st Inf.	Corinth, Miss., July, 1863	Mooreville
A.J. Lewis	Capt.	P. Cav.	Clayborne Co., Ms., Feb. '64	Port Gibson
J.L. Purgason	Capt.	32d Inf.	Corinth, May, 1863	Port Gibson
H.T. Coffee	Capt.	48th Inf.	Spottsylvania C.H., 1864	New Orleans
T.Q. Munner	Capt.	12th Inf.	Petersburg, 1864	Natchez
Chas. L. Barrett	Lieut.	P. Cav.	Port Hudson, 1863	Port Gibson
W.H. Frizzle	Lieut.	12th Inf.	Spottsylvania C.H., 1864	Holmes Co.
J.C. Carson	Lieut.	A.D.C.	Trevillian Station, 1864	Natchez
Wm. T. Jeffreys	Lieut.	P. Cav.	Clayborne, Feb., 1864	Port Gibson
Wm. L. Barton °	Lieut.	2d Inf.	Tupelo, Miss., May, 1863	Tupelo
Jno. R. Casson	Lieut.	27th Inf.	Gettysburg, July, 1863	Holly Sprgs.
Joel W. Jones	Lieut.	1st Inf.	Port Hudson, July, 1863	Smithville
R.J. Howard °	Lieut.	1st Inf.	Port Hudson, July, 1863	Byhalia
B.S. Grant	Lieut.	42d Inf.	Fallng Waters, Va., July, '63	Pontotoc
T.M. Bassonett	Lieut.	12th Inf.	Chester Gap, Va., July, 1863	Union Chrch
J.M. Allen	Lieut.	29th Inf.	Chickahominy, Va., 1863	Grenada
Wm. M. Bullock	Lieut.	48th Inf.	Spottsylvania C.H., 1864	Bovina
Timothy Foley *	Lieut.	19th Miss.	———	———

° Exchanged.   * Took oath of allegiance 1864.

Louisiana

Name	Rank	Regiment	Captured – Date	Residence
P.F. DeGurney	Lt Co	C.S. Artil.	Port Hudson, 1863	New Orleans
E.S.M. LeBreton	Lt Co	C.S. Mil.	Port Hudson, 1863	New Orleans
E.J. Hall °	Capt.	1st Cav.	Port Hudson, 1863	New Orleans
J.G. Angell	Capt.	5th Inf.	Rappahannock, Va., 1863	New Orleans
Wm. B. Kemp	Capt.	9th Cav.	Port Hudson, 1863	Greensboro
H.E. Henderson	Capt.	AAG 3d Bg	Wilderness, May 6, 1864	Alexandria
L.M. Malchor °	Capt.	7th Inf	Wilderness, May 6, 1864	New Orleans
Jno. Elliott	Capt.	2d Inf.	Spottsylvania C.H., 1864	Carrol Prsh.
L. Jestremeska [8]	Capt.	10th Inf.	Spottsylvania C.H., 1864	Alberville
Jno. L. Lemmon	Capt.	14th Inf.	Spottsylvania C.H., 1864	New Orleans
W.A. Martin	Capt.	7th Inf.	Spottsylvania C.H., 1864	Baton Rge.
Boliver Edwards	Lieut.	M. Legion	Port Hudson, 1863	Covington
J.C. Bartholmy	Lieut.	20th Inf.	Port Hudson, 1863	St. James Pr.
J. Fickisen	Lieut.	14th Inf.	North Anna, Va., 1864	New Orleans
P.H. Cavanaugh	Lieut.	1st Inf.	Wilderness, 1864	Liberty
J.B. Fitzpatrick	Lieut.	14th Inf.	Wilderness, 1864	New Orleans
J.D. Bowerman	Lieut.	15th Inf.	Spottsylvania C.H., 1864	Bastrop
T.E. Kelly	Lieut.	5th Inf.	Spottsylvania C.H., 1864	Bastrop
T.J. Henderson	Lieut.	9th Inf.	Spottsylvania C.H., 1864	Evergreen
J.M. Burgess	Lieut.	8th Inf.	Spottsylvania C.H., 1864	Holmesville
Dan Mahony	Lieut.	10th Inf.	Spottsylvania C.H., 1864	New Orleans
R.M. Fletcher	Lieut.	2d Inf.	Spottsylvania C.H., 1864	Vernon
C.A. Chisholm	Lieut.	10th Inf.	Spotts. C.H., May 12, 1864	Atachalalgo
C.J. Bachelor	Lieut.	2d Inf.	Spotts. C.H., May 12, 1864	Red Rvr Ldg
John Kilmartin	Lieut.	7th Inf.	Spotts. C.H., May 12, 1864	New Orleans
J.R. Collingham	Lieut.	3d Inf.	Haynes Blff, Miss., Apr., '63	Columbia
A.V. Duralde	Lieut.	9th Inf.	Port Husdson, 1863	Baton Rge.

Texas

Name	Rank	Regiment	Captured – Date	Residence
W.A. Collier	Lieut.	7th Inf.	Raymond, Miss., 1863	Cofferville
J.E. Cobb [9]	Lieut.	5th Inf.	Gettysburg, July, 1863	Liberty
F.J. Duval	Lieut.	32d Cav.	Deer Creek, Miss., Jan., '64	Anderson
H. Coffee	Lieut.	1st Legion	Franklin, Tenn., 1863	Dangerfield
S.G. Anderson	Lieut.	11th Cav.	McMinnville, Tenn., 1863	Weston

Arkansas

Name	Rank	Regiment	Captured – Date	Residence
Van H. Manning	Col.	3d Inf.	Wilderness, 1864	Hanbury
M.R. Willson	Major	1st Bat. Inf.	Port Hudson, 1863	Hanbury
W.E. Stewart	Major	15th Inf.	Port Hudson, 1863	Easton, Md.
D. Arbuckle	Major	17th Inf.	Port Hudson, 1863	Fort Smith
J.L. Brent	Major	18th Inf.	Port Hudson, 1863	Louisvl., Ky.

° Exchanged.   [8] Escaped.   [9] After the war member of U.S. Congress

Arkansas *continued*

Name	Rank	Regiment	Captured – Date	Residence
D.B. Coulter	Major	12th Inf.	Port Hudson, 1863	Centre Pnt.
Geo. K. Cracraft	Capt.	23d Inf.	Port Hudson, 1863	Chicot
J.C. Patterson	Capt.	14th Inf.	Port Hudson, 1863	Yellville
A.B. Israel	Capt.	1st Inf.	Missouri, Dec. 25, 1863	Ponchoton
J. McG. Jones	Capt.	B. Cav.	Arkansas Line, Oct. 4, 1863	Berryville
W.A. Hancock	Lieut.	Neat's Bty.	Arkadelphia, Oct. 30, 1863	Marion
D.S. Branaugh	Lieut.	16th Inf.	Port Hudson, 1863	Liberty
P.H. Benson	Lieut.	23d Inf.	Port Hudson, 1863	Jonesboro
J.B. Baxter	Lieut.	23d Inf.	Port Hudson, 1863	Monroe Co.
Geo. W. Carter	Lieut.	23d Inf.	Port Hudson, 1863	Arkadelphia
M. Hixon	Lieut.	16th Inf.	Port Hudson, 1863	Shoal Creek
R.Y. Dillaird	Lieut.	2d Cav.	Port Hudson, 1863	Nashville
C.M. Allen	Lieut.	2d Cav.	Cold W. Ford, Miss., 1863	New Orleans
O.H.P. Caldwell	Lieut.	19th Inf.	Big Blk Rvr, Miss., May '63	Magnolia
D.M. Coffman	Lieut.	Sheff. Cav.	Missouri, Dec., 1863	Smithville
W.E.D. Evans	Lieut.	17th Inf.	Natchez, Miss., Dec., 1863	Wshngtn Co

Kentucky

Name	Rank	Regiment	Captured – Date	Residence
J.B. McCreary	Major	7th Cav.	Cheshire, Ohio, 1863	Richmond
C.L. Miner *	Capt.	Shelby Cav	Cheshire, 1863	Waco, Texas
A.A. Norris	Capt.	Mrgn's Cav	Cheshire, 1863	Burksville
R.D. Logan °	Capt.	6th Cav.	Cheshire, 1863	Danville
M.D. Logan °	Capt.	3d Cav.	Cheshire, 1863	Lancaster
Jno. B. Austin	Capt.	2d Cav.	Dixon Co., Tenn., 1863	Charltte, Tn
T.M. Hammack	Capt.	10th Cav.	Rutland, Ohio, 1863	Morganfield
J.A. Fox	Lieut.	7th Cav.	Buffington, Ohio, 1863	Richmond
Geo. C. Nash	Lieut.	6th Cav.	Buffington, 1863	Owen Co.
Benjm. S. Drake	Lieut.	2d Cav.	Buffington, 1863	Lexington
H.P. Dunlap	Lieut.	10th Cav.	Cheshire, 1863	Paris, Tenn.
F.G. Eakins	Lieut.	12th Cav.	Cheshire, 1863	Hudson Co.
W.P. Crow	Lieut.	6th Cav.	Cheshire, 1863	Hudson Co.
W.T. Dunlap	Lieut.	2d Cav.	Cheshire, 1863	Marshall
W.A. Kendall	Lieut.	3d Cav.	Cheshire, 1863	Lenton
H. Moles	Lieut.	7th Cav.	Cheshire, 1863	Albany
B. Logsdon	Lieut.	1st Cav.	Charleston, Tenn., Dec. '63	Sturgis
W.T. Leathers	Lieut.	7th Cav.	Buffington, 1863	Lawrencebg
L.D. Newton	Lieut.	3d Cav.	Buffington, 1863	Union Co.
R.B. Haynes	Lieut.	6th Cav.	Buffington, 1863	Lincoln Co.
J.S. Hughes	Lieut.	6th Cav.	Buffington, 1863	Lincoln
W.B. Ford	Lieut.	8th Cav.	Buffington, 1863	Winchester
J.D. Morris	Lieut.	8th Cav.	Buffington, 1863	Winchester
A.B. Chinn	Lieut.	8th Cav.	Cheshire, 1863	Lexington
C.E. Richards	Lieut.	5th Cav.	Cheshire, 1863	Warsaw
B.F. McNeer	Lieut.	6th Cav.	Cheshire, 1863	Owenton
G.W. Hunter	Lieut.	8th Cav.	Cheshire, 1863	Bardstown
S.M. Cowan	Lieut.	6th Cav.	Cheshire, 1863	Summerset

* Took the oath of allegiance.   ° Exchanged Hilton Head, 1864.

Kentucky *continued*

Name	Rank	Regiment	Captured – Date	Residence
D.N. Prewitt	Lieut.	6th Cav.	Cheshire, 1863	Perryville
J.O. Meddows	Lieut.	3d Cav.	Syracuse, Ohio, 1863	Benham, Tx.
M.S. Aldridge	Lieut.	3d Cav.	Syracuse, Ohio, 1863	Dallas, Tx.
S.P. Allensworth	Lieut.	2d Cav.	Salensville, Ohio, 1863	Todd Co.
S.S. Atkins *	Lieut.	10th Cav.	Mt. Liberty, Ohio, 1863	West Liberty

Tennessee

Name	Rank	Regiment	Captured – Date	Residence
Abe Fulkerson	Col.	63d Inf.	Petersburg, June, 1864	Roysville
F.N. Daughterty	Lt Co	8th Cav.	Lexington, Tenn., 1864	Lovington
W.H. Craft *	Capt.	Mrry's Cav	West Tennessee, 1864	Nashville
J.P. Burke	Capt.	2d Cav.	Corinth, 1863	Knoxville
J.W. Boyd *	Capt.	6th Cav.	Corinth, 1863	—
L.P. Carson	Capt.	35th Inf.	Seymour Valley, Tenn., '63	McMnnsvlle
G.R. Campbell	Capt.	Scout	Shelbyville, Tenn., 1863	Manchester
T.T. Perkins	Capt.	11th Cav.	Williamson Co., Tenn., 1863	Franklin
J.P. Lyttle	Capt.	23d Inf.	Bean Station, Tenn., 1864	Unionville
Jno. Hicks	Capt.	Scout	Hickman, Tenn., 1863	Hickman Co
J.H. Polk °	Capt.	1st Cav.	Meridian, Tenn., 1863	Ashwood
S.J. Johnson	Capt.	25th Inf.	Drury's Bluff, 1864	Sparta
J.R. McCallum	Capt.	63d Inf.	Petersburg, 1864	Knoxville
W.N. James	Capt.	44th Inf.	Petersburg, 1864	Carthage
E. Boddie	Lieut.	7th Inf.	Wilderness, 1864	Gallatin
J.D. Jenkins	Lieut.	14th Inf.	Wilderness, 1864	Clarksville
H.C. Flemming	Lieut.	25th Inf.	Drury's Bluff, 1864	Spencer
J.F. Landerdale	Lieut.	2d Cav.	Spring Place, Ga., 1864	Clayborne
S.A. Morgan	Lieut.	25th Inf.	Petersburg, 1864	Sparta
J. Ledford	Lieut.	25th Inf.	Petersburg, 1864	Livingston
C.L. Hutchison	Lieut.	63d Inf.	Petersburg, 1864	Georgetown
M.A. Douglass *	Lieut.	44th Inf.	Petersburg, 1864	Gallatin
Thos. J. Goodloe	Lieut.	44th Inf.	Petersburg, 1864	Winchester
C.D. Covington *	Lieut.	45th Inf.	Lebanon, Tenn., 1863	Lebanon
Thos. E. Bradly	Lieut.	23d Inf.	Chickamauga, Ga., 1863	Dixon Sprgs
W.H. Anderson	Lieut.	1st Cav.	Columbia, Tenn., 1863	Maury Co.
W.E. Knox	Lieut.	4th Cav.	Wilson, Tenn., 1863	Shelbyville
W.H. Adams	Lieut.	51st Inf.	Ringgold, Ga., 1863	Covington
Joseph Irwin	Lieut.	11th Inf.	Missionary Ridge, 1863	Nashville
J.B. Lewis	Lieut.	1st Inf.	Union, Tenn., 1863	Tazewell
W.B. Easley	Lieut.	48th Inf.	Hickman, 1864	Vernon
Y.R. Elliott	Lieut.	4th Cav.	White County, Tenn., 1864	Albany, Ky.
J.A. Irvin °	Lieut.	9th Cav.	Maury, Tenn., 1863	Columbia
J.H. Henderson	Lieut.	3d Inf.	Monroe, Tenn., 1864	Madisonville
B. Arnold	Lieut.	31st Inf.	Huntsville, Ala., 1864	Sparta
W.E. Allen	Lieut.	60th Inf.	Big Black River, 1863	Newport
H.H. Cook	Lieut.	44th Inf.	Drury's Bluff, 1864	Franklin
W.A. Cameron *	Lieut.	25th Inf.	Drury's Bluff, 1864	Sparta
J.G.S. Arrants	Lieut.	63d Inf.	Petersburg, 1864	Zollicoffer

* Took the oath of allegiance.   ° Exchanged, 1864.

Tennessee *continued*

Name	Rank	Regiment	Captured – Date	Residence
J.H. Hastings	Lieut.	17th Inf.	Petersburg, 1864	Shelbyville
Z.W. Ewing	Lieut.	17th Inf.	Petersburg, 1864	Lewisburg
A.J. Elzy (died)	Lieut.	17th Inf.	Petersburg, 1864	Columbia
Jno. M. Hooberry	Lieut.	44th Inf.	Petersburg, 1864	Nashville
Jno. M. Henry	Lieut.	44th Inf.	Petersburg, 1864	Hartsville
W.C. Campbell	Lieut.	25th Inf.	Petersburg, 1864	Cookeville

Died and Buried on Morris Island

Name	Rank	Regiment	Captured – Date	Date Death
W.P. Callahan	Lieut.	25th Tn Inf	Petersburg, 1864	Sept. 26, '64
Frank P. Peake	Lieut.	Bryn Artlry	Cheshire, 1863	Oct. 2, '64
J.C.C. Cowper	Lieut.	33d NC Inf	Gettysburg, 1863	Oct. 15, '64

Recapitulation

Recapitulation	In Stockade	In Hospital	Died	Exchanged	Escaped	Sent to Beaufort, S.C.	Died at Beaufort
Maryland	6						
Virginia	171	1				14	
North Carolina	102	1	1			7	
South Carolina	21	1	1	1		2	
Georgia	58	1				1	
Florida	9					1	
Alabama	22				1	3	
Mississippi	19					2	
Louisiana	27					4	
Texas	5						
Arkansas	21	1	1			4	
Missouri	8						
Kentucky	32	1				1	
Tennessee	45	2	1			1	1
Total	546	8	4	1	2	39	1

Under fire: 558.   Not under fire: 42.
Total number sent from Fort Delaware: 600.

This list was made October 16, 1864; changes not noted except removal of Captain Boyd and the wounding of Captain Blair and Lieutenant Harris by Negro sentinel at Morris Island, S.C.

Prisoners of War of 600 Sent From Hilton Head to the Hospital at
Beaufort, South Carolina, August 30, 1864, Before the Balance
Were Placed Under Fire on Morris Island

Name	Rank	Regiment	Captured – Date	Disease, Etc.
Evan Rice	Lt Co	55th Va. Inf.	Falling Waters, Va.	Chronic diarrhœa
A.A. Sumdler	Major	7th Va. Inf.	Rappahannock, 1864	Lost left leg
E. Carter	Capt.	8th Va. Inf.	Gettysburg, 1863	Wounded right leg
J.B. Fitzgerald	Capt.	B.W.R.	Gettysburg, 1863	Mental, died Ft. Pul.
W.T. Johnson	Capt.	18th Va. Inf.	Gettysburg, 1863	Wound in right thigh
Geo. Hopkins	Capt.	10th Va. Cav	At Home	Lost eye
E.D. Camden	Capt.	25th Va. Inf.	Spotts. C.H., 1864	Erysipelas
R.S. Elam	Capt.	22d Va. Inf.	Gettysburg, 1863	Lost left leg
N.A. Haskins	Lieut.	25th Va. Inf.	Wilderness, 1864	Erysipelas
C.D. Chadwick	Lieut.	33d Va. Inf.	Spotts. C.H., 1864	Chronic dysentery
C.R. Darricut	Lieut.	Stewart's Art	Hanover C.H., 1864	Wounded left arm
J.P. Chalkey	Lieut.	14th Va. Inf.	Gettysburg, 1863	Lost right leg
G.B. Long	Lieut.	11th Va. Inf.	Gettysburg, 1863	Wound in shoulder
L.C. Leftwich °	Lieut.	C.S.N.	At Sea, May 7, 1864	Wound in left lung
R.M. Atkinson *	Capt.	2d N.C. Cav.	Hanover C.H., 1864	Chronic diarrhœa
A.S. Critcher	Capt.	37th NC Inf.	Spotts. C.H., 1864	Chronic diarrhœa
J.C. Garman	Capt.	2d N.C. Inf.	Spotts. C.H., 1864	Billious fever
A.A. Cathey	Capt.	34th N.C. Inf	Gettysburg, 1863	Lost left leg
I.H. Gilbert	Capt.	37th N.C. Inf	Gettysburg, 1863	Chronic diarrhœa
E.W. Dassey	Lieut.	11th NC Inf.	Gettysburg, 1863	Lost left leg
R.A. Glenn *	Lieut.	22d N.C. Inf.	Hanover C.H., 1864	Chronic diarrhœa
J.W. Burt	Lieut.	7th S.C. Inf.	Gettysburg, 1863	Lost left leg
F.M. Boughman	Lieut.	1st S.C. Inf.	Hanover C.H., 1864	Chronic diarrhœa
J.S. Green	Lieut.	4th Ga.	Wilderness, 1864	Wound rt arm, side
Jas. Collins	Lieut.	5th Fla.	Wilderness, 1864	Chronic diarrhœa
J.D. Meddows	Lieut.	1st Ala. Inf.	Port Hudson, 1863	Both legs wounded
W.A. Ledyard	Lieut.	3d Ala.	Gettysburg, 1863	Lost left leg
W.H. Bedell	Lieut.	1st Ala. Cav.	Tennessee, 1863	Wounded in foot
A.H. Farrar	Lieut.	13th Miss.	Gettysburg, 1863	Wounded in left leg
Lamar Fontaine	Pvt.	10th Miss.	Lexington, Ala., 1863	Wounded thigh, knee
W.E. Oriely	Lieut.	9 th La.	Rappahannock, 1864	Wounded left ankle
Jas. Martin	Lieut.	1 st La.	Gettysburg, 1863	Wounded left arm
Sam E. May	Lieut.	10th La.	Gettysburg, 1863	Wounded left arm
W.A. Fernney	Capt.	3d Ark.	Arkansas, 1863	Wounded left thigh
H.L.W. Johnson	Capt.	12th Ark.	Port Hudson, 1863	Lost leg
J.L. Greer	Capt.	23d Ark.	Port Hudson, 1863	Lost arm
W.B. Burnett	Capt.	10th Ark.	Port Hudson, 1863	Lost right foot
M.S. Bradburn	Capt.	16th Ark.	Port Hudson, 1863	Chronic diarrhœa
J.M. Cash	Capt.	4th Tenn.	Lexington, Ky., 1863	Chronic diarrhœa
R.C. Bryan	Capt.	2d Tenn.	Salem, Miss., 1863	Died Oct., 5, 1864

° Exchanged, 1864.   * Took oath of allegiance.

This list of officers were exchanged Dec., 1864, from Beaufort, S.C., except
Lieutenant Leftwich, who was exchanged at Hilton Head. Lieutenants Glenn and
Atkinson took the oath of allegiance.

Escaped

Name	Rank	Regiment	Captured – Date	Location
G.W. Woolford	Col.	S.C. Cav.	Tallahassee River	*Crescent City* ship
G.H. Ellerson	Capt.	3d Ala.	Fredricksbrg, Va., '64	*Crescent City* ship
W.E. Stewart	Major	15th Ark.	Gettysburg, 1863	Hospital, Ft. Pulaski
W.H. Hatcher	Lieut.	42d Va.	Spotts. C.H., 1864	Hospital, Ft. Pulaski

Exchanged Morris Island

Name	Rank	Regiment	Captured – Date	Date Exchanged
Henry Bruist	Capt.	27th S.C.	Petersburg, 1864	Sept. 27, 1864

Taken Out of Stockade Pen After This List Was Made

Name	Rank	Regiment	Captured – Date	
J.W. Boyd	Capt.	6th Tn. Cav.	Corinth, Miss., 1863	

Confederate Officers Placed in Convict Prison at Hilton Head For Cutting Buttons Off Coat of Oath-Takers and Making Plan to Escape

Name	Rank	Regiment	Date of Confinement	Date Released
Van H. Maning	Col.	3d Ark.	Jan. 20, 1865	Feb. 16, 1865
Thos. T. Perkins	Capt.	11th Tenn.	Jan. 20, 1865	Feb. 16, 1865
W.H. Kitchens	Capt.	12th N.C.	Jan. 20, 1865	Feb. 16, 1865
G.R. Campbell	Capt.	Scout	Jan. 20, 1865	Feb. 16, 1865
Peter B. Akers	Capt.	11th Va.	Jan. 20, 1865	Feb. 16, 1865
Jno. R. Casson	Capt.	17th Miss.	Jan. 20, 1865	Feb. 16, 1865

On February 28, 1865, the following officers attempting to escape from Fort Pulaski prison, were betrayed by one of the party – R.C. Gillespie – and recaptured, put in a dark cell in their wet clothes and kept there without fire for five days; Capts. W.H. Griffin, Md.; Kent, Ga.; J.O. Murray, Va.; D.N. Prewitt, Ky.; W.H. Chew, Ga.; H.P. Dunlap, Tenn., W.W. George, Va. Gillespie took the oath of allegiance when captured.

The Officers Who Took the Oath of Allegiance to United States, 1865

Name	Rank	Regiment	Captured – Date	Location of Oath
Jno. A. Baker	Col.	3d N.C. Cav.	Petersburg, 1864	Fort Pulaski
R.W. Atkinson	Capt.	2d N.C. Cav.	Hanover C.H., 1864	Fort Pulaski
R.C. Gillespie	Pvt.	45 th Va. Inf.	Millford Stat., 1864	Fort Pulaski
W.H. Craft	Capt.	Mrry's Cav.	West Tenn., 1864	Fort Pulaski
J.G. Kelly	Capt.	Eng. Hbt. Stf	Smithville, N.C., '64	Hilton Head
Chas. L. Miner	Capt.	Shlby Ky. Cv	Cheshire, Ohio, 1863	Fort Pulaski

The Officers Who Took the Oath of Allegiance, *continued*

Name	Rank	Regiment	Captured – Date	Location of Oath
W. Halliburton	Capt.	Truman Art.	Arkansas, 1863	Fort Pulaski Hosp.
L. Berry Doyle	Lieut.	5th Va. Inf.	Spotts. C.H., 1864	Fort Pulaski
R.A. Glenn	Lieut.	22d N.C.	Spotts. C.H., 1864	Fort Pulaski Hosp.
J.W. Davis	Lieut.	20th Va. Cav	Frdrck City, Md., '63	Hilton Head Prison
W.A. Cameron	Lieut.	25th Tenn.	Drury's Bluff, 1864	Hilton Head Prison
Tim Foley	Lieut.	19th Miss.	———————	Hilton Head Prison
C.D. Covington	Lieut.	45th Tenn.	Lebanon, Tenn. 1863	Hilton Head Prison
J.M. Mulvaney	Lieut.	27th S.C.	Petersburg, 1864	Morris Island
M.A. Douglas	Lieut.	44th Tenn.	Petersburg, 1864	Hilton Head
S.S. Atkins	Lieut.	10th Ky. Cav	Mt. Liberty, Oh, '63	Hilton Head
J.W. Boyd	Capt.	6th Tn. Cav.	Corinth, Miss., 1863	Morris Island

Made in the USA
Middletown, DE
20 March 2025

72986441R00125